# EVOLVING POSSIBILITIES

# EVOLVING POSSIBILITIES

## Selected Papers of Bill O'Hanlon

Edited and Compiled by
Steffanie O'Hanlon
and
Bob Bertolino

| USA | Publishing Office: | BRUNNER/MAZEL<br>*A member of the Taylor & Francis Group*<br>325 Chestnut Street<br>Philadelphia, PA 19106<br>Tel: (215) 625-8900<br>Fax: (215) 625-2940 |
|---|---|---|
| | Distribution Center: | BRUNNER/MAZEL<br>*A member of the Taylor & Francis Group*<br>47 Runway Road, Suite G<br>Levittown, PA 19057-4700<br>Tel: (215) 269-0400<br>Fax: (215) 269-0363 |
| UK | | BRUNNER/MAZEL<br>*A member of the Taylor & Francis Group*<br>1 Gunpowder Square<br>London EC4A 3DE<br>Tel: 171 583 0490<br>Fax: 171 583 0581 |

**EVOLVING POSSIBILITIES: Selected Papers of Bill O'Hanlon**

1 2 3 4 5 6 7 8 9 0

Edited by Edward A. Cilurso and Jean Anderson. Printed by Edwards Brothers, Lillington, NC, 1999. Cover design by Joseph Dieter Visual Communications.

A CIP catalog record for this book is available from the British Library.
∞ The paper in this publication meets the requirements of the ANSI Standard Z39.48-1984 (Permanence of Paper)

**Library of Congress Cataloging-in-Publication Data**

Available from the publisher

ISBN 0-87630-980-5 (case)

# Acknowledgments

We want to acknowledge Bill O'Hanlon for talking both of us into taking on this project and for good-naturedly enduring our tag-team, ego-leveling critiques of his early writing.

We especially want to acknowledge Andy Bertolino for his work on typesetting and designing the original manuscript.

Steffanie wants to acknowledge Bob for his fantastic attention to detail.

Bob wants to acknowledge Steffanie for her perseverance.

# Dedication

This book is dedicated to Bobby and Murry Shapiro for their generous support of my graduate education and to my friend Gary Bonalumi who always manages to show up in the Room of 1000 Demons (no matter how many times it relocates) to share a few irreverent jokes (which inevitably improve the atmosphere). I hope our lives and careers continue to coevolve with the uncanny synchronicity that they always have.—S. O'H.

This book is dedicated to my brothers and sisters who have collectively taught me to be a better person and to all of the wonderful people I've met at Bill's workshops and trainings who have enriched my life.—B. B.

Evolving Possibilities: Selected Papers of Bill O'Hanlon

# Preface

Bill O'Hanlon has two overall missions. The first is to change the field of psychotherapy by bringing about a therapy that is more respectful to clients and more effective in creating change. The second mission developed out of the first. In order to influence the field, Bill transformed himself from a shy, depressed dreamer into an engaging presenter and author. Along the way he learned a tremendous amount about overcoming the skepticism of others and the limitations of one's own mind. His psychotic optimism about possibilities became a mission to inspire and, if necessary, cajole others to pursue their dreams and passions. *Evolving Possibilities* reflects these missions.

The writings in this book span the period from 1986 to the present. Arranged in phases, they include his incarnations as an Ericksonian/strategic, solution-oriented, and possibility and inclusive/collaborative therapist. As you read these pieces, you can see the development of Bill's ideas, writing style, and particularly his voice. Like many young writers, his early work is somewhat stiff and formal and primarily focuses on the ideas of others. Bill says the way he got his first articles published was by "sleeping with the editor" (he included the articles in a journal he was editing) and we can believe this. We have cleaned up some of his early pieces to make them more readable but wanted to leave them close to the original as incentive for burgeoning writers who are reluctant or embarrassed to take that initial step. Many people feel they can't write or don't have anything unique to say. Bill started out a mediocre writer at best, learned what he needed as he went along, and become a more proficient writer over time. He continues to work to try to capture the unique aliveness of his presentations and the richness of his clinical work in his writing.

His ideas evolve, undergoing constant revisions and readjustments. Nothing is static; everything can be improved and made clearer. A self-described information junkie, who is always assimilating new information, he abhors boredom. Bill often expresses frustration that he can't rework the manuscripts of his published books the way he does with handouts or self-published books. While many of us limit ourselves, feeling we can't do something until it's perfect, Bill does things down and dirty and refines them as he goes along, inching toward perfection.

Sprinkled throughout the book are articles we call rants (and we won't spoil it by telling you which ones). Bill is determined to help clients (in whatever way possible) without having his or anyone else's theoretical orientations stand in the way. In his efforts to create a therapy that is more respectful, he can be strident, even fierce, about critiquing approaches he feels undermine a client's well-being. Frequently, these rants are protective of clients, but on occasion they indicate a transition in Bill's thinking, an emergence of a new idea, and seem almost a birthing process. He thinks by talking and loves a good debate (not surprising given his background as one of eight from a boisterous and strong-willed Irish family). However, at times his strident positions have left him at odds with members of the professional community. And while he is accepting and kind-hearted by nature, for Bill an exchange of ideas is an exchange of ideas. And subtlety is not one of his strong suits. Yet many of the concerns he raised over the years about psychotherapy such as nonpathologizing, client autonomy, strengths, and the importance of flexibility of method and ideas are now more widely accepted and championed by solution-based, collaborative, and narrative therapies.

Many of us think people achieve success through extraordinary talent or luck. Bill would be the first to tell you this isn't so. He lives his life by "locking onto" a particular goal, such as learning to write or teach workshops, and then lets life teach him what he needs to do to achieve it.

Bill sometimes tells a story of a friend, Jerry Jerome. Jerry was training for a marathon but every morning when it was time for him to get up and run, he found himself wrestling with feelings of tiredness or laziness or questioning his motives or ability to run a marathon. Sometimes he would win the struggle and go out and run, and other times he would lose. Unfortunately he lost often enough so that he was never in shape enough to run a marathon when it came around. The way he finally was able to condition himself for a marathon was by learning not to let his feelings or doubts determine whether he trained or stayed in bed. Bill uses a similar process: he points his feet toward the ultimate goal no matter how discouraged, tired, or frustrated he may feel at the moment. We have been inspired by Bill's process to "not know how" and to do it less than perfectly at first. We hope you will be inspired as well.

Steffanie O'Hanlon
Bob Bertolino
September 1998

# PHASE I

# Ericksonian/Strategic Approaches

# Introduction to Phase I

Bill O'Hanlon

I met Milton Erickson in 1973 at an art gallery on the campus of Arizona State University, where I was working part time to help finance my education. One of my coworkers pointed out an article about Erickson that was in *Time* magazine that week. I read it and was instantly fascinated with his work. Some years later, after reading what I could of his and going to workshops with others who were attempting to explain his work, I finally was able to work with him. Since I had little money, he arranged for me to work for him as a gardener while I learned.

My time with Erickson warped me quite a bit but also confused me. Since I dislike confusion, I felt compelled to make sense of Erickson's work. I obsessively read and listened to anything I could lay my hands on to help me in that quest. After about seven years, I finally had a sense I had a handle on the basics of his ideas and had even developed some insights into his approach that no one else had offered. I taught a number of workshops on Ericksonian therapy and related approaches (strategic/interactional/hypnotic therapies) and ultimately wrote a definitive overview and introduction to Erickson's work (*Taproots*, W.W. Norton, 1987). I also began to develop my own style and ideas, influenced by Erickson, but sometimes different and occasionally in disagreement with Erickson.

I disliked the rather heavy-handed manipulation that characterized some of these approaches, as well as the slavish gurufication of Erickson himself. As I ended this period, I became more critical of Erickson and the Ericksonian movement, a trend which ultimately got me banned from ever teaching for the Milton Erickson Foundation, the main representatives of the official Erickson legacy. The papers in this section reflect this era of my thinking.

# Chapter 1

# Milton Erickson

## An Uncommon Therapist—Part I

**Bill O'Hanlon**

Milton Erickson (1901–1980) was a seminal figure in family therapy. Although he was not strictly a family therapist, he greatly influenced the family therapy field, mainly through his effect on two of his students, Jay Haley and John Weakland. Both Weakland and Haley were research associates of Gregory Bateson, the biologist and anthropologist, who was another seminal figure in the development of family therapy. Erickson was one of the few American psychiatrists in the mid-1900s to have practiced and studied the uses of clinical hypnosis. When Bateson and anthropologist Margaret Mead (who were married at the time) needed an expert to help them understand the trance rituals they had observed and filmed in Bali, they were put in contact with Erickson. Bateson and Mead were impressed with Erickson's knowledge and skills in the area of hypnosis. So when Haley and Weakland decided that they wanted to study hypnosis as part of the Bateson research project on communication, Bateson arranged for them to meet and study with Erickson. This research project later became an important force in the development of family therapy, yielding the "double bind" hypothesis of schizophrenia and other severe emotional and mental disturbances.

After the research team disbanded, two main clinical groups emerged from it. One was the group in Palo Alto at the Mental Research Institute (MRI). The other was Jay Haley, who emerged as a theorist in his own right. Both of these groups developed interactional models for explaining psychopathology; however, initially neither had come up with much of a clinical approach for how to intervene via these interactional models. Psychoanalysis was the main model of the day and it did not lend itself to the interactional models they had developed. As

This unpublished article represents some of the early influence Milton Erickson had on Bill.

they began their practice, Weakland and Haley decided to consult with Erickson, as he had the only alternative approach to therapy they knew about. The two began traveling monthly to Erickson's office in Phoenix, Arizona, and getting consultation on cases they were seeing.

What Erickson had developed, they realized after some time, was an approach to therapy that was very different from psychoanalysis. It was comparatively very brief in duration. It was not aimed at developing awareness or insight as the curative factor. It was directive while often being very indirect. It sometimes involved seeing more than one person in the office at a time, yet just as often it would involve the use of hypnosis with an individual. Haley and Weakland had some difficulty understanding what Erickson was doing and how he approached cases, but gradually they were able to emulate and articulate parts of Erickson's therapy.

When the Bateson group studied pathogenic double binds (those types of communications that contradict each other at different levels and are given repeatedly in some families) as a key factor in the genesis of schizophrenia, they had been influenced by Erickson's use of similar contradictory messages given in the context of therapy. It was these therapeutic double binds to which Haley gave his attention.

Essentially, Haley saw that Erickson was putting patients into a bind to cure them. In the pathogenic double bind, it was "damned if you do, damned if you don't," with no way for the victim of this family bind to escape except through madness. Erickson used similar binds in therapy, but with him it was "cured if you do, cured if you don't." Again, he did not put a lot of emphasis on insight as a curative factor. He was more interested in getting his patients to think and act differently. He often accomplished this by using therapeutic binds. He would, for example, tell a patient whom he wanted to put into a trance, "You could go into a light trance or a deep trance." This technique is called the "illusion of alternatives," because it gives the patient the sense that he has a choice but really presents a bind in that either of the choices taken will lead to trance.

Erickson was also known for his use of paradoxical injunctions in hypnosis and therapy. He once told a skeptical subject in a hypnosis demonstration to "stay more and more awake" and to "keep your eyes open wider and wider." Of course, the more the subject resisted, the more he was following Erickson's directions. He quickly went into a hypnotic trance.

Erickson also used metaphorical communication to effect change in therapy. He maintained that since patients use multiple levels of meanings in their symptoms and communication, therapists had a perfect right and, indeed, a responsibility to do the same. He used stories, puns, riddles, jokes, and his own nonverbal communication to give multiple messages to patients.

Was Erickson a family therapist? He was one of the first clinicians in the United States to see families as whole groups (the first reports put his use of conjoint family therapy at about 1948), and, in fact, it was common for him to see whole or parts of families in therapy. He seemed to have an interpersonal view of problems, often rearranging the patient's social context to effect change. But as previously mentioned, he did not always see the whole family and sometimes saw only the individual. One reason for this was that he was a pragmatist, who preferred to work in the briefest manner and concentrate on where he thought change was most possible. Another reason for his not being a "pure" family therapist is perhaps more interesting and will be detailed below.

Although Erickson thought that the context surrounding the problem was important, he also thought the internal context was important. He did not attempt to get the patient to discover the origin and meaning of the symptom; instead, he wanted to direct the person to change his thinking, sensations, feelings, or experience in relation to the problem. He seemed to think systemically; that is, if you change one part of the system, the other parts will be affected and will have to adjust as well. But his systemic thinking included the patient's internal experience, not just his or her family environment. For this reason, he may have been a harbinger of a new direction for family therapy. There has been a dichotomy between internally oriented psychodynamic therapists and externally oriented family therapists. Erickson was a psychotherapist who successfully integrated both internal and external orientations.

One way Erickson was able to integrate these two seemingly incompatible ways of working was that he was uninterested in explanations and focused mainly on solutions. *How* the problem came about was not relevant for the solution in most cases. Family therapists tend to view the origin and maintenance of symptoms as matter of family interactions and patterns. Psychodynamic practitioners view symptoms as a product of an individual's intrapsychic structure, history, or conflicts. Erickson was much more interested in making changes in the internal and external environments of his patients and then noticing their response to those interventions. From those responses, he would get more information in order to intervene and start to shape the patient's behavior and experience in the direction of his or her goals.

Other contributions Erickson made to therapy include the technique of matching the therapist's language and behavior to the language and therapy of the patient and the family. This technique later became well known in Salvador Minuchin's work as "joining." Another Minuchin technique, that of changing the seating arrangement in the family session, was derived from Erickson's technique of using space as a metaphor in the therapy session.

Erickson was part of the origin of the family therapy movement, mainly through the adaptation of his techniques and ideas by influential family therapists like Weakland, Haley, Minuchin, Paul Watzlawick, Richard Fisch, and Cloé Madanes. Since his death in March of 1980, there has been a steady increase in interest in his work. This has lead to the organizing of three international congresses and the publication of 30 books dedicated to exploring the implications of his approaches to therapy. Perhaps, as his original work becomes more well known without the filtering of interpreters, he will have a direct influence on future generations of family therapists as well.

# Chapter 2

# Milton Erickson

## An Uncommon Therapist—Part II

**Bill O'Hanlon**

There's something about Milton Erickson. . . .

Recently, an upsurge of interest in the work of Milton Erickson has occurred, as evidenced by the proliferation of books, tapes, workshops, and conferences on his approaches. Indeed, there have been three International Congresses on Ericksonian Approaches to Hypnosis and Psychotherapy (held in 1980, 1983, and 1986), with each drawing approximately 2,000 attendees. Who was this man and why are people so interested in his work?

Milton Erickson was a psychiatrist (he also held a master's degree in psychology) who developed many innovative ways of dealing with resistance in therapy, of doing hypnosis and psychotherapy, and (most importantly perhaps) of utilizing the skills and abilities that people already possess to accomplish therapeutic results. Erickson had polio twice and spent his last years in a wheelchair, finally succumbing to complications resulting from muscular deterioration in March of 1980. Since his death, there has been even greater interest in trying to replicate and understand his techniques and approaches. Some said he was an eccentric genius whose work can never be replicated by others, but more and more have been able to understand, practice, and teach his approaches. This effort has given rise to the "Ericksonian" movement, people who work in Erickson's tradition and legacy.

Erickson's work was often characterized (by himself and others) as *natural-*

---

This manuscript was originally published in 1984 in the now defunct newsletter, *Assert*. At that time it was titled, *Uncommon Sense in Therapy: Milton H. Erickson and Ericksonian Therapy*. We feel that the article is a good representation of Bill's early thoughts on the work of Milton Erickson and the evolvement of what has been deemed *Ericksonian* psychotherapy.

*istic*, *directive*, and *indirect*. Cornerstones of his approaches were the use of task assignments, stories, analogies, and metaphor, and the utilization of client resources, resistance, beliefs, and symptoms in the service of change. Each of these approaches will be discussed in more detail below.

## THE NATURALISTIC APPROACH

Erickson viewed clients as having all the necessary resources available within themselves or their social systems or both to make the changes they need. The therapist's job is to access these resources and help the client put them to use in the appropriate areas of their life. Erickson didn't view people as fundamentally flawed or in need of fixing. Additionally, he wasn't oriented to discovering the "roots" of the client's difficulties. His interest was in getting people to use their own abilities to make changes in the present. Erickson had a great faith in nature and people's natural abilities to be healthy. Sometimes it was a matter of accessing their skills and abilities, and sometimes it was a matter of unblocking the expression of these natural abilities. He had confidence that if people had access to and could use those abilities, they would be fine. To Erickson (1980), therapy "was predicated upon the assumption that there is a strong normal tendency for the personality to adjust if given an opportunity" (p. 505).

Erickson also approached therapy as more of a natural situation than do many therapists. His interventions, even his hypnotic inductions, were often indistinguishable from ordinary conversations. At times, he had social interactions with clients, and they often interacted with his family, as his waiting room was his living room (often occupied by one of his eight children or his wife).

## DIRECTIVE THERAPY

Jay Haley's books, *Uncommon Therapy* (1973) and *Ordeal Therapy* (1984), skillfully and entertainingly describe Erickson's ability to get people to do something in order to improve their situation or to break out of previous restrictive patterns. Erickson remarked, "The thing to do is to get your patient, any way you wish, any way you can, to do something" (Zeig, 1980, p. 143). Then, "once you break through rigid, fixed patterns of behavior patients are forced to reorient; they are forced to pick up the pieces to put them together; and they are forced to function in a totally different way" (Rossi, 1980, p. 210).

Erickson's task assignments were often the vehicle for his directive therapy. He didn't try to teach people skills to practice, but instead he gave them assignments that would naturally lead to the accessing of personal or social resources. He would also give assignments designed to break up symptomatic or interactional patterns surrounding the symptom (e.g., family interactions). These tasks were often unusual. Erickson (Haley, 1973) once told a patient who was ashamed of a gap in her teeth to practice squirting water through the gap. In another case (Haley) he had a young boy who wet the bed practice his handwriting under his mother's supervision in the middle of the night. Erickson wasn't directive about how people should ultimately live their lives, but he had no qualms about directing people's behavior in order to move them beyond the dilemmas that confronted them.

## THE INDIRECT APPROACH: TIPTOEING AROUND RESISTANCE

Erickson frequently used indirect communication in language and action to suggest or imply rather than to directly request or state things. He created a context for the person to cooperate and to learn things implicitly rather than explicitly. He used words and his own nonverbal communication to indirectly communicate an expectation of change and to make therapeutic interventions. Rarely did he use awareness or insight as the prime means of effecting therapeutic results.

### The Use of Metaphor and Multilevel Communication

Erickson was well known for his story-telling abilities in therapy and teaching. This is well represented in Sidney Rosen's (1982) book, *My Voice Will Go With You*. It is another area in which Erickson used implicit communication rather than explicit. He might use planning and eating a meal together as a metaphor for a couple who had sexual difficulties without ever mentioning their sexual difficulties during the course of treatment. This approach not only brings forth the creativity of the therapist but also allows clients to project their own meanings and solutions. This allowed him to personalize interventions.

### The Utilization Approach: Matching, Participation, and Alteration of Clients' Realities and Symptoms

When a colleague recently asked which techniques of Erickson's would last the longest, the utilization approach immediately occurred to me. Erickson was firmly committed to using everything the client brought to therapy as grist for the therapeutic mill. Like a good organic gardener, everything is considered part of the compost to grow plants and harvest the fruits of one's labors. Erickson would accept, match (by his behavior or words or both), and participate with what other people saw as resistance or uncooperativeness. He didn't interpret resistance, he encouraged it, and then got the person to modify the expression of it to lead in useful directions. Erickson was able to work with many people who had "defeated" a number of therapists or who were generally not good candidates for therapy. Sometimes he was even able to accomplish this in a very brief period. He would accept, participate with, and alter clients' realities and behavior.

Erickson was very adamant about treating each client as unique and individual. He espoused no theory of therapy, but he had a general approach of utilizing clients' behavior, beliefs, and symptoms. He thought rigid categories of diagnosis or techniques in therapy were counterproductive and disrespectful of the individual.

## What About Hypnosis?

Erickson was one of a few who helped bring hypnosis into modern times, by updating the techniques and training in the area. In addition, he helped to get hypnosis recognized as a legitimate medical, dental, and psychological tool. His hypnotic technique was as innovative and individual as the rest of his work. He emphasized flexibility and observation rather than ritual as the main tools of the hypnotist. Erickson also stressed the importance of the ethical and knowledgeable use of hypnosis. He wrote many articles and helped to found one of the major journals and professional societies in the field. Interest in his work is one of the factors surrounding the recent renaissance of hypnosis in psychotherapy.

## Erickson's Contributions

Erickson made seminal contributions in the areas of brief therapy, hypnosis, strategic therapy, family therapy, and cybernetics. He was a curious, experimental psychiatrist who didn't accept the dogma of his profession. He counted among his admirers famed anthropologists Gregory Bateson and Margaret Mead, as well as numerous therapists. One of his former students, family therapist Jay Haley, himself regarded as a master of therapy, remarked,

> Not a day passes when I do not use something that I learned from Erickson in my work. Yet his basic ideas I only partially grasp. I feel that if I understood more fully what Erickson was trying to explain about changing people, new innovations in therapy would open up before me. (1982, p. 5)

Most of his former students feel this way. One of them, Jeffrey K. Zeig, set up the Milton H. Erickson Foundation in Phoenix, Arizona, to further his work and to form an archive for therapists to come and unravel the genius of Milton H. Erickson.

A reference list, by no means complete, follows to help those who are interested in further investigating Erickson's work. But I offer a warning, as it is easy to get hooked like the rest of us Ericksonians. After reading Erickson, I can promise that your therapy (and perhaps your life) will never be the same. There's something about Milton Erickson. . . .

## REFERENCES

Erickson, M. H. (1980). The hypnotherapy of two psychosomatic dental problems. In E. L. Rossi (Ed.), *The collected papers of Milton H. Erickson on hypnosis: Volume IV: Innovative hypnotherapy* (Ch. 56, pp. 499–506). New York: Irvington. (Original work published 1955.)
Haley, J. (1973). *Uncommon therapy: The psychiatric techniques of Milton H. Erickson, M.D.* New York: Norton.
Haley, J. (1982). The contribution to therapy of Milton H. Erickson, M.D. In J. Zeig (Ed.), *Ericksonian approaches to hypnosis and psychotherapy.* New York: Brunner/Mazel.
Haley, J. (1984). *Ordeal therapy: Unusual ways to change behavior.* San Francisco: Jossey-Bass.
Rosen, S. (1982). *My voice will go with you: The teaching tales of Milton H. Erickson.* New York: Norton.
Rossi, E. L. (Ed.). (1980). *The collected papers of Milton H. Erickson on hypnosis: Volume 4: Innovative hypnothearpy.* New York: Irvington.
Zeig, J. K. (1980). *A teaching seminar with Milton H. Erickson.* New York: Brunner/Mazel.

# Chapter 3

# What Constitutes
# an Ericksonian Approach?

**Bill O'Hanlon and Bob Bertolino**

A debate within the field of psychotherapy over the use of the term "Ericksonian" has lingered for years. Some have expressed their concern that Erickson's work was uniquely his; therefore, he was the only one who was truly Ericksonian. While acknowledging the dangers of distortion and reification inherent in any label, our view is that there is a distinct, recognizable approach that can be called Ericksonian. That is, Erickson's work had a unique "fingerprint." In this paper, we intend to identify the basic assumptions and principles that constitute that fingerprint, thereby laying a foundation for an Ericksonian approach.

While Ericksonian practitioners might disagree on certain aspects of therapy and hypnosis, there are some basic elements and orientations that are shared by all. These common denominators will be delineated below.

## AN INTRODUCTION TO ERICKSON'S WORK

Milton Erickson was trained as a psychiatrist and a psychologist, completing his training in 1929. His early interest in hypnosis was stimulated while he was a student at the University of Wisconsin. During this time, he observed a Clark Hull demonstration that profoundly influenced him. Erickson went on to explore the subject of hypnosis both experimentally and clinically while holding initial professional positions at state asylums (mental hospitals). It was at these institutions that many of the experiments that led to the development of his innovative approaches were carried out. At the time, there were few successful approaches

This unpublished, unfinished manuscript was written with Bob Bertolino and completed for this book. It attempts to outline some of the essential aspects of an *Ericksonian* approach to therapy. In addition, it is representative of Erickson's influence on the field of psychotherapy in general.

and techniques for doing therapy with severely disturbed individuals. The psychotropic drugs that later became popular as management tools for these people were not yet available. This led Erickson to develop many innovative approaches to managing and treating these disorders.

Hypnosis was Erickson's primary, but by no means only, tool. It becomes clear in his writings that after some time he started to generalize from the hypnotic experiments, experiences, and techniques, from which evolved a broader approach to psychotherapy. What Erickson developed was a way of doing therapy that did not involve formal trance, yet incorporated elements of hypnotic communication and interpersonal influence. Essentially, he transferred his ideas that previously had been associated with purely hypnotic work to a wider context.

## BASIC PRINCIPLES

Various words have been used to characterize and describe Erickson's approaches: *naturalistic, indirect, directive*, and *utilization*. Each of these terms refers to a specific principle that typifies his work, hypnotic or otherwise.

### The Naturalistic Approach

Erickson believed that people had within themselves or their social systems the natural abilities to go into a trance, experience all trance phenomena, and, subsequently, overcome difficulties and resolve problems. His approach was to elicit those natural abilities, as he was very much opposed to trying to "teach" people things in psychotherapy. In a 1966 lecture Erickson remarked,

> Now, too much has been written and said and done about the reeducation of the neurotic and the psychotic and the maladjusted personality. As if anybody could really tell any one person how to think and how to feel and how to react to any given situation. Everybody reacts differently, according to his own background of personal experience.

Erickson felt that nothing needed to be added from the outside as all the answers were within. He stated, "Patients have problems precisely because they don't know how to utilize all their abilities" (Rossi, 1980, p. xix). He had a basic view of human beings as being capable and of nature as maintaining health if allowed to: "Therapy . . . was predicated upon the assumption that there is a strong normal tendency for the personality to adjust to a given opportunity" (p. 505).

He did not see trance as an esoteric skill or ability. Instead, along with trance phenomena, he considered it to be part of common, everyday experience. The therapist's task was to create a context where the client could access already existing abilities and resources they had not previously been using in their situation. Erickson commented, "In therapy, the patient actually does the therapy, you only furnish a favorable climate" (Zeig, 1980, p. 52).

The other side of this coin of the naturalistic approach was that psychotherapy and hypnosis could be carried out in such a way that they appeared to be very natural situations and conversations. Hypnosis didn't need to be a ritual and the subject didn't need to be aware that the trance induction had begun or was happening. The same was true of therapy. Erickson often told anecdotes and gave assignments that were not easily recognized as therapeutic interventions. Therapy could be a very natural, nonritualistic process.

## The Indirect and Directive Approach

It is often said that while Erickson was directive, he used indirect techniques and suggestions. This seems to be a contradiction in terms but actually is not. Erickson told the following story in a teaching seminar,

> I was returning from high school one day and a runaway horse with a bridle on sped past a group of us into a farmer's yard . . . looking for a drink of water. The horse was perspiring heavily. And the farmer didn't recognize it, so we cornered it. I hopped on the horse's back . . . since it had a bridle on, I took hold of the rein and said, "Giddy-up" . . . headed for the highway. I knew the horse would turn in the right direction. . . . I didn't know what the right direction was. And the horse trotted and galloped along. Now and then he would forget he was on the highway and start into a field. So I would pull on him a bit and call his attention to the fact that the highway was where he was supposed to be. And finally about four miles from where I had boarded him he turned into a farmyard and the farmer said, "So that's how that critter came back. Where did you find him?" I said, "About four miles from here." "How did you know he should come here?" I said, "I didn't know . . . the horse knew. All I did was keep his attention on the road." I think that's the way you do psychotherapy. (Gordon, 1978, p. 6)

Erickson was directive in that he wanted to get people to DO things and block the old patterns that maintained the symptom. Conversely, he didn't ever try to tell people how to live or handle life in general.

A key part of his therapy was the use of assignments and suggestions. These would often provide a loosening of rigidities, just enough for the person to discover other ways of thinking and behaving that would eliminate the symptom. Such suggestions and directions (often in very ambiguous "hypnotic" language) allowed clients to find their own meanings and ways to solve their own problems.

Erickson was direct in dealing with the symptom and equally as indirect in matters pertaining to the way the person should live his or her life after the symptom was resolved. In addition, he was very indirect as far as how the person would resolve his or her symptom. He related,

> Too many hypnotherapists take you out to dinner and then tell you what to order. I take a patient out to dinner and I say, "You give your order." The patient makes his own selection of the food he wants. He is not hindered by my instructions, which would only obstruct and obscure his inner processes. (Rossi, 1980)

Erickson's indirect approach involved many techniques, but it was a general approach as well. He communicated indirectly through the use of puns, symbols, jokes, riddles, ambiguous language, and behavior. Often times he communicated on several levels at once, leaving the client to find his or her own meaning or solution. The need for awareness and insight in solving therapeutic difficulties seemed unnecessary to Erickson. He remarked, "If you look over the lives of happy, well-adjusted people, they have never bothered to analyze their childhood or their parental relationships. They haven't bothered and they're not going to" (Haley, 1973, p. 246).

## The Utilization Approach

Most therapists and hypnotists have prerequisites without which their treatment and techniques would not be successful. Erickson seemed to have very few prerequisites or expectations for what constituted a workable situation in hypnosis and therapy. Whatever the client presented with was utilized in service of the therapy. He used rigid or difficult beliefs, behaviors, demands, and characteristics in a way that didn't interfere with the desired results in therapy. In fact, these things often facilitated therapy.

The things that Erickson often utilized in treatment included *presenting problems* and *symptoms*, *rigid beliefs* and *delusions*, and *rigid behavior patterns*. In order to clarify his use of each type of utilization, some examples will be provided.

**Utilization of Presenting Problems and the Symptom.**   Erickson utilized the symptom in a case at the state hospital in which a man had only been able to use word salad, very disjointed phrases, and had therefore never been able to be treated. He learned how to speak word salad by studying transcripts of the man's speech patterns. He then conversed with the man in word salad in a seemingly meaningful way until gradually more and more understandable phrases began to emerge in the patient's communication (Rossi, 1980).

**Utilization of Rigid Beliefs and Delusions.**   Erickson approached a man at the state hospital who claimed to be Jesus Christ and told him that he understood that the patient had experience as a carpenter. Knowing that Jesus did indeed help his father, Joseph, who was a carpenter, the man could only reply that he had. Erickson said that he also understood that the patient wanted to be of service to his fellow man. To this, the patient also answered in the affirmative. Erickson then informed him that the hospital needed help building some bookcases and asked for his cooperation in the matter. The patient agreed and was able to start participating in constructive behavior rather than continuing his symptomatic behavior (Haley, 1973).

**Utilization of Rigid Behavior Patterns.**   A nervous man appeared in Erickson's office talking rapidly—almost nonstop—claiming that he was too nervous to sit down. Erickson instructed the man to continue his pacing. During this, he matched his rate of speech to the man's pace, gradually slowing his speech.

The man gradually followed suit and slowed down, almost waiting for the next instruction. Eventually, Erickson structured the situation so that the man ended up in trance sitting in a chair. Most therapists would have had difficulty dealing with this presenting situation without the use of medications or without securing the man's conscious cooperation in having him calm down.

The main point to be emphasized here is that there are no prerequisites for the presentation, personality, behavior, or beliefs that the person brings to the therapist or the hypnotist. Whatever the person presents with is adopted as the starting point for therapy. In addition, the symptom or complaint is used, if possible, in service of the desired goal. Erickson again and again emphasized the importance of treating each individual as such, while developing a different approach in each case. He subscribed to this idea rather than using a general theory or typology to guide treatment.

## Pattern Intervention

Erickson often gathered very specific information about the exact expression of the symptom. When did it occur? How often did it occur? How long did it last? After gathering this sort of information, he would often prescribe an activity or task that would interfere with the performance, experience, or pattern of the symptom. Erickson noticed that

> maladies, whether psychogenic or organic, followed definite patterns of some sort, particularly in the field of psychogenic disorders; that a disruption of this pattern could be a most therapeutic measure; and that it often mattered little how small the disruption was. (Rossi, 1980, p. 254)

Once a pattern was broken, Erickson felt that people would adjust accordingly: "Once you break through rigid, fixed patterns of behavior, patients are forced to reorient; they are forced to pick up the pieces to put them together; and they are forced to function in a totally different way" (Rossi, 1980, p. 210).

It is apparent throughout his work that Erickson did not limit the use of pattern intervention to task assignments or symptom modification. He would constantly alter patterns of communication and behavior to affect hypnotic trance or to elicit certain feelings, behaviors, or associations. These patterns might be those of the client, those of others around the client, or the therapist/hypnotist's patterns.

## BASIC ASSUMPTIONS

There are various underlying assumptions or presuppositions that one can extract from Erickson's work. Some of these he stated very explicitly and some are inherent in the approaches he used. The basic assumptions that are discussed in this section include *responsiveness, patient activity, present orientation, natural healthiness,* and *flexibility.*

## Responsiveness

Erickson didn't discuss the topic of whether a person had the trait of hypnotizability very often, and since this is such a common concern for hypnotists, one might be curious about that. Likewise, he seemed to be able to work with people who most therapists or hypnotists might have found extremely difficult, if not impossible. Both of these phenomena are related to the "responsiveness" frame that Erickson seemed to hold. People are not fixed as they express themselves currently. They are able to respond to different stimuli in different contexts with different responses. Instead of attributing unworkability to rigid personality characteristics, Erickson would take it upon himself to learn what individual patterns of behavior and response the person would exhibit. He would then utilize these in service of change, rather than treating them as blocks.

## Patient Activity

As previously mentioned, Erickson stressed the importance getting the patient to DO something in psychotherapy. When clients engaged in forms of action, often times repetitive sequences could be disrupted, hence, the dissipation of the symptom.

## Present Orientation

An important distinction for Erickson was his emphasis on the present (and the immediate future) and a deemphasis on the past and the search for causes and reasons of present difficulties. As discussed above, his view was that activity by the person in the present was the most important element of success in psychotherapy. Therefore, time spent in examining the unchangeable past was considered time wasted, for the most part.

## Natural Healthiness

Erickson had a real respect for nature and viewed it as essentially good. The associated belief was that people would naturally develop if not blocked. He usually acted as if he did not assume the worst about people. Unlike many therapists, he didn't posit symptom substitution or resistance as primary aspects of therapist posture. Instead, Erickson (Erickson & Rossi, 1979) conveyed the notion of flexibility: "Each person is an individual. Hence, psychotherapy should be formulated to meet the uniqueness of the individual's needs, rather than tailoring the person to fit the Procrustean bed of a hypothetical theory of human behavior."

## Flexibility

The flexibilities that are inherent in Erickson's work are in making hypotheses and in the therapist's behavior. These will be explained more fully in the following sections as we discuss *flexibility in hypotheses* and *flexibility in the therapist's behavior.*

**Flexibility in Hypotheses.**  Despite almost a century of experimental inquiry into the matter, there is still very little agreement about the causes of human behavior and experience. Many profess to know the rhyme and reason to human behavior, but their ideological opponents argue just as persuasively and vociferously for opposing explanations and conceptualizations. There is no certainty in this realm given our present state of knowledge. An appropriate stance for the therapist, therefore, is one that is able to consider alternate explanations, meanings, and motivations for human behavior and experience. It has been suggested that, given the current state of understanding in this realm, perhaps a better criteria than "true/false" for evaluating hypotheses in a clinical setting would be "more/less useful" (Bandler & Grinder, 1975). One group of therapists has even written about "hypothesizing" as a crucial element in therapy (Selvini Palazzoli, Boscolo, Cecchin, & Prata, 1980).

**Flexibility in the Therapist's Behavior.**  Erickson conducted a great number of hypnotic studies that yielded fascinating results. Many of these experiments demonstrated the effects of changing his own behavior and communication on his subject's experiences. He discovered that, sometimes, slight changes in the therapist's or hypnotist's words, behavior, and communications could lead to dramatic alterations in the experience of trance subjects. He subsequently extended this orientation to his therapeutic work.

Erickson would do something different or differently if what he had previously done had not attained the appropriate response. He wasn't bound by any theory in making these changes, just a sense of curiosity and flexibility combined with a keen sense of observation. He remarked, "When you want to find things out about your patients, observe. Observe their behavior" (Rosen, 1982).

Erickson often stressed to his students the importance of observation. As Rossi has stated, "Erickson was a lucid naturalist who felt no need to go much beyond the sense observations of what was immediately present" (Rossi, Ryan, & Sharp, 1983, p. 51).  As discussed in a previous section, he also stressed that you don't know for certain what the things you observe mean. He seemed to emphasize the use of all the therapist's sensory modalities, especially watching and listening for clues related to how the therapy was working with a particular client. Listening to the patient's language, changes in their vocal dynamics, alterations in their muscle tonus, and the gestures they used were also identified as key elements in determining a client's responsiveness.

## CONCLUSION

While this is by no means a complete description of Erickson's work, we believe it covers the essential elements that those who work in his tradition share in common. Some emphasize one element more than others or use principles not mentioned here, but at the core we all share the use of these principles in our work. As Erickson warned, we should not attempt to mimic him, but we can adapt the principles he used in our own work.

## REFERENCES

Bandler, R., & Grinder, J. (1975). *The structure of magic: A book about language and therapy*. Palo Alto, CA: Science and Behavior Books.
Erickson, M. H. (1966). *Advanced psychotherapy*. Unpublished transcript of lecture for the American Society of Clinical Hypnosis. Des Plaines, IL: ASCH.
Erickson, M. H., & Rossi, E. L. (1979). *Hypnotherapy: An exploratory casebook*. New York: Irvington.
Gordon, D. (1978). *Therapeutic metaphors*. Cupertino, CA: Meta Publications.
Haley, J. (1973). *Uncommon therapy: The psychiatric techniques of Milton H. Erickson, M.D.* New York: Norton.
Rosen (1982). *My voice will go with you: The teaching tales of Milton H. Erickson*. New York: Norton.
Rossi, E. L. (Ed.). (1980). *The collected papers of Milton H. Erickson on hypnosis: Vol. 4. Innovative hypnotherapy*. New York: Irvington.
Rossi, E. L., Ryan, M. O., & Sharp, F. A. (Eds.). (1983). *The seminars, workshops, and lectures on Milton H. Erickson: Vol. 1: Healing in hypnosis*. New York: Irvington.
Selvini Palazzoli, M., Boscolo, L., Cecchin, G., & Prata, G. (1980). Hypothesizing-circularity-neutrality. *Family Process, 19,* 73–85.
Zeig, J. K. (1980). *A teaching seminar with Milton H. Erickson*. New York: Brunner/Mazel.

# Chapter 4

# Custom Reframing

## The Use of Analogies for a Change

**Bill O'Hanlon**

"You know my tendency to use analogies, and they work."
—*Milton Erickson* (Haley, 1985a, p. 120)

The work of Milton H. Erickson shows many examples whereby a new orientation and frame of reference is provided for clients to facilitate the resolution of therapeutic problems. This type of reorientation is termed "reframing" in family, brief, and Ericksonian therapies. This paper will discuss Erickson's use of analogies to provide frames that create a context for change in therapy.

## EXEMPLIFICATIONS

Below are some analogies that Erickson used that can give a sense of the therapeutic application of this technique.

Erickson used the following image to show the power of gradual change:

> Folklore is full of examples of that sort. You all know the camel and the Arab in the sandstorm.
>
> "Please, master," said the camel, "my nostrils are very tender. May I put them inside the tent? . . . Please, master, my eyes are very tender, may I put them inside the tent? . . . Please, master, my ears, my neck, my shoulders, are very tender. . . ."

This article was originally published in 1986 in Steve de Shazer's now defunct newsletter, *The Underground Railroad*.

It wasn't long before the Arab was outside of the tent, the camel was inside the tent and now the Arab was saying, "Please, camel, my nose is very tender . . . may I put it inside the tent"! (Rossi & Ryan, 1985, pp. 161–162)

The following analogy was used by Erickson with Harold, a young man who had little self-esteem but who was at least proud of being a good farm laborer:

A piece of farm machinery [is] unsuited for anything except manual labor. Then I pointed out that a tractor needed the right kind of care. It needed to be kept oiled, greased, cleaned and protected from the elements. It should be properly fueled with the right kind of oil and gas, . . . and the valves should be ground, the spark plugs cleaned, the radiator flushed out, if the tractor was to be a useful manual laborer. (Haley, 1973, p. 129)

This analogy was pivotal in getting Harold to start taking good care of himself.

In discussing the task of getting couples in marital therapy to accept new-found positive changes in their relationships, Erickson gave an example of an analogy that is particularly apt for married couples:

I tell them, "How do you really handle a brand-new set of dishes? Because you're worried about breaking some. . . . Handle with care because it's valuable. They're tremulous about handing that brand-new set of dishes, and they've had plenty of experience. Take your own reaction when you get a new pair of eyeglasses. You never put them down like that (tossing them down)." (Haley, 1985a, p. 86)

This is a good example of the multilevel communication Erickson often used. The analogy subtly provided associations and memories of being newly wedded.

The next analogy was for a man who constantly asked his wife whether she was enjoying sex during the sex act, which was interfering with both her and his pleasure:

If you went to see a show and it was a show you wanted to see very much, . . I want to go and I want to enjoy that show, and I'm going to enjoy it with absolute intensity. But I'll swear at anybody who says, "Isn't that good? Isn't that good?" Do you want me satisfied?

Let me alone. Let me enjoy it to the utmost. (Haley, 1985a, p. 121)

In talking with a couple who had differing sexual desires, Erickson might use this analogy to facilitate the negotiations:

Suppose Joe invites you to have dinner in a restaurant. You know what you want when you pick up the menu. Joe knows what he wants. There's one thing that's really going to decide it—the money in the wallet. A reality situation. So you both accommodate your wishes to the reality possibilities. Joe has so much capacity to love in the way that you want; you have so much capacity to love in the way that he wants. An intelligent attitude in a restaurant in which you can get a meal. (Haley, 1985a, p. 164)

For a couple who had just gone through the crisis of an affair, Erickson suggested this analogy:

I see no sense in a rehash. They had all the facts, so did I. The only question was, "Is this the termination of your relationship or is it the beginning of a new one?" If it's termination, period. If it's the beginning of the new, what do you want in this new relationship? In other words, are you moving out of the old house into a new one? If you're moving out, all right, let's not talk about scrubbing the kitchen, the basement, and so on. What do you want in the new house? Now that's a figure of speech, or an analogy, I use quite often. "So you're going to move out of the old house, and leave all of the old furniture there. What kind of view do you want from the new one? It ought to be in a different part of town, with a different view, a different house entirely, with different furniture, different arrangements. Now what do you want in the new house?" (Haley, 1985a, p. 164)

Here is a snippet of dialogue from a case that Erickson was treating in which the man was depressed. Erickson reframes the depression as not such a terrible thing, suggesting that it may even be valuable. The man, understandably, has a tough time initially accepting this new frame, but Erickson cites an everyday experience to facilitate its acceptance:

*Erickson*: And what are the particular values in each depression that you have? Because I suspect you have the mistaken idea that depression is wrong.

*Patient*: Well, when I'm depressed I'm, I think, less productive.

*E*: Mmmm hmmm. And when you get the rear wheels of your car caught in a ditch, and you can't go ahead in first gear or second gear, third gear, well, I think it's awfully nice to shift into reverse, and then into first, and reverse, and first, and reverse, and first, and rock yourself out of the ditch.

*P*: Mmmm hmmm.

*E*: And I think you ought to enjoy it and really rock yourself out of it. And not regret going into reverse. You've learned an awful lot about driving, handling a car. (Haley, 1985b, p. 306)

## SUMMARY

This paper has given an introduction to Erickson's use of analogies for reframing. Erickson used analogies and metaphors for other purposes as well in various aspects of hypnotic and nonhypnotic treatment, but those uses are to be the subject of future communications.

# REFERENCES

Haley, J. (1973). *Uncommon therapy: The psychiatric techniques of Milton H. Erickson, M.D.* New York: Norton.

Haley, J. (Ed.). (1985a). *Conversations with Milton H. Erickson, M.D.: Changing couples* (Vol. 2). New York: Norton/Triangle.

Haley, J. (Ed.). (1985b). *Conversations with Milton H. Erickson, M.D.: Changing individuals* (Vol. 1). New York: Triangle/Norton.

Rossi, E., & Ryan, M. (Eds.). (1985). *The seminars, workshops, and lectures of Milton H. Erickson: Life reframing in hypnosis* (Vol. II). New York: Irvington.

Chapter 5

# The Use of Metaphor for Treating Somatic Complaints in Psychotherapy

**Bill O'Hanlon**

Some years ago, while I was teaching a workshop on Ericksonian approaches, someone asked me what criteria I used to decide when and when not to use hypnosis. In answering that question, I thought back on my experience of doing psychotherapy and using hypnosis so far. What gradually emerged for me was a guideline, a rule of thumb, that I use for deciding whether or not to use hypnosis and metaphorical approaches in therapy.

## THE ACTION/EXPERIENCE DISTINCTION

This is a heuristic distinction for the therapist's use only. I divide presenting complaints into two groups: *action complaints*—those which involve behavior by the person who is seeking the therapist's help; and *experience complaints*—those which involve affective or somatic difficulties.

For *experience complaints*, I typically use an indirect approach (usually involving hypnotic and metaphorical methods), one that does not involve the person in doing some deliberate action. For *action complaints*, I typically use a more directive, action approach (O'Hanlon, 1982; O'Hanlon & Wilk, 1987) termed *pattern intervention*. Of course, this is only a general guideline, and one that I feel free to ignore in particular cases when I deem it appropriate.

What rationale do I have for using this guideline? One is that I discovered

---

This article originally appeared in the book, *Indirect Approaches to Therapy* (Aspen), edited by Steve de Shazer, and published in 1986.

that this was roughly how I divided my cases when I looked at the threads that ran through my use of hypnosis and metaphorical approaches. Another is that I treat actions as if they are voluntary and experience as if it is involuntary. If a client reports that he is having arguments with his wife, I would assume that he was doing some actions that he could deliberately alter to effect the arguments. That is an "action" complaint and I would typically try and solve it by getting the client (or clients) to do some different actions. If, however, a client reported that she got a rash every time she went to the supermarket, I would assume that she could not stop the rash by doing anything different (aside from avoiding the supermarket). Therefore, I would typically use indirect interventions that do not involve getting the person to deliberately do anything different.

## WHAT'S A META FOR?

As this chapter will concern the use of metaphor and analogy for treating somatic complaints, the use of metaphor in general will be discussed first.

### Transferring Know-How Across Contexts by Indirect Means

The etymological meaning of the word "metaphor" gives a clue to the function of metaphor in therapy. The word is derived from the (Greek) roots "pherein," which means "to carry" and "meta," "which means "over" or "beyond." The thesis of this chapter is that metaphor carries knowledge across contexts, beyond its initial context into a new one. The purpose of metaphor in therapy, it is suggested, is to transfer skills (or, more colloquially, know-how) across contexts from the context where the person developed or uses it to the context where it would solve the problem that brings the person to therapy.

### About Metaphor

Metaphor is a literary device which includes simile (something spoken of as "like" or "as" something else: e.g., "cheeks like roses") and analogy (a computer's disk drive is like a cross between a tape recorder and a record player). Any time one thing is likened to another, or spoken of as if it were another thing, metaphor is involved. For instance, "We seem to have reached a *dead end* in this discussion," and "Your smile is like the *summer sun*" are common metaphorical phrases. In fact, phrases such as these are so common we sometimes fail to recognize a metaphorical phrase as metaphor. These devices are used to *cast a different light* (another metaphor) on the subject. We know what a dead end is when we are traveling along a road, so we can understand the analogy when it is used to characterize a discussion. We have experienced a summer sun, so we can imagine that a smile likened to it would be bright. Metaphor helps us to use understandings or experiences that we already have to understand and make sense of new experiences.

## The Assumption of Competence

In this model, derived in part from the work of Milton H. Erickson (well known for his use of metaphor and other indirect approaches), there is an assumption that people already have the abilities, or know-how, to solve problems that have been troubling them. They have developed and mastered these abilities in certain contexts, but are not currently using this know-how in contexts of the problem. The task of therapy, then, is to transfer this know-how across contexts from the one(s) in which the client currently has it, to the context in which he or she doesn't. This is accomplished by using metaphor, primarily in the form of analogies and anecdotes.

## Experiential and Physiological Competence

To solve somatic problems, clients can use their previous physiological and experiential knowledge or competence. Almost everyone has blushed some time in his or her life. He or she has the ability to alter his or her blood flow. This ability can be extremely useful in eliminating or ameliorating a headache (as in the well-known biofeedback technique of getting people to warm their hands to eliminate a headache). Most of us have experienced easing into a hot bath and feeling our muscles relax automatically as the warmth of the water surrounded our bodies. We usually do not think of this as an ability, but it can be useful in helping people with chronic muscle tension or spastic colitis. Our bodies know how to relax our muscles, to alter blood flow and body temperature, to fight and eliminate infections, and to alter our body chemistry—just to name a few. We have physiological know-how, but we do not always use it where and when we need it.

In addition to physical competence, we all have a variety of experiential abilities and know-how. These abilities mainly involve how we interpret what we perceive and where we direct or focus our attention. Many people have had the experience of being absorbed in a good book and not hearing someone who is calling their name. That ability, called *negative hallucination* in hypnosis circles, is a good method of pain control. Some who have lived in colder climates might have experienced the unusual sensation of putting cold hands under running water and not being able to tell whether the water is hot or cold. This ambiguity of sensations is another useful resource for effecting pain control.

## SOLVING SOMATIC PROBLEMS

To illustrate the use of analogies and anecdotes to solve problems, some case examples and interventions will be provided. The first several cases will be taken from the work of Milton Erickson and the rest will be from the author's clinical work.

## Case A—Erickson's Treatment of a Husband With Phantom Limb Pain and his Wife With Tinnitus

A man sought Erickson's help for persistent pain in a leg that had been removed. In addition, his wife reported ringing in her ears (tinnitus). Erickson began the session by telling the couple about a time when he was traveling around during his college days and he slept the night in a boiler factory. As he slept during the night, he learned to blot out the sounds in the factory. By morning, he was able to hear the workers conversing in a normal conversational tone. The workers were surprised to learn of Erickson's adjustment as it had taken them much longer to master this ability. Erickson related that he knew how fast the body could learn. Next he told about seeing a television special the night before about nomadic tribesmen in Iran who wore layers of clothing in the hot desert sun, but seemed very comfortable. During the session he told a number of stories illustrating the ability that people have to become habituated to any constant stimulus so that they could tune it out after awhile. This is the know-how that could solve both problems.

## Case B—Erickson's Treatment of a Boy With Enuresis

Erickson, in his treatment of a boy who wet his bed, used analogies to access abilities the youth had developed in other contexts for him to use to solve his bedwetting. He found out that the boy played baseball and proceeded to launch into a long dissertation about the fine muscle control that was necessary to be a good baseball player. The outfielder must open his glove at just the right time, and clamp down at just the right time. To throw the ball to the infield, he must release the ball at just the right time. If he releases the ball too early or too late it will cause the ball to go where he does not want it to go. Next Erickson told the boy about his digestive tract and how the food goes into a chamber where muscles at either end close down for the proper amount of time, relaxing and releasing the food when it is time to move it to another chamber. He talked to the boy about the focusing of the eye, and the muscles in the eye that are involved in archery. All these analogies had a common theme of automatic muscle of control, just what the boy needed to use to stop wetting the bed.

## Case C—Treatment of a Case of Warts

A woman sought therapy from the author for persistent warts, which were mainly located on her hands. She had been to a dermatologist for 18 months on a regular basis to have the warts removed by freezing. Despite this treatment, the woman suffered painful aftereffects, and the warts kept returning. The woman sought hypnosis, as she had heard that it could cure warts. After helping her into trance, I told her about irrigation ditches used in Arizona to water the plants and how pipes were used to irrigate each crop row. When the pipe was removed from the row, the hot desert sun would wilt the weeds, which were more fragile than the crops. In a similar way, I told her, her body knew how to regulate the blood flow and withdraw nutrients from the warts, but to still keep her skin alive. I gave her the task assignment of soaking her feet in the hottest water she could stand for fifteen minutes followed by soaking them in the coldest water she could stand for another fifteen minutes. Several other analogies were offered, like how she blushed automatically, and how the blood went to her digestive area after she ate a meal. All these were to transfer her ability to alter her blood flow and thereby eliminate the warts. Three sessions of this type of treatment were sufficient to clear up the warts and regular follow-up of several years has indicated no recurrence.

## Case D—Treatment of Asthma

A woman was referred to the author for treatment of a "pregnancy phobia." In doing the assessment, it was discovered that the woman had previously been pregnant and had almost died several times during and after the pregnancy due to asthma and bronchitis. She was late for her expected menstrual bleeding and had become quite anxious, with accompanying difficulty in breathing. I told her that I did not think she had a phobia at all, but a quite realistic fear, and I suggested that we use hypnosis to see if we could help her to "breathe easier." After inducing trance, I reminded her that she had probably experienced automatic muscle relaxation when in a hot bathtub. I suggested a complete body dissociation, as well as hand levitation (both involving automatic muscle control). I recalled a well-known commercial on television for a breathing medication that showed "blocked bronchial tubes" opening up and the muscles around the bronchi relaxing. I told her that her body had previously ended bronchitis and asthma attacks and that it knew from that and other experiences how to relax her bronchial muscles. The woman was seen several times and experienced significant relief. She had found out that she was not pregnant soon after treatment started. After she experienced such improvement through treatment, however, she and her husband decided to have the other child they had wanted. She came in irregularly through her pregnancy (for "booster shots") and experienced none of the previous breathing difficulties.

## Case E—Treatment of a Cluster Headache

I told a man who had sought my help that I had never heard of cluster headaches, though I had treated many people with migraines. He told me that cluster headaches are like migraines, except they come in groups. A phase might last days, weeks, or months, with one severe headache following another. One never knew how long they would last. "They call 'em .45 caliber headaches," he said with a finger to his temple, "cause when you have one you want to blow your head off." After doing a trance induction (he was never convinced that he was in fact in trance throughout our work—two sessions), I used the analogy of being so absorbed in a movie or a good book that one did not notice that one had to urinate (to suggest dissociation or negative hallucination). He might have experienced that particular ambiguity of sensations that accompanied cold hands put under running water; one could not really tell if the water was hot or cold (to suggest reinterpretation of the sensations). I talked about that peculiar sensation (or rather lack of sensation) when one's leg falls asleep (to suggest anesthesia). I reminded him that he had probably waited for some anticipated event, like the clock in the schoolroom to show that it was time to go home, or a check to arrive in the mail, and experienced time slowing down and stretching out subjectively. I suggested that he slow down and stretch out the times when he felt good and comfortable. He had all these abilities and more, I said, and I didn't know which one or ones he would use. Neither of us knew how quickly he could get relief or whether that relief would be total or only partial. (These last suggestions are examples of another type of indirect intervention, using presupposition or implication to create an expectation of success.) Follow-up indicated that he experienced the beginnings of a headache the day after the second session, which quickly dissipated. No further recurrence of the headaches were reported. A year later, he sent me a coworker who also suffered from cluster headaches.

## HOW TO GENERATE METAPHORS FOR TREATMENT

The first step in generating metaphors for treatment of somatic problems is to think of possible solutions that could happen physiologically or psychologically. There is no focus here on explanations, no search for psychological or interpersonal causes or functions. What type of physiological change or shift in focus of attention would solve the problem and help the person to feel better? It might be that they would be distracted from feelings of discomfort (a shift in focus of attention). It might be that their body would change the blood flow so that the pressure in their head was relieved and they no longer had a headache (a physiological change). It could be that they "develop calluses" for their pain so that they no longer attend to it (again, a shift in focus of attention). They might relax their muscles involuntarily to be able to breathe easier or rid themselves of a spastic colon (a physiological change).

The next step is to think of a common everyday experience that involves the physiological change or shift in focus of attention. If the goal was to change the blood flow so that more blood would flow into the person's hand (for the treatment of Reynaud's disease or migraine headaches, for example), one could use analogies like having one's hands in warm water, holding them up to a fire, wearing mittens into a warm building in the winter, or holding your date's hand and getting sweaty.

The third step is to connect the analogous experience or understanding to the actual problem context. Sometimes this is done by implication, merely using the analogy while doing therapy or hypnosis for the somatic complaint may be enough to connect the two. Other times, an explicit connection can be made, giving a punchline, such as Erickson's (Erickson & Rossi, 1979) Case A above, when he said,

> What people don't know, is that they can lose that pain and they don't know that they can lose that ringing in their ears. . . . All of us grow up believing that when you have pain, you must pay attention to it. And believing when you have ringing of the ears that you must keep on hearing it. (p. 105)

## SUMMARY

A model for using metaphor (mainly analogy and anecdote) to solve somatic problems has been detailed, along with case examples (from the work of Milton H. Erickson and the author) to illustrate its use. The main focus of this model is on transferring abilities, competence, and know-how from contexts in which the person has experience and mastery to the somatic problem context. The types of know-how that are mainly used to solve somatic problems involve changes in physiological processes and shifts in focus of attention.

## REFERENCES

Erickson, M. H., & Rossi, E. L. (1979). *Hypnotherapy: An exploratory casebook.* New York: Irvington.

O'Hanlon, B. (1982). Strategic pattern intervention: An integration of individual and family systems therapies based on the work of Milton H. Erickson, M.D. *The Journal of Strategic and Systemic Therapies, 1,* 26–33.

O'Hanlon, B., & Wilk, J. (1987). *Shifting contexts: The generation of effective psychotherapy.* New York: Guilford.

# Chapter 6

# The Tape Recorder Cure

**Bill O'Hanlon and Jeffrey Rifkin**

One of the world's leading therapists, American advice columnist Ann Landers, published a letter some time ago in her column that serves as a perfect introduction to this method.

> Dear Ann Landers,
> This letter is for wives whose husbands snore. When I complained to "Gus" about his snoring, he always denied it. Then one night I said, "I'm going to tape you so you can hear for yourself." I set up the recorder and told him to go to sleep and snore to his heart's content. The joke was on me. He was quiet as a mouse, and what's more, he didn't snore for three years after that. Then he started again, but it was soft and dignified, a snore that wouldn't wake a fly. It never got loud like before. I lost Gus last winter. How I wish I had taped him when he snored like an elk. It would be music to my ears. God bless his memory.—San Jose
> (*Omaha World Herald*, December 13, 1987)

Some years ago, a friend of Bill's told him about a conflict she had had with her daughter. Jane was a single parent who was struggling to raise two children, aged 6 and 9, alone. She was very close to the 9-year-old, but they had recently developed a pattern of arguing in the morning. Jane had to get the kids ready for school and get herself to work by 9:00 a.m. The 9-year-old, Susan, had started to oversleep, go back to sleep when awakened, dawdle over dressing and breakfast, and in general make the mother late most mornings, putting her job in jeopardy. Jane would nag Susan from the moment she woke her up and Susan would defend herself until they escalated into screaming at each other every morning. They both felt ashamed about the way they talked to each other in the mornings, but

---

This article was coauthored with Jeffrey Rifkin and was originally published in the international journal, *Family Therapy Case Studies*, in 1989.

were at a loss as to how to prevent it. Finally, in desperation, over the dinner table one night when they were discussing their morning problems and the rift it was causing between them, Jane came up with an idea. They would record their morning interactions on an audio cassette recorder and listen back to it at night for clues as to how to change it. The next morning, Jane put her plan into action. As Jane and Susan listened to the tape over dinner that night, they were both so shocked and ashamed at how they screamed at each other that the problem never again occurred.

This paper offers a simple intervention: introducing an audio tape recorder into the problem or symptom context to alter or eliminate the symptom. Several cases are described to illustrate the use and limitations of this technique. Some discussion on why this intervention works is offered.

## DEMON SEED

Anna appeared in Bill's office and said that she needed some help because she hated her daughter. As Anna described her, the girl sounded like a demon. There were two other children with whom Anna got along very well, one younger than the "problem child" and one older. The girl's father saw nothing wrong with the girl. Anna, however, reported that when Father wasn't home the girl would give her the most hateful looks and fight her on every little thing. She had come to hate the girl and felt very guilty about it. She wanted to know if Bill thought he could do anything to help change her feelings about the girl or to reform the girl. She was reluctant to bring the girl in to see Bill because both her husband and the girl thought there was no problem. Remembering his friend and how she had resolved her conflict with her daughter, Bill suggested Anna record the daughter on an audio tape recorder, especially during their struggles in the morning, when she was trying to get the children off to school and Father was not around. Due to the Christmas season, a session was scheduled one month later. Anna was to bring the tape for Bill to review so he could give her some consultation.

When she returned a month later, Anna had very little of interest on the tape. She said that she had been so busy with the Christmas activities for a few weeks that she had not had a chance to buy any blank tapes to make the recording. Finally, one day when her daughter was being particularly hateful, she decided that she would just go ahead and record over an old tape. When she got out the tape recorder and turned it on, the daughter noticed it and asked what it was for. When her mother explained that it was for a counselor she was seeing, the daughter refused to talk. Anna was a bit frustrated at first, but then recognized the blessing in disguise. She started turning on the tape recorder every time the daughter was giving her trouble and the trouble immediately ceased. Bill expressed his amusement at the situation, but said he would need a tape of the daughter being hateful if he were going to be a consultant to her.

Another session was scheduled for the next month. Of course, Anna again appeared with an uninteresting tape. She guiltily confessed that she had occasionally turned on the tape recorder even when she had already run out of blank tape, just to stop her daughter from acting up. The month had been trouble-free and she and her daughter were starting to get closer. After a brief discussion, she was sent on her way with solemn instructions to get Bill something juicy on the next month's tape.

When she appeared with no juicy material on the next month's tape, Bill discussed the futility of their efforts and both he and Anna agreed that the situation had improved so much that further consultation was unnecessary. Anna said that she had realized during the past month that she may have been part of the problem, because in listening to the tapes she made, she noticed that she always spoke more considerately to her daughter when the tape recorder was on since she knew Bill would be listening to it. Bill agreed that it usually takes two to tango, but dismissed all that as irrelevant speculation now that the problem was gone.

Some years later, Bill and Jeff were discussing their shared interest in the treatment of bulimia and Jeff described the following case.

## THE BULIMIC'S GREATEST HITS

Barbara was a 20-year-old, single woman who was living at home with her mother and stepfather who was an alcoholic. Barbara's mother was seen by Jeff for depression, which was the result of "being in a rotten marriage for the second time." Some time after the resolution of the depression, Barbara's mother referred Barbara for treatment of her three-year difficulty with bulimia.

Barbara presented herself as an extremely attractive, coy woman who felt very much out of control with food. She regularly (daily) binged at lunch as well as dinner and induced vomiting when she could no longer put any more food in her stomach. One of the key factors in her bulimic pattern was after confessing her "sins" to her family members and friends, they would regularly chastise her and plead with her to refrain from continuing her "self-destructive behavior." Jeff intervened by instructing her to continue the binge-and-purge pattern with one difference. Whenever she induced vomiting, she was to record it on her audio tape machine and bring the tape to the next session so that therapist and client could review it. Jeff reframed her purging as "giving your stomach an opportunity to refuse discomfort" and said he wanted to be sure she was "throwing up the right way." Upon hearing this, Barbara stated she was not interested in recording "The Bulimic's Greatest Hits" and she would rather not throw up at all. Jeff said that that was her prerogative but that whenever she threw up she was to follow the prescription. Barbara agreed, and she has neither binged nor purged since (some four months at the time this was written).

Recognizing the similarities in the two cases, we decided to write a joint paper on the intervention. What follows are two more case examples in which the intervention was helpful in the therapy, but did not have the dramatic effect it did in the above two cases.

## UP IN SMOKE

Since the tape recorder intervention had worked so well for Jeff with Barbara, he decided to use it again with similar clients. Laura was a 19-year-old woman who, previous to her six-month history of bulimia, used to model. She was a very attractive woman who, like Barbara, placed a great deal of importance on the opinions of others, especially with regard to her appearance. The "Bulimic's Greatest Hits" intervention was used, yet unlike Barbara, Laura refused to comply with the prescription. After much discussion about her refusal to follow the directive, Jeff and Laura agreed on another intervention that worked just as well. A portion of their conversation is presented:

*Laura*: I just don't want to do it.

*Jeff*: What would happen if you did?

*Laura*: I guess I wouldn't want to binge and vomit again.

*Jeff*: What's wrong with that?

*Laura*: I don't know, but maybe my mother and I won't have much to talk about if I'm not bulimic.

*Jeff*: And if not, what else could you talk about?

*Laura*: Well, I'm worried about the fact that she smokes three packs of cigarettes a day and, according to her doctor, she's going to get emphysema.

Utilizing Laura's concern for her mother and Mom's concern for Laura, Jeff was able to assure Laura that since she's able to control her eating and vomiting (she had agreed that she wouldn't want to binge and vomit again if she taped the vomiting), he would use hypnosis to assist her mother in controlling her addiction to cigarettes. Once Laura agreed to stay abstinent if her mother agreed to stop smoking, Jeff got the same commitment from her mother. At the time of writing, Laura had been abstinent for six weeks (a relatively long time for her) and felt confident about her continued success. She agreed to tape a vomiting episode if she ever relapses, but has stated: "There's no way I'll ever do that again." This case underlines the importance of maintaining flexibility in the face of a client's objections. Solutions are negotiable, and it makes little sense to prescribe an intervention that a client will not comply with, unless of course you paradoxically intend them to defy the intervention.

## NEW ASSOCIATIONS

Susan was a 28-year-old aerobics instructor and a recovering alcoholic (she has been sober for the past seven years). She had binged and purged for the past 12 years. Initial interventions included scheduling the bulimia, which helped Susan develop a greater sense of control and reduced her episodes from three times a day, seven days a week, to one time per day, three times a week. From this point on, Susan's "symptoms" were gradually reduced to one episode a month, yet Susan grew impatient with her progress. Susan was offered the taping intervention with the choice of bringing in the tape for us to listen to, or listening to it at home. Inasmuch as Susan often binged and vomited in restaurants as well as at home, she was instructed to bring her tape recorder with her whenever she went out. As other clients before her have, Susan stated: "That's great! I'll never throw up again." Susan was wrong in her prediction and did binge and purge during Thanksgiving dinner (as do most of us, but for her it was a problem). She did, however, tape the episode and was amazed to discover how violent her vomiting was. Though the intervention did not prevent Susan from bingeing and vomiting during Thanksgiving, the intervention did interrupt her dissociative process by having her tape and listen to the tape. Now whenever Susan feels like bingeing, she listens to her tape. She had been abstinent for a month at the time this was written.

Those who are familiar with benevolent ordeals (Haley, 1963, 1973, 1984) and symptom-contingent tasks (O'Hanlon, 1987; O'Hanlon & Weiner-Davis, 1989; O'Hanlon & Wilk, 1987) understand how this intervention could be viewed as interrupting symptomatic patterns. Clients are given tasks that they are to do in conjunction with the performance of their symptoms. These tasks are so burdensome or abhorrent that clients would rather avoid the symptom than to do the task. We also think that this intervention recontextualizes the "symptom." Clients are able to experience their same old symptom in a new context, which may change the significance of it for them (O'Hanlon & Wilk, 1987; Rifkin, 1986). We offer these as only our explanations, knowing that others looking through different theoretical lenses would have entirely different explanations for the effectiveness of this intervention. We look forward to hearing how other clinicians fare with this intervention.

## REFERENCES

Haley, J. (1963). *Strategies of psychotherapy*. New York: Grune and Stratton.

Haley, J. (1973). *Uncommon Therapy: The psychiatric techniques of Milton H. Erickson, M.D.* New York: Norton.

Haley, J. (1984). *Ordeal therapy: Unusual ways to change behavior.* San Francisco: Jossey-Bass.

O'Hanlon, W. H. (1987). *Taproots: Underlying principles of Milton Erickson's therapy and hypnosis.* New York: Norton.

O'Hanlon, W. H., & Weiner-Davis, M. (1989). *In search of solutions: A new direction in psychotherapy.* New York: Norton.

O'Hanlon, B., & Wilk, J. (1987). *Shifting contexts: The generation of effective psychotherapy.* New York: Guilford.

Rifkin, J. (1986). *Unity and beliefs: A treatment for bulimia.* Unpublished doctoral dissertation. LaSierra University, Riverside, CA.

Chapter 7

# Contextual Pattern Intervention

## Integrating Individual and Interactional Approaches to the Treatment of Bulimia and Bingeing

**Bill O'Hanlon**

Once you break through rigid, fixed patterns of behavior patients are forced to pick up the pieces to put them together; and they are forced to function in a totally different way.

—Milton H. Erickson

Contextual pattern intervention is a method of resolving presenting complaints in therapy by altering patterns of action and interaction involved with and surrounding these complaints. It seeks to integrate individual and interactional approaches through the unifying notion of altering "symptom"[1] contexts. The thesis of this approach is that by altering the contextual patterns (regularities and redundancies) involved in or surrounding the bulimic or bingeing behavior, the presenting complaint can be successfully resolved in a brief manner.

---

[1]"Symptom" is used in this context as a shorthand term for undesired behavior and/or experience (the presenting complaint) and not as the observable tip of an "underlying problem."

This is an unfinished, unpublished manuscript (circa 1986) that was completed for this book. Many of the ideas represented here later appeared in Bill's book, *Taproots: Underlying Principles of Milton Erickson's Therapy and Hypnosis* (Norton, 1987).

## PATTERNING IN CONTEXTS

This model holds that "symptoms" (presenting complaints) occur in contexts and are dependent for their continuation on those contexts. Contexts are in turn maintained by and contain patterned aspects. Patterns are defined as regularities or recurring sequences or aspects of a situation. The patterns that are the focus of this model are observable, specifiable patterns. These are patterns of action, interaction, and context (including elements of time and space).

Automatic patterns seem to be a necessary and desirable aspect of contexts. Some therapists and therapies seem to view any automatic invariant patterns as "unhealthy" and strive to abolish any automaticity in the client's behavior or in their family interactions. In this approach, however, patterns are not viewed as necessarily symptom producing and at times are quite useful. They help people organize experience, perceptions, and behavior, and improve efficiency in behavior. For therapy purposes, it is important to alter automatic patterns only when they contain or accompany undesired experiences or behaviors (symptoms).

## OBTAINING A SPECIFIED PRESENTING COMPLAINT

In order to intervene in symptom contexts, it is helpful to obtain a sensory-based description of the symptom pattern. This description is like a "video description" (O'Hanlon & Wilk, 1987), in that it ideally should contain only those aspects verifiable with the senses (especially the eyes and the ears). That means that the description must be free of unverifiable hypotheses and unverified explanations. How, when, where, with whom, and under what circumstances does the person binge eat? What times of the day would the person never binge? Always binge? Do they always binge at home? In which room in the house do they binge? Do they always binge when alone or do they binge with other people around? What foods would they usually eat on a binge and what foods would they never or rarely eat? Do they binge on salads? And so on.

The therapist's task here is to discover the range beyond which the pattern never occurs or within which it always occurs. Each client will be different, but with each client a range and regularity in one or more aspects of the bingeing or purging or both can be delineated and discovered. The therapist is to gather only the facts of the matter, leaving out the hypotheses and speculations, and then abstract a descriptive pattern from the data.

In addition, obtaining a specified presenting complaint entails asking for specific instances rather than generalities. While the therapist will be searching for regularities in the context (invariant patterns of action and interaction involving and surrounding the symptom), he or she should not accept the client's generalizations and ideas about the patterns, but should instead ask for specific "video" descriptions of specific instances of symptom occurrence and abstract a pattern from this data (O'Hanlon & Wilk, 1987).

## PATTERN INTERVENTION

The process of pattern intervention consists of gathering sensory-based information (observation or description) about the symptom and then altering any part of the pattern involved with and surrounding that symptom.

Once the therapist has gathered specific sensory-based information on the pattern and the range of the pattern, he or she begins (in conjunction with the client) altering the patterns. Specific therapists will have specific stylistic preferences and skills available. The author's bias is usually to use directive task assignments to accomplish the pattern intervention.

### How and Where to Intervene in Symptom Contexts

**Symptom Pattern Intervention.**    Frequently the easiest and most straightforward way to intervene in a context containing a symptom is to alter the pattern of the symptom itself. The therapist arranges for the client(s) to alter the performance of the symptom in some small or insignificant way. The work of Milton Erickson contains many examples of this type of contextual intervention (Haley, 1973, 1984; Rossi, 1980). Erickson might direct a compulsive hand washer to change the brand of soap he uses to wash his hands. Or, he might get a person who smokes to put her cigarettes in the attic and her matches in the basement. He told a thumb sucker to suck her thumb for a set period of time every day. He directed a couple who argued about who was to drive home after a party (at which they'd both had a few drinks) that one was to drive from the party to one block before home; then they were to stop the car, switch places, and the other was to drive the rest of the way home.

It seems as though an alteration of the performance of the symptom often changes the patterns around it and thereby alters the context. Often with this alteration of the context, the symptom (either gradually or abruptly) disappears. Again, the therapist may accomplish this alteration directly or indirectly, with authority, or in a cooperative venture with the client.

The classes of interventions that are used in this realm can be summarized in the list below:

1) Change the frequency of the performance of the symptom.
2) Change the rate of performance of the symptom.
3) Change the duration of the performance of the symptom.
4) Change the location of the performance of the symptom.
5) Add (at least) one new element to the symptom pattern.
6) Change the sequence of elements/events in the symptom pattern.
7) Break the symptom pattern into smaller pieces or elements.
8) Link the symptom performance to the performance of some burdensome activity.

## PERSONAL AND INTERPERSONAL PATTERN INTERVENTIONS

When direct pattern intervention with the symptom does not work or would be inadvisable, one might work to alter the personal or interpersonal patterns surrounding or accompanying the symptom (O'Hanlon, 1982). Individual and interpersonal approaches are often viewed as being at odds with one another. One is either a "systemic" therapist or an "individual, linear" therapist. This approach, however, finds no conflict between the two. The unifying concept of pattern is used to bridge the (apparent) gap. What the two approaches have in common is the discovery and alteration of patterns of action surrounding the symptom. If causal, functional, and other explanatory hypotheses are avoided, no conflict need arise. How and why the patterns came to be, what function or meaning they have, and other such speculations are viewed as irrelevant and distracting to the main task, that of discerning the patterns of action and interaction surrounding the symptom and altering them.

### Personal Pattern Intervention

Personal pattern intervention consists of altering patterns that do not directly involve the performance of the symptom. For example, a person who binges on food may avoid going out with friends on the days when she has been bingeing. Another "binger" might never get dressed on the days on which she binges. Although not directly involved in the bingeing, altering these accompanying regular patterns might bring about an alteration in the symptom context that would lead to the resolution of the presenting complaint. The therapist should ask for descriptions of actions not directly involved in the symptom performance and alter those that seem to be regular accompaniments to the symptom.

### Interpersonal Pattern Intervention

Of course, many family therapy interventions would be included. The field here is limited to those interventions that alter (by whatever means) observable patterns of interactions (verbal and nonverbal) not directly involving the performance of the symptom. Things such as who is around when the symptom is performed and what others (those not directly involved in the performance) say or do about the symptom with the person or persons directly involved are included in this category. In this approach, there is no particular "right" or "healthy" pattern of interaction. The task is to discover and change current patterns of interaction. In some interactional approaches, evaluative criteria are applied to interaction (e.g., "too enmeshed," "triangulation," "poor communication," "disqualification of other family members," and so on). These patterns are viewed as inherently undesirable and symptom producing. This model avoids the evaluative approach and does not consider the question of cause, functions, or other speculative matters. This keeps the approach simple and checkable. Just find any regular pattern of interaction surrounding the symptom and alter that. The symptom will either disappear or it will not. If the first intervention doesn't lead to successful results, the therapist and client(s) can experiment until a successful pattern intervention is found.

## CASE EXAMPLES

**Case A.**   A woman sought therapy from the author to stop bingeing on food. She was given the assignment to put on her favorite shoes before she binged. In addition, she was to eat one of her "binge" foods (ones which she ate only when on a binge and never in front of anyone else) in front of her father. After she ceased bingeing, she was instructed to throw the shoes away. She asked if she could just give them to the Salvation Army, but was firmly told she must throw them away.

**Case B.**   A "bulimic" was told to step into the bathtub and wash her feet after bingeing and before vomiting.

**Case C.**   A client was instructed that she could binge all she wanted, as long as she did so while naked and sitting or standing in front of a mirror.

**Case D.**   A bulimic agreed that when she got the impulse to binge, she would walk five times around the block before doing so.

**Case E.**   A binger was told that she could binge all she wanted, provided she ate all her food with Tabasco sauce on it.

**Case F.**   A binger who reported that she hated housework agreed to do an hour's worth of housework if she binged. During the assessment, we discovered that she usually binged after an argument with her husband. Her husband enjoyed arguing (or "having a good debate," as he called it), while she did not and was in fact quite upset by it. She was first instructed to time the debates, then spend that amount of time the next night doing something he found objectionable and she found pleasurable but that wasn't really bad. She decided to spend time either alone or with her girlfriends, both activities of which he disapproved. She reported that she never had to do the housework, as the thought was enough to keep her from ever bingeing.

**Case G.**   A bulimic who binged in her pajamas was instructed to take a shower, dress up for the day, fix her hair, put on her makeup, and then she could binge if she still wanted to.

## SUMMARY

What has been presented here is a model for intervening in contexts that contain symptoms by altering the symptom performance patterns or the personal and interpersonal patterns surrounding the symptom. Contextual interventions provide a unifying concept for the seemingly disparate individual and interactional approaches. This model describes interventions that might be characterized as "paradoxical," but here they are viewed as merely another variety of pattern intervention.

The steps to using this approach are (1) gather specific descriptive or observational data regarding the performance of the symptom and the patterns of action and interaction surrounding the symptom, and (2) arrange for the symptom performance patterns or the patterns of action and interaction surrounding the symptom to be altered in such a way that the context no longer contains the undesired experience or behavior (symptom). The model posits no need for causal, functional, or other explanatory hypotheses or diagnosis.

## REFERENCES

Haley, J. (1973). *Uncommon therapy: The psychiatric techniques of Milton H. Erickson, M.D.* New York: Norton.

Haley, J. (1984). *Ordeal therapy: Unusual ways to change behavior*. San Francisco: Jossey-Bass.

O'Hanlon, B. (1982). Strategic pattern intervention: An integration of individual and family systems therapies based on the work of Milton H. Erickson, M.D. *The Journal of Strategic and Systemic Therapies, 1*, 26–33.

O'Hanlon, B., & Wilk, J. (1987). *Shifting contexts: The generation of effective psychotherapy*. New York: Guilford.

Rossi, E. L. (1980). *The collected papers of Milton H. Erickson on hypnosis* (4 volumes). New York: Irvington.

# Chapter 8

# Not Strategic, Not Systemic: Still Clueless After All These Years

**Bill O'Hanlon**

I sometimes tell people the story of how I got my first papers published. "I slept with the editor of the journal." Before they have time to react, I quickly assure them that there was nothing improper involved, "*I* happened to be the editor of the journal." Ten years ago, Don Efron invited me to be the first guest editor of *Journal of Strategic and Systemic Therapies* (*JSST*) and I slipped two of my papers into that issue. I do not think they were great papers, but others over the years have told me they enjoyed them, so I guess they weren't quite as awful as I thought.

Don has invited some early *JSST* authors to reflect on the changes in themselves, their viewpoints, and the field of strategic/systemic therapy in the ensuing years. So here's my offering.

## FROM CLEVER TO CLUELESS: NOT STRATEGIC, NOT SYSTEMIC

The first and most radical change is that I no longer think of what I do as strategic or systemic. That does not mean that I don't think I fit in with *JSST* anymore—I think the field has changed.

Strategic therapy has several aspects to it. One is Haley's classic definition that a therapy can be called strategic if the therapist defines the direction and takes charge of making things happen in the therapy. The other connotation that

This was an invited paper for the Tenth Anniversary issue of the *Journal of Strategic and Systemic Therapies* (now the *Journal of Systemic Therapies*). The editor, Don Efron, asked early contributors to the journal to revisit ideas they held 10 years earlier. This was Bill's response.

strategic therapy has, or at least had when I was doing it, is that of being tricky and manipulative (you cannot not be manipulative, Bandler and Grinder and the MRI folks would remind us again and again). There was a sense that since everything is constructed, deceit in the name of change was okay, since considerations of truth do not matter in a constructed world.

On the first count, I would say that my sense of what I am responsible for in therapy has shifted a bit. I used to come into therapy with many clever ideas. I was a pretty good strategic therapist. These days I don't have many clever ideas anymore, but I trust that my clients and I will come up with many ideas in the course of our conversation. Steve de Shazer (1985) wrote a book called *Clues: Investigating Solutions in Brief Therapy.* I've been thinking of writing a book called *Clueless: On the Value of Not Knowing in Brief Therapy.* I certainly have a sense of direction, toward empowering clients in the present and the future, but I let my clients lead me as well, and even change my direction at times.

On the second count, the thing that always disturbed me about strategic approaches was how therapists using these approaches played fast and loose with the facts and the truth. Just because social meanings are constructed does not mean that there is no truth or facts. If a strategic thief stole your car, you wouldn't want them to get away with it because they could show that stealing is just a social construction. I complained about this trickiness and deceit once to John Weakland, the MRI brief therapist. He thought for a moment, tamped down his pipe and said, "Bill, sometimes you're so forthright, I think you're being tricky!" When all is said and done, though, I think clients can tell when the therapist is being deceitful and sometimes they go along because they recognize the dramatic license that a therapist needs in order to get a point across, but at other times I think deceit damages the trusting relationship between therapist and client. In any case, I never felt comfortable being deceitful and I think there are less tricky ways to help clients change.

In the matter of systemic therapy, I no longer buy a central premise of most systemic approaches—that symptoms derive from familial/social processes and serve an interpersonal function. These beliefs are causal hypotheses that distract from the main purpose of therapy—to help people change what they came in to change. I've argued this one out with Jay Haley, who thinks, I suspect, that I am deluding myself when I eschew explanations in therapy. He argues that one must have an explanation to guide treatment, albeit a simple one. I argue that explanations are not necessary. On this, I think Haley differs from Erickson, who often worked without formal or consistent explanations. In the *Conversations* books, Haley is often heard trying to get Erickson to see that symptoms serve an interpersonal function. Erickson, who first proposed this interpersonal function idea in the mid-1940s, at the first Macy conference that led to the development of cybernetics, chides Haley and suggests that symptoms may be merely habits.

I think strategic and systemic theories and methods were important steps in the development of an emerging approach to therapy that could be called conversational and collaborative. That emerging approach has no name yet.

## THE FOURTH WAVE

I was talking to Tapi Ahola, a therapist friend from Finland, about the emergence of this new approach. He nodded in agreement and said, "Oh, yes, the Fourth Wave." When I looked confused, he explained, "The First Wave was pathology and therapist-explanation driven. The Second Wave was problem focused. The Third Wave was solution oriented. The Fourth Wave is what is coming out of the solution-oriented approaches. There's no clear name for it yet."

I was involved in organizing a conference of some of these Fourth Wavers in Tulsa, Oklahoma, in late June 1991. The key words for this new approach are collaboration, respect, coconstructing, stories, narrative theory, conversation, empowering, resources, strengths, and possibilities.

## HERETIC OF THE FIRST CHURCH OF ERICKSONIANISM

In that issue that I guest edited for *JSST*, the theme was Ericksonian approaches. I have taught Ericksonian workshops and methods for many years and have written two books about Erickson's work. I was never a good guru follower, however, and was always irreverent about Erickson and the Ericksonian movement. Lately that has gotten me in trouble.

I read a book called *The February Man: Evolving Consciousness and Identity in Hypnotherapy* some years ago (Erickson & Rossi, 1989). I was excited to read it, as it was one of the few complete case transcripts of Erickson's therapy that we have. Furthermore, this case was done in the 1940s, when we have even fewer records of what Erickson actually did with patients, and the case involved one of Erickson's most innovative techniques, hypnotic reparenting, to treat childhood trauma. When I read it, however, I was appalled. Here was what I considered the worst side of Erickson. A nurse had been invited to attend a hypnosis demonstration and was, in my view, manipulated in a disrespectful way into being Erickson's patient. She was then given amnesia for the experience. I was so disgusted that I wrote a scathing review, which Rich Simon agreed to publish in the *Family Therapy Networker*. I mentioned the review to Jeff Zeig, the President of the Erickson Foundation, and Steve Gilligan, prominent Ericksonian workshop presenter, while we were having dinner at one of the Erickson conferences. They had both liked the book but seemed accepting of my different opinion.

After he returned home, Gilligan called and asked me if I thought Rich Simon would let him do a counterreview, expressing why he liked the book and how he thought I misread it. I encouraged Gilligan to contact Rich. He did and the counterreview was subsequently published. I was excited to be part of the opening of the Ericksonian field to good, healthy criticism and debate. Then the feces hit the fan. A letter was distributed among various Erickson family members, board members, and Ericksonian trainers deriding my review and suggesting that perhaps I was no longer a patriotic Ericksonian and therefore perhaps should not be invited back to the Erickson Foundation seminars and conferences.

The next, and final, straw for my official involvement in the Erickson movement came after I was interviewed by Michael Yapko for the *Erickson Foundation Newsletter*. In the course of the interview, Yapko asked me about some of my recent criticisms of the Ericksonian field and I answered that I had several. One was that the field had gurufied Erickson a bit much, but I thought this was diminishing and was happy about it. Fewer people were wearing purple or acting as if they were paralyzed. My criticisms of Erickson, after studying his work in depth for 15 years, were threefold: (1) he sometimes manipulated people into treatment without their clear request for it (as in the *February Man* book); (2) he seemed to give up on couples too easily. A reading of Haley's three *Conversation* books shows that the most cases he gave up on or refused related to working with couples. Perhaps because he had been divorced, this was one of his blind spots; and (3) he had females expose parts of their bodies (breasts, thighs, etc.) as part of treatment a bit too often to think of it as a fluke. He never reported having males do the same thing. He was a creative enough therapist that he could have found other ways to do treatment in these cases, I thought.

When Yapko sent the interview transcript to the Erickson Foundation to have it printed in the newsletter, we were both sent an angry letter, outraged that we would consider that the Foundation would publish such an attack on Dr. Erickson. The upshot was that I was permanently disinvited from teaching at the Erickson Foundation.

Oh, well, as Groucho Marx said, I don't want to be a member of any club that would have me as a member. I doubt my actions will have much positive influence on the Erickson field, but I can always hope that it will be a slight opening in their defensive posture. I think that if a field cannot criticize itself or allow criticism, it is dead. So, I haven't nailed any proclamations on the Wittenburg Doors of the First Church of Ericksonianism, but I've left a few Post-it notes there. It was time for me to move on anyway.

## AGAINST TIME-LIMITED THERAPY: THE QUESTION OF BRIEF THERAPY

Another thing that has become clearer to me over the past 10 years is that time-limited therapy is different from brief therapy. I have become known as an advocate of brief therapy, through my writings and teaching. I am a brief therapy evangelist, to be sure, but above and beyond that, I am an advocate of respecting clients. Therefore, I stand opposed to time-limited therapy. I certainly influence my clients in the direction of completing therapy briefly, but I also attend to their responses and let those influence me. What some clients have taught me over the years is that they won't complete their therapy briefly. Not that they are resistant or dependent, but that therapy takes differing amounts and lengths of time for different people. Erickson used to see people for sessions lasting three or four hours or for 15 minutes. Modeling that, I have completed therapy with some in one session and I have completed therapy with others in three years of regular sessions.

My experience is that the vast majority of people will complete their therapy in a relatively short time, three or four sessions, and a few, perhaps five percent, will take longer.

## STANDING AGAINST THEORY COUNTERTRANSFERENCE AND DELUSIONS OF CERTAINTY

As I have become a convert to several different therapeutic approaches over the years (nondirective/Rogerian, family/systems therapy, neurolinguistic programming (NLP), Ericksonian, solution-oriented), it has become clear to me that most therapists are suffering from what I call delusions of certainty. They believe that the things they hear about and see from their clients and the problems they "discover" in therapy exist independently from the therapy conversations.

When I was nondirective, clients would talk about feelings quite a bit. When I was a family systems therapist, I was discovering family and systems issues in every case, I was seeing and hearing neurological/linguistic patterns when I was NLPing on people, and I was discovering unconscious resources as an Ericksonian.

I think that the problems therapists discern are selected from among many possible issues. Then the therapist wittingly or unwittingly convinces the clients of the correctness of the assessment. I call this *theory countertransference.* So I continue to try to alert therapists to the idea that what they are expecting influences what they get in therapy.

While there is no getting away from this, there is a way to be open to clients influencing you as a therapist. You can listen to them instead of your theories. You can validate their experience and let them teach you what works and doesn't work for them.

I have enjoyed my association with strategic and systemic therapies but no longer identify with them as my main theoretical orientation. In fact, I'm not sure what my main theoretical orientation is. I'm still clueless after all these years.

## REFERENCES

de Shazer, S. (1985). *Clues: Investigating solutions in brief therapy.* New York: W. W. Norton.
Erickon, M. H., & Rossi, E. L. (1989). *The February man: Evolving consciousness and identity in hypnotherapy.* New York: W. W. Norton.

# Solution-Oriented Therapy

# Introduction to Phase II

**Bill O'Hanlon**

I was warped by Erickson's influence into paying attention to the resources and capabilities my clients had. Erickson viewed everything as an ability, even the ability to experience symptoms. Studying with Bandler and Grinder was also a big influence. They stressed identifying the "best practices" and best moments of clients and others and then finding ways for the clients to use those as solutions when they were faced with future problems. Around this time, I went through the est training. The emphasis in that training of distinguishing between one's stories about events and the events themselves also shaped the development of the solution-oriented approach. I found that my clients had spontaneously begun to tell me more about their resources, strengths, abilities, and solutions, so I thought that there must be something I was doing differently during the assessment and interviewing processes. I met Jim Wilk, an American expatriate living in England, and we told each other about these unusual one-session treatments we had begun to have in our practices. We made a vow to articulate how this could be. Out of that collaboration came a book (*Shifting Contexts*, Guilford, 1987) and the beginning of the articulation of solution-oriented therapy. I found that therapy naturally became briefer when I was solution oriented. I also found that I didn't have to be quite as clever as when I did primarily Ericksonian, strategic, and interactional therapies. My clients, it turned out, were clever enough to solve their own problems much of the time. This was a great relief to me. I needed to merely be better and better at creating a context in which my clients' competencies emerged and better and better at listening carefully for any hint of solution that I could pursue.

This section contains my writing from the solution-oriented period of my work and thinking. There is some controversy on the origins of solution-based approaches. Steve de Shazer and his colleagues at the Milwaukee Brief Family Therapy Center (BFTC) often write and speak as if they solely derived this approach, but I differ in that writing of the history. It appears the ideas were first and most completely articulated at a presentation given by a therapist named Don Norum in 1978 in Milwaukee. He read a paper called, "Brief Therapy: The Family Has the Solution," in which he argued that it was preferable to ask families about their own solutions, rather than focus on their problems or the therapist's ideas of the solution. He also articulated ideas about clients making positive pretreatment change, which were later reflected and developed in solution-based approaches. (The paper was submitted for publication in *Family Process* but turned down as "shaky, dubious and unsupported.") It is reported that Steve de Shazer, his wife, Insoo Kim Berg, and others who would later become part of BFTC were present at the lecture and also worked with Don Norum at Family Service, but to my knowledge they have never acknowledged the debt we all owe to this unsung hero. In any case, my idea is that the ideas of solution-focused therapy and the ideas of solution-oriented therapy codeveloped and had mutual influences on each other through the years. Many of my basic ideas that led to this approach were codeveloped directly with Jim Wilk, who took many of these ideas to BFTC when he worked there for a year before the solution-focused model was formally spelled out, and Michele Weiner-Davis, who also worked at BFTC after the model was developed. To be fair and inclusive, I call the generic approach solution-based.

Chapter 9

# Solution-Oriented Therapy

## A Megatrend in Psychotherapy

**Bill O'Hanlon**

*The otherwise-impossible can be made to happen under the stimulation of a
comprehensive plan and program focused on finding solutions instead of
attacking a problem. By looking at the best that might be and determining
how to get there, problems that might have been formidable are evaporated
by the larger vision.* (Rouse, 1985, p. 15)

Several years ago, John Naisbitt published his popular book, *Megatrends* (1982),
which detailed some sweeping trends that he saw emerging in our society but
were, perhaps, not obvious to others. In a similar manner, I have observed and
experienced a "megatrend" in psychotherapy that is detailed in this chapter. Stated
simply, psychotherapy is moving away from explanations, problems, and pathology and toward solutions, competence, and abilities.

    This megatrend has gradually emerged for me mainly as a result of my
practice of "Ericksonian" therapy, that is, therapy in the tradition and spirit of
Milton Erickson. Doing Ericksonian therapy has warped me in a particular direction. After some time, I noticed a similar warp in the work of others, most notably
the recent work of Mara Selvini Palazzoli and her colleagues at the Nuovo Centro per
lo Studio della Famiglia in Milan, Italy, and that of Steve de Shazer and his group at
the Brief Family Therapy Center (BFTC) in Milwaukee, Wisconsin. While they

    This manuscript originally appeared in Jeffrey Zeig and Stephen Lankton's edited book,
*Developing Ericksonian Therapy: State of the Art* (Brunner/Mazel), published in 1988. It preceded
Bill's book with Michelle Weiner-Davis, *In Search of Solutions: A New Direction in Psychotherapy*
(Norton, 1989).

are not really Ericksonians, and in some ways work quite differently from the way in which Erickson did, there was something that smelled vaguely familiar in their work. Following that scent led to the articulation of this megatrend for me.

## THE PATTERN THAT CONNECTS

There is a thread that connects the work of Selvini Palazzoli, de Shazer, and Erickson (and perhaps others with whose work I'm not familiar). Here I describe the work of Palazzoli and de Shazer that shows evidence of this thread.

### Milan Invariant Prescription

Mara Selvini Palazzoli is an Italian psychiatrist who became interested in family therapy after she started working with people with anorexia. Her training was biologically and psychoanalytically rooted, but she found these approaches entirely inadequate to the task of treating these patients. The people with anorexia had an annoying habit of dying before their analysis was complete! Dr. Selvini Palazzoli's (1978) book about her work with people with anorexia is recognized as one of the seminal clinical works in the field. In the transition to working systematically, she gathered three psychiatric colleagues who worked as a team observing sessions from behind a one-way mirror.

After working with people with anorexia for a number of years, the team became bored because they were able to resolve most of the "hopeless" cases with their methods. So they turned their attention to schizophrenia and began to develop similar methods and report similar consistent successes. As was bound to happen, they became quite well known, especially in Europe, and were sought-after speakers and workshop presenters. This eventually led to the splitting of the team across gender lines, with the two men (Boscolo and Cecchin) choosing to do more teaching and training along with their clinical work and the women (Prata and Selvini Palazzoli) choosing to set up their own institute (the Nuovo Centro mentioned previously) to concentrate more on clinical research and practice.

The Nuovo Centro team once treated a family with an anorexic member with whom they were stymied. The 21-year-old eldest daughter, Mary, had made several suicide attempts, nearly succeeding at times. The team saw little hope for curing this case and at best resigned themselves to rescuing the parents from the tyranny of their children, who constantly interfered in the parents' personal lives. Accordingly, they dismissed the children from therapy and saw the parents on their own. They gave the parents a directive that involved them going out together one night, not telling the children where they were going, but only leaving a note telling the children that they would be back at an appointed hour. The resulting disruption in the family system led to some amazing results. The daughter who had been anorexic began to improve dramatically, attending nursing school and becoming active in sports, eventually marrying a widower and becoming a "good, happy wife and loving stepmother."

The team was flabbergasted by these reported changes. How had they come about? In an effort to investigate exactly which part of the intervention had the dramatic impact, they decided to use this intervention with every family that sought their help. They have to date given the intervention to 114 families. The dramatic results in many of these families have led them to develop an invariant prescription (Selvini Palazzoli, 1986). One interesting aspect of this research is that the team is not interested in solution-oriented therapy. Although they have come across a widely applicable solution, they are on a quest to understand why the solution works—they are on their way back to explanation-land.

## de Shazer's Skeleton Key Interventions

The recent work of Steve de Shazer has focused on interventions for solutions. In his latest book, *Keys to Solution in Brief Therapy* (1985), he details several invariant prescriptions that his team has found useful across a wide range of presenting complaints. He writes that he has become more interested in the nature of solutions than in the nature of problems. He gives five skeleton key interventions. They are as follows:

1)  The therapist tells the client (or clients) that "between now and the next time we meet, I would like you to observe, so that next time you can describe to me what happens in your (family, life, marriage, relationship) that you want to continue to have happen."
2)  The therapist tells the client that he does not know what will help but that the client should do something, anything, different about the problem than what was done before.
3)  The therapist tells the client to "pay attention to what you do when you overcome the urge to (binge, drink, yell at your children, get depressed, etc."—whatever the presenting complaint involved).
4)  When a client is obsessed with some unhappy event (e.g., the breakup of a relationship), he or she is told to write about the subject for a certain amount of time on odd-numbered days, to read it over on even-numbered days and then burn it. If the obsessive thoughts occur at any other time, he or she is to put them out of mind until the "regular time."
5)  Couples or families that have been fighting are told that they should have a structured fight in which each person gets to have his or her say for a set amount of time with no interruptions from the others. They are to toss a coin to see who goes first; then the other people get their turns. If they decide to go another round, they are to spend a certain amount of time in silence between rounds (de Shazer, 1985; de Shazer & Molnar, 1984).

Again, the team reports quite dramatic and impressive clinical results with these interventions. There is something afoot here.

## The Birth of a Nation: Identifying the Common Thread

At first blush these interventions seem to be going in the exact opposite direction from Erickson, who emphasized not having an invariant approach to anything, much less clients in therapy. There was something familiar in these reports, however. It was the emphasis that Erickson placed on focusing on solutions rather than on problems. In conversation with Haley and Weakland (Haley, 1985a) in the 1950s, it comes across that Erickson had a solution orientation and Haley and Weakland lived in explanation-land. When they would suggest that getting rid of a symptom would just lead to symptom substitution because the interpersonal function was not taken care of, Erickson challenged that assumption: "Your assumption is that it served other purposes. Have you ever thought about symptomatology wearing out in serving purposes and becoming habitual pattern?" (Haley, 1985a, Vol. 1, p. 15). Notice here that Erickson is not asserting that symptoms are habits, but he is challenging the "symptoms serve a function" idea and suggesting a more solution-engendering frame of reference.

This was the warp that I had gotten from working with Erickson and using his approaches for some time—the emphasis on solutions rather than explanations. It was what I responded to in the work of de Shazer and Selvini Palazzoli. Do not pass go; do not collect $200; do not go after explanations; proceed directly to solutions.

While I call this a megatrend, it may just be wishful thinking on my part, as I certainly hope this is a direction that therapy will take in the future. Time must be the ultimate judge, however, as to whether this is a trend or merely a phase or a fluke. Meanwhile, I will present a summary of how solution-oriented therapy developed and some of the differences in thinking and practice that this way of working entails.

## FROM EXPLANATIONS TO SOLUTIONS: THE EVOLUTION OF PSYCHOTHERAPY

What follows is a brief history of the broad trends in therapy, a sort of *Cliff Notes* or *Reader's Digest* version of the history of therapy in my eyes. This will trace the steps we have taken to get to where we are in the therapy field and point the way for the future trend that I am describing.

### The Etiology of Therapy

Therapy was spawned in a sea of different disciplines, with tributaries from psychology, medicine, and philosophy. These disciplines very much concern themselves with explanations, diagnoses, and understanding the nature of human beings. While they are worthwhile endeavors, time has shown, I have come more and more to suspect that therapy involves a different set of assumptions and approaches than those provided by these systems. Therapy involves intervention to produce a change. As many of our clients can demonstrate, having a good explanation does not necessarily produce the desired therapeutic outcomes. Psychoanalysis is, of course, the archetypal approach that emphasizes that insight leads toward change. One assumes that sometimes it does indeed produce results, but more often it leads to situations like Woody Allen describes when he tells a friend that he has been in analysis for 13 years. As she expresses amazement that he has been in treatment that long with no results, he quickly counters by telling her that he intends to give it 20 years and quit if he has not gotten better by then.

## The Emergence of Therapy as a Separate Discipline

Recently, since about 1960, therapy has emerged as a separate and distinct discipline practiced by nonphysicians and nonpsychologists. Perhaps those account to some extent for the trend that therapy is emerging as a separate discipline concerned with change and solutions rather than one concerned with understanding and explanation.

It is by now apparent that there are many different ways to do therapy. However, the advocates of the different methods and schools often are diametrically opposed to one another about the crucial elements and techniques involved in a successful therapy. Witness the Evolution of Psychotherapy conference (Phoenix, December 1985). The faculty members for that conference represented a number of major schools and approaches to therapy and yet little agreement on assumptions or working methods was evident in the presentations. Some might think that this is bad news, but I think it is the good news. Many different theories and many different techniques and approaches seem to produce change and results. Perhaps we should search in another direction rather than for the right theory of therapy.

At first, therapy was primarily oriented to the past, searching in the client's childhood for the roots of present symptoms. Then, in the 1960s, a greater concern with the present prompted the emergence of behavior therapy, ego psychology, gestalt therapy, family therapy, and so on. Past-oriented therapy was dismissed as time wasting and too speculative by these brash new approaches. These contemporary approaches were concerned with the generation or maintenance of the symptom in the present, with data that could be confirmed in the present. What I am suggesting here is that therapy has begun to evolve to a more future orientation that is unconcerned with how problems arise or even how they are maintained, but instead is concerned with how to resolve problems.

From the sea of psychology, medicine, and philosophy, we emerge into the dry land of intervention. In intervention-land there is no right or wrong diagnosis, no right or wrong theory, just data about what works or is useful in particular cases. The stress here is on the *particular*. Erickson's work shows a strong bias against general theories, explanations, and techniques and toward individualized treatment plans and approaches for each person. The latest data on successful results in therapy show that therapy does work and that each school seems to have approximately similar success rates (Gurman & Razin, 1977). The newest research therefore focuses on which therapists or approaches work best with which clients or types of problems. We have, in the words of Ashleigh Brilliant (1980), given up our search for truth and are now looking for a good fantasy.

## THE UNCERTAINTY PRINCIPLE IN THERAPY: NEGOTIATING A SOLVABLE PRESENTING PROBLEM

As I have tried and believed in different models and approaches for therapy, I have noticed that not only do I get different results with different models and approaches, but I get different data during the assessment process, which leads to different definitions of the problem. In other words, problem definition in therapy is a function of the assessment process. The assessment process is influenced by the therapist's metaphors and assumptions with regard to people, the nature of problems, and the theory of resolution he or she holds. It seems that the way one observes alters the data that are being observed. We could call this the Uncertainty Principle in Therapy.

At our house we make spritz cookies every year at Christmas—it's a family tradition. We use a cookie press to make these cookies. If you've never seen a cookie press, I'll explain it to you. Once the dough is made up, it is put into a tubular device with a mold on the end. The dough is forced through the mold at the end so that it comes out looking like a camel or, if the mold is changed, like a Christmas tree or a Santa Claus. The dough is the same; the shape changes. The cookies are then cooked and harden into that mold's shape. This is the type of process that I think happens in therapy. The raw data of the client's complaint is the same. It is shaped by the therapeutic interaction during and after assessment into a more solid "presenting problem." If the client walks into a behaviorist's office, he or she will leave with a behavioral problem. If a client goes to a psychoanalyst's office, her or she will leave with unresolved issues from childhood as the focus of the problem. If a client seeks help from an Ericksonian, he or she is likely to get a problem that can be treated most effectively with hypnosis.

It is not that therapists randomly assign problems to clients. The problems are derived from the raw data of the client's complaints. They are interpersonally negotiated, or cocreated. It is uncanny, though, how similar the clients of a therapist of one particular persuasion will look and how different they will look from those of clients of a different school. I remember chiding Ernest Rossi in a seminar I presented in which he was in the back of the room. I told him I thought that his clients probably talked about dreams very often in therapy, while my clients rarely discussed them. I wondered aloud about whether that might have had more to do with the fact that Dr. Rossi had been trained as a Jungian analyst and written a book about dreams (Rossi, 1985) than the differences in our client population. Of course, I think it does.

The implications of this point are exciting to me. If problems are negotiable, one might as well negotiate a problem that is easy or possible to solve. If you do not know how to do hypnotic pain control, it would be detrimental to negotiate a problem that requires that for a solution. It would be better to negotiate "stress" or problems in interpersonal relationships or something else that you know how to solve and that the client agrees fits with the facts of his or her situation.

Usually clients have already come up with some sort of problem definition that has not sorted out the situation. I prefer to negotiate a problem definition that is both within the client's and my own power to solve. I often offer new, more workable problem definitions or listen for some hint of something in the client's complaint that can be solved or both.

A beautiful illustration of this principle of offering a new, more solvable problem definition is provided in an example taken from the book *Tea With Demons* (1985), written by Carol Allen with her psychiatrist, Herbert Lustig. Carol is afraid she is going insane and brings this concern to Dr. Lustig. (This excerpt has been edited for the sake of brevity. The ellipses indicate where material has been deleted.)

> "Last night I felt so out of control," I explained. "I was so afraid."
>
> "Afraid of what?" he asked.
>
> "Afraid that if all that force were released, I would disintegrate. Explode into a million pieces."
>
> "That sure would be messy, wouldn't it?" Dr. Lustig answered cheerfully. He looked over to the wall across from us, motioned toward it with his head, and continued, "You—splattered over the whole universe."
>
> "Well, not really that," I said. "It was more of a feeling, really. The feeling that I wouldn't be able to contain the anger."
>
> "Oh . . ." he replied musically, as if he was understanding the issue in a new light. "Not able to contain it? Well," he said, "that's different."
>
> He took out his wallet as he spoke, and removing a twenty-dollar bill, handed it to me. "I want you to take this money and go out and buy yourself a sweater." He glanced briefly at the navy-blue and red scarf around my head that day. "Buy either a dark blue or a red sweater. And make sure it fits very tightly. Get a sweater that fits so snugly that you can feel the edges of yourself—your physical limits. Then, anytime you feel that you're about to lose control of your feelings, or even if you feel that you're losing control, go immediately and put on that sweater. This will allow you to accurately perceive your outer limits and to comfortably contain any emotion that you are experiencing—even if the emotion is a very frightening and powerful one."
>
> I did in fact go out and buy a tight, navy-blue sweater several days later. And on several occasions during the next month, I put it on to calm my alarm. But gradually I found that I didn't need it anymore. Dr. Lustig's words had given me some of the inner control that I sought. I no longer needed, for the moment at least, a symbolic container for my fears. (pp. 86–88)

## THE ANSWER WITHIN: GETTING CLIENTS TO SOLVE THEIR OWN PROBLEMS

### Starting From the End or Nothing Succeeds Like Success

Erickson used to have a task he would give to trainees. He would challenge them to read the last page of a book and then speculate on what must have come before to have led to that ending. In a similar manner, the solution-oriented therapist can start from the end goal and work backward from there until he or she connects with the current state of affairs in the client's life. Erickson's "pseudo-orientation in time" technique (Erickson, 1954) provides an example of this approach. Erickson would have the client hallucinate (usually in an imaginary crystal ball) meeting Erickson some time in the future after his problem had been resolved. He would ask the patient to relate to him how the problem had been resolved and would inevitably get some description of the brilliant task or insight that resulted in the alleviation of the problem. Erickson would then suggest amnesia for the hallucination and send the client on his or her merry way. The client did not always use the hallucinated solution, but would often report success in resolving his problem.

Michelle Weiner-Davis (1986), a solution-oriented therapist in Illinois, discussed a small research project she conducted recently in a report published in Steve de Shazer's newsletter, *The Underground Railroad* ("a newsletter for therapists who work . . . this way"). This report provides some preliminary data that are quite interesting. Reproduced below is her description of the project and the results.

Clients come to therapy thinking that they have an insurmountable problem which occurs "all the time." Their "black and white" perceptions are very apparent. Our task then becomes to ask questions regarding when the problem does not occur and explore what is different about those times. Clients often realize for the first time that much of their life is problem-free and that they have, in some way, been doing something right to make that happen.

Our research team noticed that clients would often mention changes they made in between the call for an appointment and the first session. Although they placed little significance on these changes, we wondered whether pre-session change could be viewed as the beginning of the change process. If so, this offered both client and therapist a great deal of information about exceptions to the problem. When clients begin to change prior to treatment, our job would simply be to help them continue the changes and avoid relapses.

Since clients who told us about pre-session change placed little significance on it, we wondered whether there were many more clients who did not think to mention their successful efforts to eliminate the problem. After all, clients do not expect to begin therapy discussing how well they are managing their lives. However, from our perspective, this is exactly the information we want.

We devised three questions and began to informally survey clients beginning therapy. (This survey was conducted with the help of the staff at the McHenry County Youth Service Bureau in Woodstock, Illinois.) We informed them that "our agency is doing some research, and before we begin our session, we have some questions we want to ask you."

1) Clients often notice in between the call for an appointment for therapy and the first session that things already seem different. What have you noticed about your situation?
2) Are these changes in the problem area?
3) Are these the kind of changes you would like to continue to have happen?

Of the 30 clients asked these questions 20 reported experiencing changes prior to treatment. Of the 20 reporting changes, all answered "yes" to questions #2 and #3. Later in the session several of those who initially responded "no" to question #1 reported changes that had occurred before therapy had begun.

Perhaps the reader can make the connection between this report and Erickson's technique of "pseudo-orientation in time." Both start with getting the clients to provide the data that will lead to successful resolution and getting the clients to focus on solution. The work of Lankton and Lankton (1986) on ambiguous function assignments, an extension of some of Erickson's work, shows a similarity to these interventions as well. Clients are given an ambiguous task and challenged to find a therapeutic meaning for the assignment. When they come back to therapy with a meaning they have derived for the task, they are challenged again to come up with a deeper, more profound meaning. In this way, clients will often sort out their own problems without the interference of the therapist's interpretations.

## CREATING A CONTEXT OF COMPETENCE

### Accessing Abilities and Transferring Them Across Contexts

A woman who came to see me was upset with her husband and the way he interacted with her. She attributed the problems in their relationship to his moodiness and felt helpless to do anything that would alter this. She happened to be a skilled horse trainer, one whose expertise was often sought to work with impossible-to-train horses. I asked her what her secret was for training impossible-to-train horses. She brightened considerably and proceeded to give me a detailed account of the principles of horse training. I took notes, as I quickly saw that not only could she use her know-how from the horse area in her marriage, but that I could use these same principles in psychotherapy with good result. I will list the principles she provided:

1) Be consistent.
2) Reward small changes and progress.
3) Give up some small controls to keep the overall control (e.g., let go of one of the reins if the horse is fighting you).
4) Do not get discouraged. Do not get hooked in unhelpfully (e.g., getting angry).

I told her that we should pretend that her husband is a horse, but not to tell him that as he might take it the wrong way. (I think we were both thinking about what kind of four-legged animal he was, though.) She went off with the new enthusiasm and ideas about making changes in her marriage.

### What Does the Client Do Well?

A colleague once asked me what contributions of Erickson's would last once the "Erickson fad" had passed. I responded without hesitation, "The utilization approach." Erickson cooperated with clients and discovered and used what clients were already doing well, even "resistance" and "symptoms." This principle seems to have been incorporated into many contemporary therapies, especially family therapies. In service of change, one of the therapist's tasks in solution-oriented therapy, then, is to discover and use what the client does well—even if it looks like it is useless or will be an impediment to change.

> A couple came to therapy with Erickson. They had been married less than a month and the husband was insisting on a divorce due to the "outrageous behavior" of his bride. Erickson accused the man of being a coward and ordered him to shut up while his bride talked. The woman gave an account of their sexual relationship, which had to be done according to the husband's rather stringent standards of what constituted proper lovemaking. The lights had to be off, the curtains had to be drawn tightly, and she was to wear a nightie during the sex act. He would not kiss her or touch her in any way except to insert his penis in her vagina. The husband said that breasts were for babies only and served utilitarian purposes. Erickson told the man that his sympathies were with the wife and that the man probably wouldn't like what Erickson said. Therefore he was to sit there and listen with his jaws clenched and his arms folded while Erickson discussed in some detail with the wife how a husband ought to approach sex with his wife and how she, as a healthy female, ought to enjoy it. Erickson then pointed out that people have a tendency to give pet names to things. They name their guns "Old Betsy," their boats "Stay-Up," and their cabins "Do-Come-In." He suggested that the husband ought to come up with pet names for his wife's breasts, since he loved her. Erickson suggested that her twins really ought to have names that rhymed. If the husband did not name them by the next session, Erickson would name the first and the husband would be stuck with naming the second, which would immediately come to the man's mind. At the second session, the wife reported that her husband's sexual behavior had been more flexible, but that he had vowed he would never name the twins. Erickson then christened the right breast "Kitty." Six months later Erickson got a Christmas card from them, signed with both their names and K. and T., along with a note from the wife relating the great improvement in their sex life and relationship. (Haley, 1973, pp. 162–164)

In this approach, one assumes that the client has the know-how needed to solve the problem. The therapist's job is to create a situation in which the client can transfer that know-how from the context in which she or he already uses it to the problem area.

## CHALLENGING ASSUMPTIONS: FURNISHING PREMISES FOR SOLUTION-ORIENTED THERAPY

To contrast an explanation- and pathology-oriented approach with a solution-oriented one, an examination of the assumptions of both is provided below. To make my point more clearly, I may have drawn the differences as too black and white and perhaps shortchanged some therapies in the process.

## Assumptions of Many Contemporary Therapies

**Deep, Underlying Causes for Symptoms.** A common assumption for many psychodynamic approaches and of many family/interactional approaches is that there is some underlying dynamic not readily perceived by the untrained eye that is creating the problem. Problems are thus "symptoms" of some deep, underlying cause; only the tip of the iceberg is seen, but the largest part of it is out of view. This "iceberg" theory seems to arise directly from medicine, where systemic processes give rise to specific symptoms. In medicine, it is often viewed as inadequate or even dangerous to treat only the symptom. Many therapies have transferred this notion and this caution to their models and approaches.

**Awareness or Insight Is Necessary for a Change or Symptom Resolution.** Following the medical metaphor again, it would be unwise to treat the "symptom" without an understanding of the underlying causes for the problem. Many therapies attempt to provide the client with an awareness of both the nature and the origin of the problem in order to resolve it.

**Amelioration or Removal of Symptoms is Useless or Shallow at Best and Harmful or Dangerous at Worst.** Jay Haley (personal communication, 1985) likes to say, perhaps only a bit tongue-in-cheek, that he thinks that psychoanalysts do not like to focus on eliminating the symptom because they do not know how to. I think that it is not necessarily so insidious. Again, it follows from the models of explanation- and pathology-oriented therapies that it is not only impossible to eliminate the real problem by removing the symptom, but that it could be dangerous, because it might mask the problem and reduce the client's motivation to seek "treatment."

**Symptoms Serve Functions.** Most therapies assume that symptoms occur because they serve some function or purpose in the person's life. If they did not serve a purpose, they would not persist. This idea exists in both individual and family therapies. The psychodynamically oriented therapist assumes that the symptom serves some intrapsychic function, and the interpersonally oriented therapist assumes a family or interactional function. Although they may not like to be lumped together, I find that both psychodynamically and interactionally oriented therapists around the world share this fundamental conviction. It follows from this belief that if the symptom is removed without somehow taking care of the function it serves, then symptom substitution can arise.

**Clients Are Ambivalent to Change and Resistant to Therapy.** In supervising the teaching therapists of many persuasions, I have noted a fundamental attitude that holds that clients do not really want to change, or that at least they are fundamentally ambivalent about the possibility of change. Therefore, one has to either wait them out or get around their defenses. This position lends itself to an adversarial model at times, with attendant military metaphors ("attacking the defenses," "being defeated by clients," "strategies of resistance," etc.). One recent author characterized "resistant" families as "barracudas" (Bergman, 1985).

**Real Change Takes Time and Brief Interventions Are Shallow and Do Not Last.**   Since problems and pathology are deep rooted or entrenched, repetitious patterns ingrained in individual or social systems, little can be expected with brief interventions and contacts, other than the possibility of better social or life adjustment. Brief intervention changes do not last. Real change takes place the same way the pathology arose, over a long period of time. In relationship-oriented therapy, where the relationship between the client and the therapist is the focus of treatment, it takes quite a while to build up this relationship.

**Focus on Identifying and Correcting Pathology and Deficits.**   The emphasis is on pathology and deficits. I recently attended a workshop where a tape of solution-focused work was shown. It was a "one-shot cure" and the tape showed the techniques and follow-up very clearly. I was certain that even the skeptics in the audience could not fail to be swayed by the clear evidence and impressive results on the tape. After it was shown, a member of the audience commented on the rather bubbly mother in the family and inquired whether the therapist did not notice something strange about her affect. She appeared to the questioner as if she were "on uppers." I remember thinking that therapists look for pathology under every possible rock.

## Assumptions of Solution-Oriented Therapy

**It Is Not Necessary to Know the Cause or Function of a Symptom to Resolve It.**   Erickson was articulate on this topic. "I think that the cause of many problems is very often buried under an accumulation of a lifetime of experience, so that it is very difficult to excavate. . . . In many psychiatric cases the real problem is that of delivering the 'baby' of mental health to patients so that they can get along satisfactorily; the problem is not that of digging into the past in a frantic endeavor to discover possible causes" (quoted in Rossi & Ryan, 1985, pp. 208–209). "Etiology is a complex matter and not always relevant to getting over the problem" (Haley, 1973, p. 106).

**Rapid Change or Resolution of Problems Is Possible.**   One only has to have the experience of seemingly intractable situations being resolved rapidly with no symptom substitution and no further occurrence of the difficulty to know that this is possible. Solution-oriented therapists not only think it is possible to rapidly resolve problems, but that the therapist can create the conditions to make it likely. Mara Selvini Palazzoli (1978) has said, "If we change the rules, we change the organization. . . . It should, moreover, be stressed that this interaction does not demand hard or protracted work on the part of the therapist but only the ability to seize the right moment at the right time" (p. 199).

**Focus Is on What Is Changeable; Focus on Solution and Abilities Rather Than Pathology.**   Our project elaborated the systems view as an explanation of human interaction in families and larger systems. As we applied the notion to families in therapy, it took the form of resistance to change. When we offered these ideas to Dr. Erickson, he responded with polite irritation. He thought, correctly I believe, that a theory that encouraged the notion that people resist change was a noxious theory for a therapist, since expecting resistance encourages it (Haley, 1985b).

**Get the Client to Do Something.**   "In therapy, the first thing I want to do with a patient is to get that patient to do something" (Haley, 1985a, p. 203). One of the things that I constantly get accused of when teaching workshops is being a behaviorist. At first this annoyed me a great deal, as I consider behavioral theory just as full of speculation as any other psychological theory and I do not agree with much of it. After a time I realized that any therapy that got people to take action was characterized by psychodynamic therapists as "behavioral." Erickson was very oriented toward getting people to do things that would encourage them to discover solutions. I follow his lead. My father used to say that if I wanted to work, I would have to go out and look for it, because no one was going to walk up, knock on the door, and offer me a job. He was partly right. If you take actions to put yourself in the way of a job, you are much more likely to get one. I've noticed a correlation in my practice when working with the unemployed client. Those who go out and apply for jobs get them a lot faster than those who do not go out and apply for jobs, regardless of which clients work the hardest or have the most insight in the therapy room. (My father was partially wrong, as people often call up and offer me jobs teaching workshops, sometimes people I've never met. It took me a lot of effort to get to that position, though.) In any case, there is an orientation toward getting people to take action, most often of the observable kind, but occasionally of the internal variety, in the service of change in solution-oriented work.

**Find a Trend Toward Positive Change and Encourage It.**   Out of the raw data of the client's complaint, there are often facts that can serve to create the frame that the client has been going in some positive direction. The therapist's task is to presume this trend and encourage the client to further this change. Just as I was writing this paper, I saw a client and had a supervisee sitting in. The client had been in once before, complaining of severe nightly headaches that would keep him awake; the problem I negotiated was twofold: (1) the client was not getting enough sleep; and (2) he was having headaches, perhaps made worse by the stress of not getting enough sleep. When he returned, he initially indicated no change. He reported that he had had several days of no headaches following the last session, but that the rest of the time he had had headaches pretty much daily. He did say that he had not had a headache at his usual time, however. They had moved to a different time of the day (to 9:30 A.M.). Since this was one of the possibilities I had suggested in the first session, I was quite happy with the response. Since he had also experienced some relief following the first session, I told him that it was now a matter of stretching out the results so that they lasted longer. I pointed out to the man that we had already taken care of one of the two problems he had sought help for. He was now getting a sound night's sleep every night. He agreed.

## SUMMARY

The purpose of this chapter is to make a case for a new, emerging positive trend in psychotherapy, one that I would like to encourage. It is a switch from a view that is focused on discovering the "real, underlying problem" and correcting the deficits and pathologies that give rise to the problem. There is another approach rising in the land that emphasizes the abilities that people have to solve their own problems. It is focused on creating solvable presenting problems and getting clients to continue to proceed toward the solution. This approach involves not only a new set of techniques, but also a different orientation and set of assumptions.

It is my fervent hope that this is a preliminary report of a new territory, as undreamed of as the creatures of the land were to sea creatures before land creatures evolved. Those first fish struggling out of the water could not have imagined eagles or elephants. In a similar manner, I hope that future generations of therapists continue to evolve in this direction, bringing forth new, previously undreamed of forms of effective therapy.

## REFERENCES

Allen, C. (with Lustig, H.). (1985). *Tea with demons.* New York: William Morrow.

Bergman, J. (1985). *Fishing for barracuda: Pragmatics of brief systemic therapy.* New York: Norton.

Brilliant, A. (1980). *I have abandoned my search for truth and am now looking for a good fantasy.* Santa Barbara, CA: Woodbridge Press.

de Shazer, S. (1985). *Keys to solution in brief therapy.* New York: Norton.

de Shazer, S., & Molnar, A. (1984). Four useful interventions in brief family therapy. *Journal of Marital and Family Therapy, 10,* 297–304.

Erickson, M. H. (1954). Pseudo-orientation in time as a hypnotherapeutic procedure. *Journal of Clinical and Experimental Hypnosis, 2,* 261–283.

Gurman, A. S., & Razin, A. M. (1977). *Effective psychotherapy: A handbook for research.* New York: Pergamon.

Haley, J. (1973). *Uncommon therapy: The psychiatric techniques of Milton H. Erickson, M.D.* New York: Norton.

Haley, J. (1985a). *Conversations with Milton H. Erickson, M.D* (3 Vol.). New York: Triangle/Norton.

Haley, J. (1985b). Conversations with Erickson. *Family Therapy Networker, 9,* 30–43.

Lankton, S., & Lankton, C. (1986). *Enchantment and intervention in family therapy: Training in Ericksonian approaches.* New York: Brunner/Mazel.

Naisbitt, J. (1982). *Megatrends.* New York: Warner Books.

Rossi, E. L. (1985). *Dreams and the growth of personality.* New York: Brunner/Mazel.

Rossi, E., & Ryan, M. (Eds.). (1985). *The seminars, workshops, and lectures of Milton H. Erickson: Life reframing in hypnosis* (Vol. II). New York: Irvington.

Rouse, J. (1985). Commencement address. *Johns Hopkins Magazine,* October, p. 15.

Selvini Palazzoli, M. (1978). *Self-starvation: From the intrapsychic to the transpersonal approach to anorexia nervosa.* New York: Jason Aronson.

Selvini Palazzoli, M. (1986). Towards a general model of psychotic family games. *Journal of Marital and Family Therapy, 12,* 339–349.

Weiner-Davis, M. (1986). What's new at BFTC? *The Underground Railroad, 6,* 7–8.

Chapter 10

# Take Two People and
# Call Them in the Morning

## Brief Solution-Oriented Therapy
## With Depression

**Bill O'Hanlon**

This is a slightly condensed transcript with commentary of a one-session consultation with a woman who had been depressed and with whom her therapist felt
stuck. The session provides good illustration of the principles of brief solution-
oriented psychotherapy, as well as highlights its differences from traditional psychotherapy. The client, Ellie, has given permission to discuss our consultation as
well as to publish this transcript.

Ellie's therapist, Mickey, had come to see Ellie as having "characterological
issues," probably dependent personality disorder. Therapy wasn't going anywhere
and Mickey was fearing that she would start to replicate some of Ellie's relationships, in which Ellie would get so needy and dependent that others would withdraw from her and then the relationship would end. Mickey was fighting her own
sense of despair and a feeling that Ellie was "sucking her blood."

The two main principles that guide brief solution-oriented therapy and our
conversation during the session are *acknowledgment* and *possibility*. Therapists
must ensure that they have given the client the sense that the client has been
heard, validated, and respected. At the same time, the therapist must be careful
not to crystallize the client's current sense of things (felt experience and points of
view) but to introduce and keep open the possibilities for change and solution

This article originally appeared in Steven Friedman's edited book, *The New Language of Change:
Constructive Collaboration in Psychotherapy* (Guilford, 1993).

(O'Hanlon & Wilk, 1987; O'Hanlon & Weiner-Davis, 1989; Hudson & O'Hanlon, 1991).

Therapy is seen as a collaborative venture to which both client and therapist bring expertise. The client is the expert on his or her feelings and perceptions and has the essential descriptive data from which the therapist can construct a workable problem definition and solution frame and plan. The therapist is an expert at creating a collaborative solution-oriented dialogue and in noting and incorporating the client's responses to what is being discussed.

Because the work that I do is fairly transparent, I have not provided a great deal of commentary. I merely highlight some of the phases of the session and the therapeutic intent of some of my talk.

*Bill*: Because we have such a short time together and I can't know everything about you, I just want to know a couple of things to orient me toward where you are and where you want to go.

*Ellie*: Okay.

*Bill*: I've asked not to know anything about you before we talked. So the question I have is, if we could wave a magic wand, and everything was wonderful and terrific, how would we know when you get there and things are resolved; and how would other people, if they were following you around in your life, or making a video tape of Ellie's life, know that the situation is resolved? That will help me understand where you are right now and where you want to go.

*Ellie*: I feel like I need more self-confidence. I go through these patterns when I'm doing fine and I'm feeling great, but I get so that I feel like I can't handle everything and I can't cope. I just kinda let go and quit my job or something like that where I'm not coping with everything, and I don't feel independent, and I really want to learn how to—

*Bill*: —make sure it's more consistent that—

*Ellie*: Yeah.

*Bill*: —confidence that you have and that—

*Ellie*: Right.

*Bill*: —independent feeling that you have—

*Ellie*: Yeah.

*Bill*: —so that you don't have these interruptions in the future.

*Ellie*: Right.

*Bill*: Like, "Oh, here I go—

*Ellie*: Yeah.

*Bill*: —two steps forward, two steps back—

*Ellie*: Yeah.

*Bill:* —or three steps back." (*Ellie laughs*)

*Ellie*: Yeah, it's been kind of this pattern, this cycle—
[*When I hear this, I immediately know that there are times when she is feeling and doing better. She is speaking about the problem and I am listening respectfully while at the same time making a mental note of her saying that it is a pattern or a cycle.*]

*Bill*: Um hmm.

*Ellie*: —where I get really depressed and can't seem to cope.

*Bill*: Um hmm. Okay, but tell me about the competent and confident times when things are going pretty well. Give me like a typical day during that time. If we could contrast the two, okay?

*Ellie*: Um hmm.

*Bill*: Unconfident, "depresso" times and the confident times. It's morning time and you've been sleeping at night or you haven't been sleeping at night, I don't know, that may be one of the differences. And it's time to get up and face the day. What's the difference between confident, competent times and depresso, no-fun times?
[*In this exchange, I have both reflected and shifted her description of the problem. I have incorporated her terms: "depression" becomes "depresso times" and later "depresso-land" and "need more self-confidence" becomes "confident and competent times." This illustrates the two basic cornerstones of this approach, acknowledgment and possibility. Usually I am doing both at the same time.*]

*Ellie*: The confident times I, get up and um, I, like. . . .

*Bill*: You get up any earlier?

*Ellie*: Um, oh, definitely (*laughs*). I get up on time. Yeah, I get up on time, it doesn't take me that long to get up, and I feel like I can handle the day, I think, you know, about what's coming ahead, and, um, you know, I don't feel like I can't handle it (*laughs*).

*Bill*: So, on those days there are different feelings and different actions.
[*Here I am acknowledging her focus on feelings and refocusing her on actions. I prefer action descriptions to help me to search for solutions and to construct task assignments, as well as to deconstruct (cast a little doubt on the reality of the fixed nature of depression, preferring to think of it as changeable).*]

*Ellie*: Yeah.

*Bill*: You get up more quickly, get ready, you look forward to the day, and think about what you've got to do?

*Ellie*: Uh huh.

*Bill*: Okay, so that's the very beginning of the morning, but contrast the depresso feeling, incompetent, and unconfident times. You would linger in bed more? You would turn off the alarm? You would what?

*Ellie*: Oh yeah, go back to sleep. (*Laughs*)

*Bill*: Okay, for how long? You know, I used to be terrible at getting up in the morning. I couldn't sign up, I discovered after a couple of semesters in college, for any classes that started before 11:30. (*Ellie laughs*)

[*Here I start to tell a little story, which has two purposes. One is to normalize having a hard time getting up in the morning and the other is to steer her toward giving an action description of how she stays in bed or does not get up in the morning.*]

*Bill*: Because I had a snooze alarm thing.

*Ellie*: Oh yeah.

*Bill*: And it went for 10 minutes, and I would press the snooze button for—three hours—

*Ellie*: Oh yeah.

*Bill*: Ten minutes, rrrrrr. Ten minutes, rrrrrrr.

*Ellie*: Yep.

*Bill*: And I would do it for three hours. So, is it more like that? You would be trying to get up, or would you just go back to sleep, or you would just say forget it, I don't want to go in? Or would that never be true unless you hadn't quit your job or have you sometimes flaked out on going to the job?

*Ellie*: Oh yeah, I've called in sick and stuff.

*Bill*: Uh huh.

*Ellie*: Yeah, and I just can't make it.

*Bill*: And how long would that last usually?

*Ellie*: Oh, I'd sleep all morning.

*Bill*: Okay, all right.

*Ellie*: You know, until, like noon or something.

*Bill*: So then why would you get up eventually? Why not stay in bed all day?

[*Although she is telling me about the problem, again I am oriented toward and orienting her toward change times and solutions. When I hear about a change, although she sees it as part of the depression, I highlight and get an expanded description of that change.*]

*Ellie*: Ah, oh, I'd get up and sit in the living room *(laughs)*. So I'll be awake. I won't be lying down the whole time.

*Bill*: I'm trying to understand the differences here between you and other people who get depressed. I've known some depressed people who just stay in bed all day.

*Ellie*: Well, I have done that too.

*Bill*: But that's not typical for you.

[*There was a possibility of exploring and expanding on the problem description here, but I refocused on solutions by guessing that staying in bed all day was not part of her typical pattern of "depression."*]

*Ellie*: Yeah.

*Bill*: And what finally gets you out of bed, do you think?

*Ellie*: Um, well, I think I should at least get up.

*Bill*: Um.

*Ellie*: Yeah, I feel like, that around noon, I should at least get up (*laughs*).

*Bill*: Um hmm. Get dressed, or maybe move to the living room. Do you get dressed then?

*Ellie*: Not always. Sometimes.

*Bill*: All right. Then give me the rest of the day. The confident, competent, doing pretty well times, not depressed, as opposed to the depresso times.

*Ellie*: You mean compare the—

*Bill*: Compare and contrast and go back to the confident time.
[*This and the next few questions and statements could be viewed as hypnotic suggestions for regression and retrieval of the sense of the nondepressed times. Note the use of the present tense, rather than the past, even though I'm speaking about the past. I did not consciously intend that, but I have a hypnosis background (O'Hanlon, 1987; O'Hanlon & Martin, 1992).*]

*Ellie*: Uh—

*Bill*: Okay, you've gotten up and gotten ready for your day. You typically go to work?

*Ellie*: Right.

*Bill*: You have a job at that time.

*Ellie*: Right.

*Bill*: You typically go to work. You go to work and things go okay at the job or things go hard, things are overwhelming, what? I mean, that could be different on different days, but. . . .

*Ellie*: Yeah.

*Bill*: Typical day.

*Ellie*: I do secretarial work, and normally I can handle it fairly well, except when it gets really busy, and there's a lot of different things happening, and I can't seem to handle, too many things happening at the same time.

*Bill*: There're those times you might be heading down the tubes into depresso-land. Then there're those times when things are pretty chaotic, difficult, busy at work and yet somehow you handle it better.

*Ellie*: I uh. . . .

*Bill*: What's the difference between those days, or those times?

*Ellie*: Uh . . . hmm. I feel. Huh. I feel more cheerful, or more, uh, as long as I have people around me. . . .

*Bill*: Um hmm.

*Ellie*: And I have some kind of a support system, like, you know, some friends, or someone that I can talk to.

*Bill*: And you can say, "Boy, it's been crazy at work."

*Ellie*: Yeah. And just kind of, you know, just have some kind of an outlet, I seem to be okay. I seem to be able to handle it.

*Bill*: Uh huh.

*Ellie*: And, um, and feel good about myself, that I can do it, that I can get through this day that's chaotic.

*Bill*: That's been crazy.

*Ellie*: Yeah.

*Bill*: So it may even help you to have a stressful day, if you've got the supports there, and if—

*Ellie*: Um hmm.

*Bill*: —And if you're feeling cheerful, but especially if you've got the supports there, it may help you, because it strengthens your muscle, because—

*Ellie*: Yeah.

*Bill*: Like "Wow, I handled this day!"

*Ellie*: Um hmm.

*Bill*: That must mean I'm doing pretty well. Okay.

*Ellie*: Yeah, and I can feel really good about myself.
[*This is a reframing. Successfully handling hard times can help build her self-confidence, I'm suggesting. She agrees.*]

*Bill*: All right, so you continue to go through the day, it's time to get off work, and then, what, on those days when you're doing pretty well, confident, competent?

*Ellie*: Um.

*Bill*: You get off work, and then what do you do? Or do you do anything different during lunch, during those days?

*Ellie*: I would go out with some friends of mine.

*Bill*: Okay. And if you're on the depresso slide, but you're still at work, what would you do that's different?

*Ellie*: I would probably go alone and get myself even more depressed—

*Bill*: Right. Uh huh.

(*talking at once*)

*Ellie*: —or get really bummed out, and I mean, can't even talk to anyone about it. Yeah.

*Bill*: Okay. So, good times, confident, you get off work, and what happens when you get off work, where do you go, what do you do?

*Ellie*: If I'm tired, I usually just go home.

*Bill*: Um hmm.

*Ellie*: And if I was really busy, and tired, I'd take a nap or something.

*Bill*: And then what would you do in the evening?

*Ellie*: Oh, sometimes I like to call friends, or just watch TV or, um, I like to do artwork occasionally too.

*Bill*: Um hmm. Okay, now it's noon, you've gotten up finally from your bed, it's depresso time, and you move to the living room, but you're still in depresso mode. You may not be dressed, you may be dressed, but you're in the living room, what do you do, are you watching TV?

*Ellie*: Yeah, sometimes I watch TV, but sometimes I can't even do that. Like it doesn't make any sense to me.

*Bill*: What else would you be doing?

*Ellie*: I usually just kind of sit around, maybe listen to music. . . .

*Bill*: You know, I used to major in depression in college—this was my thing. I was a really depressed person and I almost killed myself at one time.
[*Again I tell a little story about myself to normalize and equalize the relationship a bit, as well as to elicit a description of her process while depressed. This also has the effect of reframing depression as a process rather than being thing-like. I am also indirectly checking for suicidal ideation or impulses by mentioning it offhandedly. She does not seem to respond to the suicidal part of the story or to later indirect probes, reassuring me that suicide is probably not an immediate danger. Follow-up contact confirmed this impression.*]

*Ellie*: Um.

*Bill*: So I know how to do a good depression, because I used to do it so well.

*Ellie*: Um hmm.

*Bill*: And so, I need to tell you how I did it a little and ask you how you do it. What I used to do was sit around and think, and here's the kind of thinking I would do—"I've always felt this way, I'll always feel this way, you know, this is forever," kind of thing—

*Ellie*: Um hmm.

*Bill*: And I would get myself into this—"This is the only way I've ever been, I'm hopeless," or whatever.

*Ellie*: Um hmm.

*Bill*: And I would compare myself with other people and lose by the comparison. I'd think they were more mentally healthy or less depressed or smarter. I was a real skinny guy, so I'd think they were physically nicer or better looking than I am, and this and that. I would compare myself with other people and lose by the comparison. That would be a good way for me to do a depression. Another way I did my depression was to sit in a chair and read books about—self-help books about depression.

*Ellie*: Uh huh.

*Bill*: I would never do anything about what I read, I would just sit and read these books about—

*Ellie*: Um hmm.

*Bill*: —how I might help myself. And that was a good way to do a depression. So what do you do when you're sitting there? What kind of thinking? Like, if you were going to teach me the Ellie way to get depressed. (*Ellie laughs*)

*Bill*: I want to know the Ellie method for depresso thinking.

*Ellie*: Ah, yeah!

*Bill*: How could I do it? Give me the typical kinds of thoughts that Ellie would think—

*Ellie*: I have gone the self-help book route before, but—

*Bill*: But it's not what you're specializing in these days.

*Ellie*: Yeah, uh, yeah, I don't do that now. Sometimes I read books that are like, um fantasy, science fiction, to totally remove myself from, you know, what um, is going on, and. . . .

*Bill*: And does that help?

*Ellie*: No.

*Bill*: So, sometimes the reading, but if you're sitting there thinking, what are you thinking? Just sort of blank? Or?

*Ellie*: No, I think about, you know, how I've been through the same pattern, and. . . .

*Bill*: Yeah, the same pattern.

*Ellie*: Yeah, it's the same feeling of hopelessness, and like, you know, am I going to have to go back home to live with my dad or something or, you know, like—
[*There was an invitation to explore family relationship patterns, but I did not take that route, as it seemed a distraction from the main path we were on toward solution. I noted it mentally in case I need it later, however.*]

*Bill*: "Here I go again."

*Ellie*: Yeah, "Here I go again."

*Bill*: "What's wrong with me?"

*Ellie*: Oh definitely, yeah. Like I feel like I'm even closer to the edge of not being able to cope at all, than I ever have been before.

*Bill*: Because this time is another one that—

*Ellie*: Yep, um hmm.

*Bill*: "I thought I'd moved out of this, but here I go again, I guess"—

*Ellie*: Right.

*Bill*: —"maybe I'm more hopeless than I thought"—

*Ellie*: Um hmm.

[*Here I use a technique that I never knew I used until someone did a dissertation on my work (Gale, 1991). I talk for my clients at times. I do this to acknowledge what they are feeling and thinking and to subtly restate their feelings and points of view so they are more open to the possibility of change and solution (e.g., "maybe I'm more hopeless than I thought"). As long as clients agrees that it is an accurate enough reflection of their experience, this technique can save a great deal of time and trouble.*]

*Bill*: Okay. So how long would you sit there either reading or doing that, typically? Typical depresso day. When you're in the midst of it.

*Ellie*: Most of the day, most of the day, yeah. Um.

*Bill*: Would you eat anything?

*Ellie*: I'd eat a little bit. Just like breakfast kinda stuff.

*Bill*: Okay, so it's now late afternoon, early evening, what's happening?

*Ellie*: Uh, I decide I need to take a shower—

*Bill*: Uh huh.

*Ellie*: So I take a shower and get dressed. Around like 7:00 or so.

*Bill*: Okay, and then, in the midst of that, does that help a little?

*Ellie*: It helps a little bit.

*Bill*: Okay, all right, and then what?

*Ellie*: And then I start thinking of friends that I can call. I've been doing that a lot lately.

[*Here I missed a recent change that might have been very helpful to explore more. I could have asked her to tell me more about how she got herself to make this change, even though she was depressed and how it helped her feel better, to both gather information about it and to highlight it for her.*]

*Bill*: Uh huh.

*Ellie*: Calling girlfriends, and—

*Bill*: Does that help? I mean, does that alleviate it a little? Or a lot? Or—

*Ellie*: It alleviates it a little bit. Only when I'm talking with, you know, only when I'm talking with—

*Bill*: —Okay, would you ever go out during those depresso times, like go out with friends or do anything? Would you ever do art, would you . . . what?

*Ellie*: I've done a minimal amount of art. Um, and, I have a really close friend that I go see sometimes, my friend Steve.

*Bill*: Only when you're depressed?

*Ellie*: He's the only one I feel comfortable with when I'm depressed.

*Bill*: He's the only one you typically see when you're that depressed. . . .

*Ellie*: Um hmm.

*Bill*: Because he understands and he's okay with it, he knows about. . . .

*Ellie*: He knows what's going on.

*Bill*: But with the other friends you'd feel it would be too much of a burden on, or you feel like, oh, they don't ca—

*Ellie*: Basically I don't have the energy to even explain, you know, what's going on. So, ah, I generally don't see anyone.

*Bill*: Okay, and then there's something I'm real curious about. You've been in depresso-land, you're living there for a while, and then somehow you come out, back into confidence and competence-land—
[*Here again I am emphasizing and gathering information about a time when something changed for the better, this time the end of the larger pattern of depression.*]

*Ellie*: Um hmm.

*Bill*: Because you've gone through cycles.

*Ellie*: Um hmm.

*Bill*: What makes a difference? What happens when the cycle is ending, different from in the middle of it, and what do you think makes the difference? You think something biological shifts or is it something else? What makes the difference, how does it finally end? And also, I'm just real curious, anything under your influence that changes it, or do you just finally go, ah, I'm tired of just sitting here doing nothing, I'm going to go out and get another job, I'm disgusted? Or I'm going to try and kill myself, and then when you get to that point, you scare yourself and get up and go, what? What!
[*I'm searching for what she does to create the end of depression times. I'm also probing about the likelihood of suicide. Again she does not indicate she is suicidal, reassuring me.*]

*Ellie*: Um. . . . Well, I get to the point where I think, well, you know, I , no one else is going to help me, you know, obviously no one wants to help me *(laughs)*. So I start getting a little bit bored of sitting around, and I finally start feeling like I can do something—

*Bill*: Um hmm.

*Ellie*: —like I can at least go out of the apartment and do something.

*Bill*: Um hmm.

E*llie*: And once I start maybe going out and doing little things, then I start feeling a little bit better.

*Bill*: Um hmm.

*Ellie*: Like I, maybe I could handle, like, one step—
[*She succinctly describes the solution to her problem. I follow with a few additions to create a few new connections that she might not have come to on her own.*]

*Bill*: Um hmm.

*Ellie*: And, um. . . .

*Bill*: And that one step creates a little more energy, because—

*Ellie*: Yeah.

*Bill*: You're not stuck in your old pattern.

*Ellie*: Yeah.

*Bill*: And then that leads to the next step, or you put yourself out a little more. . . .

*Ellie*: Yeah.

*Bill*: And then how do you finally get another job? When do you get to that point, in that course?

*Ellie*: Um, I might just do like one thing a week, you know, like one interview or something and then, like, tell myself, "Wow, that was really good," you know, that I could do it.

*Bill*: Yeah!

*Ellie*: That I could do that one thing.

*Bill*: Yeah.

*Ellie*: And then I'd start realizing that maybe I'm not so bad after all, and you know, and I'd try and, um, you know, feel good about what I have done in the past.

*Bill*: Okay.

*Ellie*: But, it takes a really long time. . . .

*Bill*: Okay.
*(long pause)*

*[Next I tell a story that both mirrors many of the things she has told me about her depression and how she gets out of it and highlights some of the solutions that I am going to suggest she use. You might notice that while I talked for her quite a bit earlier in the session, here she talks for me by finishing my sentences.]*

*Bill*: I saw a woman once who was seeing another therapist at the mental health center where I worked. The woman came in depressed and in crisis and since the other therapist, Louise, was on vacation, I ended up seeing her. I told her, "I really don't know how Louise works since I just started working here and I don't want to mess up anything you two might do. So tell me, how did you and Louise work when you worked on the depression together? She told me, "I came in and I was in desperate shape. I was sleeping all day; I was really depressed. She had dropped out of college because she got so depressed, and she had lost her grants and scholarships, so she was also having financial problems. She would just sleep pretty much all day, and she had ended up seeing Louise for years. She hadn't been in therapy for the past eight months, though, because she was doing better. I asked, "Well, what did you and Louise do that worked?" And she said, "Well, the first thing was get me up by 9:00 every morning, take a shower, and get dressed. She had me walk around the block one time at first."

*Ellie*: Hmm.

*Bill*: "And it was like torture to drag myself out—

*Ellie*: Um hmm.

*Bill*: —of the bed, get showered, get dressed, and walk around the block. But," she said, "when I walked around the block one time, I had a little more energy, just that little more energy."

*Ellie*: Um hmm.

*Bill*: "And then, on my walks, I would stop and get a paper and look for jobs. You know, that kind of thing." So she had a little more energy, she could do the minimal kind of applying for jobs. She then started walking around the block two times in the morning, three times, she started increasing it. She said, "It's weird, because you're using energy to walk around the block, but the more I walked around the block, the more energy I got." So she—

*Ellie*: Wow!

*Bill*: She finally got a part-time job. She decided to go back part time to school. What she did was curious. It reminded me of you. She would recontact friends that she had before she was depressed, and she had just sort of let them drop out because—

*Ellie*: She didn't have any energy to deal with them—

*Bill*: Right.

*Bill*: And just getting up and coming to Louise's office was something. She would look forward to it every week.

*Bill*: And then gradually she really got herself back into where she would go out with friends. By the time she came in to see me, she was going to school part time and working part time, but she had gotten depressed again recently. I asked, "Well, what happened?" She said, "Well, I met this guy at school, we moved in together, and things were going pretty well, but then he started to become real critical and real controlling and"—

*Ellie*: Hmm.

*Bill*: —"he was sort of smothering me. I felt really good about myself, because I stood up to him, and I told him I don't want this relationship anymore. 'You're dominating my life, leave,' since it was my apartment, and he left."

*Ellie*: Um hmm.

*Bill*: She said, "I was feeling like—

*Ellie*: Powerful.

*Bill*: —wow, I really did get a lot out of therapy." Yeah, powerful. "I did it!"

*Ellie*: Yeah.

Bill: "But now I'm depressed, and maybe I think I need a man to be okay." I said, "Well, what have you been doing lately?" She said, "Well, I'm sleeping all the time."

*Ellie*: Oh no.

*Bill*: Then she said, "It's funny, you know, as we're sitting here talking, I realize I know exactly what to do not to be depressed, I need to (*Bill laughs*) get up—"

*Ellie*: Get up, walk around (*laughs*).

*Bill*: "Walk around the block, call my friends (*Ellie is laughing*), make sure I don't call in sick to work, go to school." She said, "You know, it isn't that I need a man. It's just that I'm doing the same things I did when I was depressed before."

*Ellie*: Um hmm.

*Bill*: "I realize I know exactly what to do not to be depressed." And so it was like, "Okay, good. I don't have to do any therapy (*Ellie laughs*) with you if you already know." So, that's what I'm curious about with you. Ellie already knows the patterns of depression and lack of confidence.

*Ellie*: Yeah.

*Bill*: You've memorized the patterns.

*Ellie*: Yeah.

*Bill*: You've got 'em down to a science (*Ellie laughs*). I work with people with migraine headaches sometimes. I do hypnosis sometimes—

*Ellie*: Uh huh.

*Bill*: With migraine headaches sometimes, I'll put people in trance and say, "Okay, you're an expert at getting rid of migraine headaches," and they'll go, "What does that mean?"

*Ellie*: (*laughs*) "What?"

*Bill*: They say, "No, I don't think so. That's why I came to see you." (*Ellie laughs*) I say, "No, I've never had a migraine headache in my life, and I've never gotten rid of one. But you've gotten rid of hundreds of migraines." But somehow the migraines have gone away. So I say to them in trance, "Okay, fine, something in your body knows how to get rid of a migraine headache, maybe changes in blood chemistry, changes in breathing, changes in the muscles of your neck or the blood vessels. I don't know what it is, but your body knows, so let your body take care of it."

*Ellie*: Um hmm.

*Bill*: With hypnosis it happens automatically, but I think the same thing about depression, so if Ellie already knows, and you've been able to teach me a little—

*Ellie*: Um hmm.

*Bill*: Here're the patterns of going into a depression—

*Ellie*: Um hmm.

*Bill*: —or a discouragement time, or feeling unconfident time, and here's the patterns of getting out of it. What I'd be curious about is, could you try an experiment? I don't know what phase you're in now.

*Ellie*: I'm in a depression—

*Bill*: You at least got out of bed today.

*Ellie*: Yeah.

*Bill*: It's 11:00 in the morning and you're out of the house!

*Ellie*: Yeah (*laughs*).

*Bill*: So, maybe today's a little better—

*Ellie*: Yeah.

*Bill*: So you're in the midst of one of those depresso phases—

*Ellie*: Um hmm.

*Bill*: So let's design a program for Ellie to walk herself out of depression. Deliberately.

*Ellie*: Um hmm.

*Bill*: Different from the migraine headaches. So I would say, tomorrow morning, you set the alarm, and no matter what you feel like, like, "I can't get up, no, I can't, I'm too depressed, I can't handle it, I'm overwhelmed." You get up, you go take a shower at 8:30, 9:00, whatever, 8:00 or 7:30, or whatever your usual wake-up time was when you had a job or when you were in the midst of good times—

[*When I am negotiating a task assignment, I usually use multiple choice options (7:30, 8:00, 8:30, 9:00) and then note my client's verbal and nonverbal responses to each option. That gives me a better sense of which options fit for them and which they are more likely to follow through on. This makes things a bit more collaborative and less authoritarian.*]

*Ellie*: Um hmm.

*Bill*: Of course, you may find a job this month, but um, you get up, you get dressed, and walk outside the house, and you go do something. I don't know what, have breakfast, go get a cup of coffee—

*Ellie*: Um hmm.

*Bill*: —go get a paper, whatever it may be. Go see a friend, make a breakfast date with a friend, you know, something that would be totally in the nondepresso pattern.

*Ellie*: Yeah.

*Bill*: Then arrange two or three things in your day that would be nondepresso activities.

*Ellie*: Um hmm.

*Bill*: Then force yourself to do them. It would have to be "force yourself to do it" at first. Like maybe you had to force yourself to get up to get here, maybe you didn't, maybe this had it's own natural energy, because of your promise to Mickey [*her therapist*] and that helped.

*Ellie*: Yeah.

*Bill*: But somehow you got yourself up today—

*Ellie*: Yeah.

*Bill*: Even though you're in the middle of a depresso pattern. So, how'd you do that? How did you get yourself up today?
[*I both wanted to highlight her ability to do the task and to find out how she got herself up during this depression time in order to build that into the assignment to increase the likelihood of success.*]

*Ellie*: 'Cause I, well, I didn't want to let Mickey down.

*Bill*: Somebody else helped you get going.

*Ellie*: Yeah.

*Bill*: So it wasn't just you thinking, "Who cares if I get up or not?" You had an appointment or an expectation—

*Ellie*: Right.

*Bill*: —from somebody else.

*Ellie*: Right.

*Bill*: So then there was just no question, it was like, ahhh, "I don't feel the energy to get up." Did you feel more energy?

*Ellie*: Um, well, I set my alarm for, like a quarter to eight, so I had plenty of time to lie there and think about (*both laugh*) getting up.

*Bill*: Uh huh.

*Ellie*: It took me almost an hour to get up. But I did it.

*Bill*: Yeah! And that's the curious part of it. That's the stuff that I home in on like a—

*Ellie*: Uh huh.

*Bill*: You know, I'm a therapist and I love this part, I go for change. So that's the moment that I'm real curious about, I mean, it's the—

*Ellie*: Um hmm.

*Bill*: —moment that . . . the hour is up, it's a quarter to nine, um or nine—

*Ellie*: Um hmm.

*Bill*: —and you're thinking, "I really need to get up."

*Ellie*: Right.

*Bill*: And you get yourself up—

*Ellie*: Go now—

*Bill*: "I've gotta go now."

*Ellie*: Yeah.

*Bill*: And you get yourself up, different from those days that you're lying there thinking, "I *can't* get up."

*Ellie*: Hmm.

*Bill*: "I just *can't*."

*Ellie*: Right.

*Bill*: Or "I don't want to."

*Ellie*: Yes.

*Bill*: It may have been the same feeling this morning, the exact same feeling that you have in the midst of all the depressions, but something was different. You made a decision differently, you did something different inside, or you just had some external constraints—

*Ellie*: Um hmm.

*Bill*: —that said to you, "Get up!"

*Ellie*: Yeah.

*Bill*: "You gotta get up."

*Ellie*: Right.

*Bill*: "There's no choice about it, you just have to get up. You promised Mickey you'd be there."

*Ellie*: Yeah.

*Bill*: "You gotta be there."

*Ellie*: Yeah.

*Bill*: So, I guess what I'm saying is, could you, *would* you, I know you could, but *would* you make some sort of plan to hasten the departure of discouragement and depression and unconfidence? That would involve breakfast dates, commitments to walk, checking in with Mickey. Maybe you would get up and go there even when you don't have an appointment, check in and go by her office at 9:00 in the morning when she comes out from a client or she's just gotten up. She'd tell you, "Okay, Ellie, you have to be at my office at 9:00 and check in with me."

*Ellie*: Yeah (*laughs*).

*Bill*: "You have to be dressed and you have to get here, and I'm expecting you every morning for the next week."

*Ellie*: Uh huh.

*Bill*: Or until you get out of depression-land—

*Ellie*: Um hmm.

Bill: Are you willing? Is that possible? What do you think about that?

*Ellie*: That sounds really hard. I mean—
[*She shows some signs of uncertainty. When I get that kind of response, I go back to acknowledgment. I take it as a message that I've been emphasizing the change part of the acknowledgment and change balance. Several times in the next few exchanges I acknowledge ("Very hard") and then I introduce the change piece again ("Not impossible") and balance it with acknowledgment again (". . . and hard, real hard").*]

*Bill*: Yeah.

*Ellie*: To do that—

*Bill*: Definitely hard—

*Ellie*: Yeah . . . to get up th—

*Bill*: No question about it.

*Ellie*: To get up and see her.

*Bill*: Not impossible, and hard, *real* hard.

*Ellie*: Really hard.

*Bill*: Um hmm.

*Ellie*: Yeah.

*Bill*: Because that feeling of not wanting to cope is—

*Ellie*: Is so strong.

*Bill*: —very strong.

*Ellie*: Yeah.

*Bill*: And you had it yesterday. Yes?

*Ellie*: Oh yeah.

*Bill*: And you had it this morning to a certain extent.

*Ellie*: Um hmm. It did feel a little different today though.
[*I seize upon this reported difference as evidence of the new frame of reference I am offering: If she has a commitment to get out of the house and see somebody in the morning, it not only changes her actions but it changes her feelings of depression.*]

*Bill*: Yeah, that's it.

*Ellie*: Yeah.

*Bill*: You had something scheduled.

*Ellie*: Yeah.

*Bill*: So you're in this slightly different frame of—

*Ellie*: I still have that scared kind of feeling—

*Bill*: —little bit scared—

*Ellie*: —but it wasn't strong.

*Bill*: But somehow it didn't dominate.

*Ellie*: Yeah.

*Bill*: So I think that can pull you out of your depression quicker.

*Ellie*: Uh huh.

*Bill*: Then, I think that, in addition to that, there are some preventative things that you can do right in the middle of confidence time, when you hit a crisis point. You can recognize these crises by now. You said it really well, if things are really stressful at work—

*Ellie*: Um hmm.

*Bill*: —and you go out to lunch alone, that's a warning sign.

*Ellie*: Yeah.

*Bill*: So, the next day, if you have one of those days, when you're feeling overwhelmed, "Oh no, I'm not going to be able to handle this, here I go again."

*Ellie*: Yeah.

*Bill*: If you have that thought, the next day, you make a promise to me, to Mickey, to Steve, to whoever it might be, whoever it matters to, whoever will keep you on track, and whoever—

*Ellie*: Right.

*Bill*: —won't let you slide out of it (*Ellie laughs*). Not just to yourself, because you may—

*Ellie*: Flake out on it (*Ellie laughs*)—

*Bill*: —you make a promise to somebody else that the next day you'll make a lunch date with somebody.

*Ellie*: Um hmm. Two different people maybe.

*Bill*: Yeah, with two different people! And also that you would talk to one person on the phone about how overwhelmed you were feeling.

*Ellie*: Um hmm.

*Bill*: You know, one of those friends in addition to Steve.

*Ellie*: Yeah.

*Bill*: I suggest that you write these things down. Here's the prevention plan for going into depression- and discouragement-land, and here's the plan for the escape from depression-land. Because when you're in the midst of it, and not sitting here talking to me, I know this because I've lived in depression-land so long, I almost guarantee you won't be able to remember (*laughs*) or put them in play, those plans—

[*I have again shifted the label just a bit to discouragement from depression. I also want to ensure her follow-through by having her write down what we work out for preventing her depression and for getting out of depression if she gets depressed in the future.*]

*Bill*: Now, having action steps is important, because if what's more likely to get you depressed and what's less likely to get you depressed is something you can't do anything about, like, "Oh, it's rainy and I'm more likely to be depressed, and when the sun's out I'm much less likely to be depressed." Well, there's not much to do about that.

*Ellie*: Ha.

*Bill*: But, if you say, "Ah, when I get up and take a shower, I feel a little bit better."

*Ellie*: Um hmm.

*Bill*: That's something you can do something about. So, on that action list, on that list would be only actions that you could do—

*Ellie*: That would work.

*Bill*: Yeah, that were, that you've already found would work.

*Ellie*: Uh huh.

*Bill*: So, that's why I asked you so many questions about it.

*Ellie*: Uh huh.

*Bill*: Because I wanted to find out in Ellie's ecology what are the natural things that occur to get her out of depression or that help her a little when she's in discouragement- or unconfidence-land.

*Ellie*: Oh, okay.

*Bill*: And then what I think happens is after a while of flexing your muscle of confidence you know you won't get stuck being discouraged again. Because part of what discourages you now is that any moment you can go back into one of these phases, and that's always sort of a like a wariness, because even when you're doing well, you're probably thinking in the back of your mind, "Yeah, I'm doing well now, but . . ."

*Ellie*: Who knows how long it will last.

*Bill*: Who knows how long it will last, and that's somewhat discouraging. If you actually had tools that you knew could pull you out of it, it wouldn't be so intimidating to think, "Oh, my god, I might go into one of those, and that time I might not make it through."

*Ellie*: Yeah.

*Bill*: So, I'm thinking that these programs strengthen your confidence muscle—

*Ellie*: Um hmm.

*Bill*: Because when you have those days that you're overwhelmed at work and it's really bad, but you make it through those days, you get a little stronger.

*Ellie*: Um hmm.

*Bill*: "I handled it!"

*Ellie*: Um hmm.

*Bill*: Wimpy Ellie, little wimpy Ellie handled it.

*Ellie*: Did it! (*Ellie laughs*)

*Bill*: So that helps your confidence in the long run, the more experiences like that you get under your belt, the better it goes in the long run.

*Ellie*: Um hmm.

*Bill*: But I think the one that you have to tackle that's much more difficult than being overwhelmed at work is starting to go into a depressing, discouraging episode or unconfident episode and actually by dint of your own effort either avoiding it or getting out of it.

[*Another subtle change of viewpoint is introduced here: these are episodes, rather than she has depression as a set, consistent internal disease or disorder.*]

*Ellie*: Um hmm.

*Bill*: Because if you're just going to be a victim of it and say, "Oh, jeez, it may came over me again, and I don't know how long it will last," then it's pretty discouraging.

*Ellie*: There's, like, no hope—

*Bill*: Right.

*Ellie*: —because it's a pattern.

*Bill*: Because it could come on at any time, and you don't know how long it will last. By now you've gotten a sense of how long they last.

*Ellie*: A couple months (*Ellie laughs*).

*Bill*: Now. But if you could cut the time short. . . . How long have you been in this one?

*Ellie*: About a month and a half.

*Bill*: Okay, so maybe it wouldn't be quite so dramatic to get out now, or in the next couple of days, but if you—

*Ellie*: Usually about now is when I start getting out of it.

*Bill*: Okay, so if you could make it a little quicker to get out of it—

*Ellie*: Yeah.

*Bill*: —maybe that would make a difference. But what would really make a difference then is the next time you started to get in, if you could prevent going in. When you could say—

*Ellie*: Um.

*Bill*: "I can tell one is coming on—

*Ellie*: Um hmm.

*Bill*: —but somehow I didn't go into it!"

*Ellie*: Um.

*Bill*: That would be real powerful.

*Ellie*: Yeah.

*Bill*: And/or, if you actually went into one, that you got yourself out quicker than a month—

*Ellie*: Yeah.

*Bill*: Or quicker than a week, you know, you could do it within a week, if you could move yourself out of it. You could even prevent the loss of the job.

*Ellie*: Yeah.

*Bill*: That would be really great, I think.

*Ellie*: Yeah!

*Bill*: It would make a difference.

*Ellie*: Oh, it definitely would.

*Bill*: Okay.

*Ellie*: Um hmm.

*Bill*: So, can you design that program? Have we talked specifically enough so you have a pretty good idea about, if you left right from here and wrote them down. Here's the program of things that have worked to avoid going into depression and discouragement and—

*Ellie*: Um hmm.

*Bill*: —unconfidence.

*Ellie*: Um hmm.

*Bill*: And here are the things that have gotten me out of it, that can get me out of it a little when I'm in the midst of it or could get me out of it. You could write down those two programs. Do you have enough specifics or enough ideas? Can you remember those from us talking, and do you know other ones that maybe we should talk about now?

*Ellie*: Like the calling—calling friends—to go out to lunch or whatever.

*Bill*: Um hmm.

*Ellie*: And what you said about getting up and taking a shower and going out-side—that would be a big one for me.

*Bill*: Okay, now, so who do you think can keep you on track about that?

*Ellie*: (*Ellie laughs*) Well, Mickey—
[*She participates in designing the task by filling in the person when I ask her.*]

*Bill*: You'd have to check with Mickey whether she'd have the time, or how this would fit with her schedule, but if you actually—if you were in the midst of one of these depression things, or started going into one—if you'd promised her that you'd get up and go over to her office, or meet her for coffee or whatever meets with her schedule. She'd be a good one—

*Ellie*: Um hmm.

*Bill*: That would be a good plan just to get you out of the house, get you dressed, and get you on to that track.

*Ellie*: Yeah.

*Bill*: So, all right, so that may be your prevention, and also get you out of it. So, what if I said, "Okay Ellie, here's your assignment: your assignment is to get you out of your depression phase more quickly, for the next five days, and the next week or whatever. Every morning you have to meet Mickey by any time before 10:00 that she says that she can meet, for two minutes, just to check in with her. And you have to be dressed, showered, um, and uh—

*Ellie*: Ah.

*Bill*: —have gotten yourself out of the house."

*Ellie*: That would work.

*Bill*: Could you, would you?

*Ellie*: That would work.

*Bill*: All right.

*Ellie*: If I had to meet her at a specific time.

*Bill*: Right. Would it be best to have the same time every morning?

*Ellie*: Probably.

*Bill*: Okay, if she can work that out. She's listening now.
[*Her therapist, Mickey, was watching and listening through a video monitor in the next room. Mickey readily agreed to participate in the task, in part, because she thought it might prevent the almost nightly phone calls she was getting from Ellie asking for help because she was so depressed and miserable.*]

*Ellie*: Um.

*Bill*: She can sort that out with you.

*Ellie*: Um hmm.

*Bill*: And, and that's the kind of thing that I'm talking about, because I think if you just make a commitment to yourself that you'll get up and walk every morning (uh uh)—

*Ellie*: Might not work.

*Bill*: Uh uh.

*Ellie*: No (*Ellie laughs*).

*Bill*: Because I make all sorts of promises to myself that I don't keep. If I promise somebody else, I'm a million times more likely to do it.

*Ellie*: Oh, definitely.

*Bill*: So, promising her, promising Steve, promising other friends, and actually scheduling it in, and making sure you can't get out of it is crucial. Maybe tell them, "Don't let me get out of this one."

*Ellie*: Oh, yeah, that would make a difference too.

*Bill*: Good.

*Ellie*: Yeah.

*Bill*: So, so, I'd say, the first task then is to get you out of this phase, or this slump, of dep—

*Ellie*: Um hmm.

*Bill*: Or discouragement and unconfidence, and I think that that makes the confidence muscle go up and gets you back. Have you got a job now or are you working on getting a job, or are you not in that stage yet?

*Ellie*: I'm working on getting a job.

*Bill*: Okay, and you're doing those minimal things, those once-a-week kind of things.

*Ellie*: Um hmm.

*Bill*: Okay, so if you could make that every day, that would be helpful, but in any case, just the things to get you out of the house—

*Ellie*: Yes.

*Bill*: —make the difference. That makes the difference in the whole day, I think, because—

*Ellie*: Um hmm.

*Bill*: You've gotten up. It's before noon, you've gotten out of the house, and it sort of sets the tone for the whole day.

*Ellie*: Gives you a little more action, or. . . .

*Bill*: That's right.

*Ellie*: Yeah.

*Bill*: Gets you out and going.

*Ellie*: I have a different feeling once I've gotten going.

*Bill*: That's right, a different feeling.

*Ellie*: Um hmm.

*Bill*: So, what I'm saying is that when you're trying to tip the balance between those scary, depressed, discouraged, unconfident feelings and the other ones, that crucial action in the morning can tip the balance that day—

*Ellie*: Um hmm.

*Bill*: —I think it's that beginning of the day—

*Ellie*: Beginning of the day. . . .

*Bill*: —that's really crucial.

*Ellie*: Yeah.

*Bill*: Very crucial.

*Ellie*: Um hmm, um hmm.

*Bill*: Also crucial is writing it down. I one time stumbled on the idea of writing a letter to myself when I was clear and not depressed and muddled to read when I got depressed and muddled.

*Ellie*: Um hmm.

*Bill*: I kept it in one of my journals, and I would read it when I was depressed and confused and think, "Ah yeah, now I remember." It was a letter to myself from a better time and a better part of myself to the stuck part of myself, and it was helpful to do that.

*Ellie*: Um hmm.

*Bill*: Oh yeah, I'm not such a shit, you know *(Bill laughs)*. I'm not such a terrible person, and things aren't as bad as I thought.

E*llie*: Yeah.

*Bill*: So what I—what I'm focusing on here is to make sure you write this stuff down—

*Ellie*: Okay.

*Bill*: —because I'm afraid that in the midst of it you'd forget it.

*Ellie*: That—it's very easy to forget. Uh. Yeah. I have written feelings down before.

*Bill*: Yeah, and that's useful in its own way, but this is different. This is an action plan.

*Ellie*: Um huh.

*Bill*: Two action plans to write down. One action plan is how to prevent going into discouragement and unconfidence, and the other action plan is how to get out of discouragement- and depression-land. All right, so that's what I have. Any other thoughts or ideas or questions that you have or things that I really haven't asked about that are probably pretty crucial that I should ask about?

*Ellie*: Um, I tend to, like, make myself feel real confused, or just like—

*Bill*: Um hmm.

*Ellie*: —you know, I have all these issues going on, and I just get really confused, and. . . .

*Bill*: And what's the Ellie technique for confusion? I want to know.

*(Ellie laughs)*

*Bill*: How would I do it if I were doing it like you?

*Ellie*: Um, oh, just worry about all these different feelings, and—

*Bill*: Um hmm.

*Ellie*: And, um, oh, I'll make myself feel bad because, you know, here I am, 34, and you know, I shouldn't be like this now. You know?

*Bill*: "I should have it more together and—

*Ellie*: Yeah.

*Bill*: —not be as confused and not be worrying about this kind of stuff?"

*Ellie*: Yeah.

*Bill*: Okay, so, in addition to thinking these things and having these doubts and all this stuff, you've gotten down on yourself, saying, "I shouldn't feel, shouldn't think these thoughts, I should have it more together than this." That kind of stuff?

*Ellie*: Yeah.

*Bill*: Well, okay, I have some ideas, but before we get to them, what helps in those situations? I mean, you're in the midst of all these confusing thoughts and feelings, and then what happens? What's helped?

*Ellie*: Um.

*Bill*: What gets you out of it? I mean, you're not there at this moment.

*Ellie*: Probably being with other people makes a big difference.

*Bill*: So, it stops going around the squirrel cage of your mind and starts coming out of the mouth?

*Ellie*: Um hmm.

*Bill*: Or, do you focus on something else?

*Ellie*: Yeah.

*Bill*: Yeah. I have this observation I made about myself and other people and life. It seems that when I'm doing the worst, I do the worst things for myself. Like, when I'm doing the worst, I'll eat sugar (*Ellie laughs*), which sends me into a sugar cycle, where I go down into feeling lethargic and wanting more sugar to pick me up.
[*Here I tell another little thing about my struggles, which equalizes the relationship a bit and also introduces an idea that I'm going to use to reinforce the task assignment.*]

*Ellie*: Yeah.

*Bill*: If somebody else is doing the worst, they do drugs, and that's their worst thing.

*Ellie*: Um hmm.

*Bill*: You know, maybe they stop doing drugs, but then they have some sort of crisis or feel bad sometime. And then they do drugs, which in the short run—in the interim—feels good or gets them away from the bad feelings, like sugar tastes good on my tongue, but in the long run, it makes things go down hill for them.

*Ellie*: Um hmm.

*Bill*: So, I think, okay, you know in your worst moments your tendency, Ellie's tendency, is to withdraw. You may have other vices as well that we haven't heard about (*Ellie laughs*), but we know your tendency is to withdraw from people.

*Ellie*: Um hmm.

*Bill*: And, in the short run, it seems to relieve you a little, to withdraw from people. In the long run, it's the worst thing you can do.

*Ellie*: Right! Exactly!

*Bill*: So, what I would say is, whenever you feel the worst, whenever I feel the worst, I should eat protein (*Bill laughs*). Whenever you feel the worst, you should head for the people.

*Ellie*: Um hmm.

*Bill*: When Ellie feels bad, my prescription for you is take two people *(Ellie laughs)* and call them in the morning.

*Ellie*: Yeah. In the morning.

*Bill*: Call Mickey in the morning.

*Ellie*: Yeah.

*Bill*: Get together with other people.

*Ellie*: Yeah.

*Bill*: Because your tendency when you're in confusion-land, when you're in doubt, when you're in depression-land, when you're in unconfidence, is to go back into yourself.

*Ellie*: Yeah.

*Bill*: And there's certainly a time for that, I admit, but if you're doing the worst, that's not the time for it.

*Ellie*: Right.

*Bill*: That's the time to go out into the world and make contact with other people. And then, later, you can spend time by yourself, 'cause there's nothing bad about that.

*Ellie*: Um hmm.

*Bill*: I can have sugar once I've had proteins.

*Ellie*: Right.

*Bill*: So, I think it's the same prescription. Get yourself out rather than in.

*Ellie*: Um hmm.

*Bill*: When things are going bad, if you go in, you're . . . likely to dwell in there for a while in a no-fun place. And, I'm not saying avoid the issues you need to deal with. Go ahead and deal with them later, but not at that moment; that's not a good time to sort out where you're going in life or who you are. That's the worst time—

*Ellie*: Um hmm.

*Bill*: —to sort it out, because all you do is go into doubt and discouragement and depressions.

*Ellie*: Um hmm.

*Bill*: Get out and be with other people, and then, later, come home and think, "Now where am I?"

*Ellie*: Yeah, yeah, a lot of times I think I need to do all this thinking, all by myself. . .

*Bill*: Yeah.

*Ellie*: And that's when it kind of spirals into—

*Bill*: Yeah.

*Ellie*: —something worse.

*Bill*: Yeah, right. And then it doesn't ever get the first thing you wanted to sort out sorted out, because you're into depression at that point—

*Ellie*: Um hmm.

*Bill*: And you're not thinking very clearly.

*Ellie*: Um hmm.

*Bill*: I think it dovetails nicely with what we are talking about. Anything else that you think is important that we haven't talked about or covered at this point that's pretty crucial?

*Ellie*: Um.

*Bill*: Have we covered the main points?

*Ellie*: Um, I think you've covered the main points. I have been feeling more scared about totally not being able to cope—

*Bill*: Uh—

*Ellie*: —like I said, more than I ever have before. . . .

*Bill*: —it's like, "Oh my God, it's even worse this time." Would you say that's true, in general, that there's been a trend and—

*Ellie*: Yeah.

*Bill*: —it's even worse each time?

*Ellie*: Yeah. Yeah.

*Bill*: I attribute that to just the discouragement of, "Here we go again."

*Ellie*: Um hmm.

*Bill*: Yeah, the discouragement of, "Is this going to happen for the rest of my life, am I not going to make it through? I mean, they're pretty terrible, I mean, am I not going to make it through?"

*Ellie*: Yeah.

*Bill*: I have a friend, a mentor, John Weakland, who's a brief therapist. He told me, "Bill, you know, you've got to be humble as a therapist, because you'll never fix people's lives forever, I mean, that's utopia. Because it's just like the old saying, you know, 'Life is just one damn thing after another.'"

*Ellie*: Huh.

*Bill*: "But for people who come into therapy, here's the discouraging thing—that life has become the same damn thing over and over again."

*Ellie*: Um hmm.

*Bill*: So I think that's what you're talking about—

*Ellie*: Yeah.

*Bill*: —is that when your life becomes the same damn thing over and over again, it's a little more discouraging.

*Ellie*: Yeah.

*Bill*: So I'm concerned that if this keeps happening, you may not make it on this planet after a while. You may check out. You may say, "It's not worth living like this anymore."

*Ellie*: Um hmm. Um hmm.

*Bill*: At the times when you're doing better, it's worth being around, but you forget about that during the midst of that tough time.

*Ellie*: Right.

*Bill*: And I think it would be a real shame if you made that decision on one of these episodes because, "Here we go again, here we go again."

*Ellie*: Um hmm.

*Bill*: So, I think it's pretty crucial to have a sense of empowerment so that you can know that you can get out of these or prevent them.

*Ellie*: That it's me that's doing it and. . . .

*Bill*: Right. Because that strengthens the confidence muscle—

*Ellie*: Um hmm.

*Bill*: —and then you don't fear so much. It's, "Here we go again and I need to do the stuff that I planned." But you won't feel like, "I'm a victim of this and there's nothing I can do, I just have to ride through it, and I'm not sure I'm up to riding through it."

*Ellie*: Um hmm.

*Bill*: "I get so scared, I get so discouraged, I get so, you know, it disrupts my life, I'm not moving on, because I keep having to interrupt my life for these things."

*Ellie*: Right, right. But if I, like, have these action plans on what to do, maybe it won't be so scary the next time.

*Bill*: If you put them into place. It (*Ellie laughs*)—that's the crucial element (*Ellie laughs*). You can have the plans, all the plans (*Ellie laughs*). You've actually got to put them into. . . .

*Ellie*: Oh yes, doing it.

*Bill*: And, again, what I would say is be gentle with yourself. So maybe you're not perfect at putting them into place, but if you do a little more than you did before—

*Ellie*: Um hmm.

*Bill*: —that's progress.

*Ellie*: Yeah.

*Bill*: And then, ultimately, putting them into play so you just don't go into that same month-and-a-half, two-month, three-month period, it's maybe a week, you know. Maybe you do have a physiology or a neurology that's more likely to get you depressed, so you may have to use these plans the rest of your life at times.

*Ellie*: Um hmm.

*Bill*: I thought I did, but to tell you the truth, over the years, I just don't go into these depressions—

*Ellie*: Hmm.

*Bill*: —anymore. So, for me, it wasn't physiological or neurological. It was pretty much emotional, psychological, and lifestyle kind of stuff.

*Ellie*: Um hmm.

*Bill*: For other people it might be more neurological, physiological, or whatever, but to me, it hasn't been. What it will be for you if you actually put this action plan into play, when you put it in play, you'll find out, I think, whether you continue to, every once in a while, be plagued by the likelihood of going into these things, or whether it just goes away once you settle it.

*Ellie*: I think, I think it'll really help.

*Bill*: Um hmm.

*Ellie*: I do. It feels like it'll really help.

*Bill*: Great (*Ellie laughs*).

*Bill*: Well, again, you have a possibility of getting a copy of this tape, and you can watch it again to remind yourself, and if you're in the midst of depression, and you don't feel like watching soap operas, you could watch the tape (*Ellie laughs*).

*Ellie*: I think that would be great.

*Bill*: Any other questions or comments or concerns you have before we end?

*Ellie*: Um, no. Thank you.

*Bill*: So I think that's all.

*Ellie*: You're great!

*Bill*: Oh, well, thank you! That's a nice thing to say.

When I called Ellie for a follow-up, I did not get her directly, so I left a message. She returned the call and left this message on my answering machine: "I'm doing fine. Meeting with you really made a difference. And it's helped me a lot." That's the short version of the follow-up.

During our subsequent conversation, she indicated that she had followed through on the plan of going to her therapist's office for a brief check-in each day at 9:30 A.M. She met with the therapist three more times after the consultation. The therapist got her to write down and follow through on a "to do" list each day. She got a temp job and started going out more with friends. She restarted flute lessons and joined a quartet that meets regularly.

When asked to compare and contrast meeting with me with other therapists and what was helpful, she said it was helpful to contrast and describe in detail the difference between depressed times and nondepressed times. She also mentioned that this was the first time she had felt that she could do something about the depression herself. Before she had always thought therapists would have to get her out of it. She also mentioned that she thought we could accomplish so much in one session because she knew that I understood her depression. "You had been there too, and that was good to know."

She said that having her describe what she did while she was depressed was hard but helpful. "Nobody had ever had me describe in such detail what I did while I was depressed. It was embarrassing." However, she was able to see while describing what she did that there were things she could do to get herself out of it. She said, "Because of the way I get depressed, many therapists have problems with me. They get discouraged or stuck."

Without any prompting from me, she gave me some history during the follow-up. She thought her trouble had started when her parents divorced. Her father was cold and distant; her mother was overinvolved and dependent on Ellie. When Ellie moved away, it had upset the balance and the mother divorced the father. Ellie had run to Chicago to escape family problems and to establish her independence. She did both and then decided it was time to return and deal with her family. She moved back to the area in which she grew up, and she moved in with her father, who had since remarried a very warm and friendly stepmother. She grew close to both of them and then found a job and moved about an hour away from where her father and mother lived. In Chicago, she had had two long-term relationships that ended badly, especially the last one, with a man who had decided after several years that he did not want to commit.

Follow-up contact with Ellie's therapist, Mickey, indicated that Ellie had followed through with the arrangement. She had checked in every morning before 9:30 A.M. between Mickey's clients, just for a minute. She came in only three times after Ellie's meeting with me. They mutually agreed to stop therapy in part due to money concerns and insurance hassles. Every once in a while, Ellie would start on some of the old patterns in therapy—those of dwelling on family of origin issues and what was wrong with her. Mickey, citing Ellie's session with me, would then steer her into focusing on what was working during those sessions. Ellie appreciated being reminded and agreed with this new focus. Ellie called a few weeks after treatment ended to tell Mickey that she had a new boyfriend and that things were going well.

Because Mickey usually worked in a much different, usually long-term, more psychodynamic and functionally oriented way, I asked her what she thought of the consultation. She told me that she did not think that this type of therapy would work for most of her patients, but that it seemed to work quite well for Ellie. I asked her if she had any concerns that she did not think were dealt with in the consultation and she said that we had not dealt with a long-standing relationship pattern of Ellie's. As mentioned above, Mickey had gathered the impression that Ellie would get into relationships with people (especially romantic/sexual relationships with men) and then get too needy and dependent. Her partner would start to withdraw and then Ellie would get even more clingy and dependent, which would ultimately sow the seeds for the dissolution of the relationship. Mickey said that she would expect Ellie to continue to have those problems, since the therapy and my consultation did not resolve those "core relationship and characterological issues." I explained that the way I would handle that issue, since Ellie did not bring it up in our meeting, was to tell Ellie that since she had now found that she could make a difference in her depressions, if she ever had any other concerns, my door was open for return visits. Building on our relationship and on her previous success, I assumed we would have an easier time sorting the relationship issues out, but I would prefer to wait until Ellie was in a relationship to deal with those issues. That way, we would get a chance to try some experiments to make a change from the old unworkable patterns, rather than just to talk about or analyze them. This reassured Mickey that my approach was not just dismissing or denying other issues.

I spoke to Ellie about Mickey's concern that we hadn't taken care of the core relationship issues. That led to a few minutes of discussion about what would be the warning signs that she was starting to go into "dependency patterns" in her new relationship, with Bruce, a guy at work—she said that when she felt a helpless feeling, similar to the feeling of depression. We agreed that she would again seek out friends and spend time away from Bruce if she felt the warning signs. She would also force herself to keep up her friendships while establishing the relationship with Bruce. I told her that I thought she had two good models for what she needed to balance in her relationship with Bruce. Her mother had showed her how to get close to people and her father had showed her how to keep a distance. Perhaps she could balance the two, since she had them both in her. She might also use her new stepmother, who was pretty balanced, in those areas, as a model and a consultant. She liked that idea.

## REFERENCES

Gale, J. E. (1991). *Conversation analysis of therapeutic discourse: Pursuit of a therapeutic agenda.* Norwood, NJ: Ablex.

Hudson, P. O., & O'Hanlon, W. H. (1991). *Rewriting love stories: Brief marital therapy.* New York: Norton.

O'Hanlon, W. H. (1987). *Taproots: Underlying principles of Milton Erickson's therapy and hypnosis.* New York: Norton.

O'Hanlon, W. H., & Martin, M. (1992). *Solution-oriented hypnosis: An Ericksonian approach.* New York: Norton.

O'Hanlon, W. H., & Weiner-Davis, M. (1989). *In search of solutions: A new direction in psychotherapy.* New York: Norton.

O'Hanlon, B., & Wilk, J. (1987). *Shifting contexts: The generation of effective psychotherapy.* New York: Guilford.

Chapter 11

# Accountability in Psychotherapy

## A Quality Assurance Method

**Bill O'Hanlon**

*We are headed nowhere, and we are moving there at a very slow pace.*
—William Dunkelberg, National Federation of Independent Businesses
(*Fortune*, 1/13/92, p. 36, Vol. 125, #1)

One of the persistent problems with the field of psychotherapy is the difficulty of defining and measuring results. In other fields, progress is achieved when a consensus is reached on measuring relevant variables and improving the results based on such measurement. So far there is no consensus in psychotherapy about how to define problems and what constitutes successful results. The Deming method of quality improvement, so successfully adopted by many Japanese industries, is based on the ability to quantify quality measures and strive to make constant incremental improvements. This monograph suggests a method for measuring and quantifying results and quality in psychotherapy.

There are four factors that make up this definition of quality and results:

1) Resolution of the presenting problem(s)
2) Client/customer ratings of satisfaction with therapy
3) Length of treatment to resolution of problems or termination
4) Percentage of fees collected compared with fees charged

This is an unpublished manuscript that was dug out of the O'Hanlon archives.

## RESOLUTION OF THE PRESENTING PROBLEM(S)

Many theories of psychotherapy disregard the client's presenting problem or consider just a surface manifestation of deeper, underlying problems or issues. In contrast, this approach takes at face value what the client (customer) complains about as the presenting problem and considers therapy successful when the client is no longer complaining about the problem or has stopped experiencing the problem. The description of the problem and the goal is subject to negotiation to ensure that it is achievable and likely to be solved rapidly.

In order to ensure feasibility and measurement of problem resolution, the problem and goal should be stated in "videotalk," that is, in terms that describe the problem and the goal in action language. The therapist and any observer must be able to imagine in detail, as if they could see and hear it on a videotape, the problem and the goal.

A basic concern is determining who the customer/client is. Sometimes the person who enters the therapist's office is not the complainant and is not a customer for therapy. In that case, it is important to determine who the customer is and what he or she is a customer for. One could also find out what the person who is in the office's goals and problems are and whether therapy is the appropriate place to solve those problems and reach those goals.

## CLIENT/CUSTOMER SATISFACTION

This variable could be measured in various ways. Was the client satisfied with the treatment overall? Some clients have reported being satisfied with treatment even when their goals have not been attained. One might assess various aspects of the treatment and strive to improve the average scores on each. For example, clients could be asked how satisfied they were about how quickly they were given an appointment when they initially sought services. They could rate their satisfaction with the timeliness of their therapist at each session.

In some cases, there is a second customer: the referral source. This might be a physician, the court, a probation officer, a school counselor or psychologist, an Employee Assistance Program (EAP) counselor, or a supervisor. It is important to ensure the referral source's satisfaction for continued referrals and for keeping or gaining a good reputation.

In most health care maintenance (HMO) and managed care settings, there is often a third customer/client. The company that buys the HMO or managed care package makes the crucial decision at contract renewal time about the cost/benefit ratio. It is important to regularly measure company satisfaction, so there is an opportunity to make improvements before contract renewal time.

These ratings of client/customer satisfaction, if high, could be used as part of the marketing and sales efforts to sell new contracts or convince contractors to renew.

Other aspects of service could be measured, such as response time after initial contact or phone call, response time for phone calls after the initial visit, lag time until initial appointment is given, courtesy/responsiveness of front desk/ receptionist/financial support staff, etc.

## LENGTH OF TREATMENT TO PROBLEM RESOLUTION OR TERMINATION

This is a relatively simple measure, determining the length of the treatment from beginning to end. The length could be measured in number of sessions (50 minutes = 1 session) or length of time (days, weeks, months, or years) or both. One would have to set a cut-off time for this measurement, e.g., six months without any face-to-face contact, because clients can return to treatment for the same or different problems at any time.

## PERCENTAGE OF FEES COLLECTED BASED ON FEES CHARGED

For some settings, this measurement would be irrelevant, as the contract sets automatic payments, but for others it is a crucial measure of the effectiveness of the therapist at collecting for services performed. Many programs have some form of copayments. These payments are handled often by collection/secretarial personnel, but the therapist can still have an influence on fees collected.

Since many therapists are notorious at not collecting fees and some therapists are quite good at collecting 100% of fees charged, this could be a measurement for quality that can be used to assess therapist competence. As the fees collected affect the financial health of the organization, this is a vital area of competence and, when measured, could be improved.

These four factors, when taken together, can indicate on an ongoing basis how the provider is doing in providing results and satisfaction in psychotherapy. This gives the opportunity for continued, incremental improvements in quality, efficiency, and effectiveness. It also provides some tools for measuring the performance of particular clinicians and offices/departments. These measurements could be used to provide guidance on where and when to give bonuses or incentive programs. They can also be used to decide who needs additional training in brief, results-oriented clinical approaches or who should be retained or perhaps even fired based on continued inability to achieve quality results efficiently.

It is important in making these measurements that we consider the potentially demoralizing or threatening impact of measuring success or quality in psychotherapy on clinicians. Dr. Deming makes an important point in claiming that individual performance appraisals are counterproductive. To minimize the threat of this demoralization, I suggest that each therapist or each clinic be measured on grouped data, for example, average stay in therapy per clinic or office or for therapist over the course of one year. It might also be important not to measure a particular therapist's statistics against a general norm, but instead against previous recorded statistics for that therapist. For example, if a therapist had a previous year's average of 17 sessions per client, the goal might be to bring that average down by two sessions (to 15 sessions) during the next year.

In addition, it is important to distinguish between limiting the number of sessions available to psychotherapy clients, which often creates dissatisfaction from clients and service purchasers, and the approach of working with service providers to ensure more timely delivery of high-quality effective therapy. There is some research to indicate that training therapists in brief therapy methods and philosophy decreases length of stay of clients in therapy. Again, Dr. Deming has stressed not blaming the workers or the customers when something is not efficient or profitable; he recommends examining the provider system and ensuring training toward consistent high-quality results.

Psychotherapy should take into account several factors that will convince third-party payers and fourth-party reviewers of the value of our services:

- Reduced cost for the entire treatment. Can we show that we are making progress on reducing the costs and effectiveness of our treatments?
- Reduced medical/legal utilization. Can we show that our treatments can significantly and measurably reduce costs and use of more costly medical services or reduce criminal behavior or recidivism in prisons?
- Reduced suicide attempts. Can we show that we have reduced attempts at suicide by those likely to attempt or commit?
- Reduced drug/alcohol misuse. Can we show we can really reduce drug or alcohol misuse or abuse, thereby reducing traffic fatalities, drug/alcohol overdoses/deaths, and alcohol and drug problems that interfere with work or productivity?
- Reduced use of hospital stays. Can we show that we are using the most cost effective and efficient treatment, rather than the most lucrative? Recent studies of alcohol treatment challenged the long-held idea that inpatient treatment is more effective than outpatient for treating this problem.

All of the considerations above point to the idea that we must be working constantly to improve our productivity and value. It is hard to bring accountability to therapy because many theories introduce vague concepts ("working through") and diagnoses (low self-esteem, depression). We need to introduce viewable/checkable operationalized diagnoses that we can all agree upon and then come to a consensus about what constitutes good results in therapy. In this chapter, I have tried to point toward some measures that could bring accountability into therapy and thus help ensure its future and improve its acceptance and effectiveness.

Chapter 12

# History Becomes Her Story

## Collaborative Solution-Oriented Therapy of the Aftereffects of Sexual Abuse

**Bill O'Hanlon**

Due in part to publicity surrounding the issue and increased therapeutic interest, a growing number of people are seeking help for having been sexually abused in childhood. Most of the approaches in the literature or taught in workshops, however, have an objectivist and pathological bias. In this paper, I will describe an alternate approach that opens the possibility for briefer treatment that does not necessarily involve catharsis or remembering the details of the abuse as a way of resolving the aftereffects. I call this approach collaborative solution-oriented therapy (O'Hanlon & Weiner-Davis, 1989).

The approach I offer here suggests that therapists cannot help but influence the memories and views the client has while in therapy, so it is important to influence clients in the direction of empowerment and moving on as rapidly as possible. I am suggesting also that each person is different—everyone is an exception—so one cannot have general principles that hold true for everyone. Treating the aftereffects of sexual abuse may involve short- or long-term treatment, it may involve remembering feelings or forgotten and repressed memories or it may not. It may involve helping the person move on and focus on the present and the future. The principles I describe below are the ones I most often bring to the table in my collaboration with clients. I stand for orienting toward solutions and com-

This manuscript originally appeared in the 1992 book, *Therapy as Social Construction: Inquiries in Social Construction* (Sage), edited by Sheila McNamee and Ken Gergen. This article along with *Frozen in Time: Possibility Therapy With Adults Who Were Sexually Abused as Children*, preceded the book (with Bob Bertolino), *Even From a Broken Web: Brief, Respectful Solution-Oriented Therapy for Sexual Abuse* and Trauma (Wiley).

petence rather than problems and pathology; for acknowledging people's experience and points of view without closing down the possibilities for change; focusing therapy on achieving the client's goals; and negotiating solvable problems. These stances interact with the values, experiences, responses, and ideas of my clients so that in therapeutic conversations we collaboratively construct our therapeutic reality and solutions.

A basic component of this approach is that assessment is an intervention; clients and therapists cocreate the problem that is to be focused on in therapy (O'Hanlon & Wilk, 1987). I think this is the case whether or not the therapist is aware of it, so it is incumbent upon the therapist to take care in the kind of problem he or she is cocreating. Not all problems are created equal. Some will take quite a long time to resolve and some a much briefer course of treatment. Some will empower people to be the experts on their problems and to have a sense of personal agency and some will invalidate and discourage clients.

Current approaches to the treatment of the aftereffects of sexual abuse hold that they are discovering and uncovering the truth about clients' childhoods. They also imply that the only way to help clients resolve these issues is to remember, feel, and express the feelings and incidents they repressed involving the abuse.

In this paper, I will provide the transcript of a brief therapeutic intervention with a woman who has been suffering aftereffects from being sexually abused. I will also provide some principles for doing this work in the form of charts and commentary on the case.

## SOLUTION ORIENTATION

If different problem definitions can be negotiated from the raw material clients bring to therapy, then it is incumbent upon the therapist to choose ways of thinking and talking in therapy that allow for the creation of problems that are solvable. Beyond that, he or she can create problems that are solvable quickly and with only the resources that clients have available to them.

Most therapists have conversations with clients that lead to the view that they are suffering from some pathological, psychological, emotional, neurological, or biochemical disorder. Focusing so much on what is wrong with people can have a discouraging effect. People tend to see themselves as sick and damaged. They often forget the resources, strengths, and capabilities they have.

What I am suggesting is that the therapist deliberately have conversations for solutions with clients. There are many aspects of human behavior and experience, then, that one could focus on in therapy. Where we put our attention and direct our inquiries will inevitably influence the course of treatment and the data that emerge. Since all successful therapy eventually comes around to finding solutions by getting people to do something different or to view things differently, I propose that we start pursuing these goals more deliberately from the start of therapy. In this view, clients are presumed to have resources and competence to make the changes they want to make. The therapist's job is to create a context in which clients get access to their resources and competence. The interviewing process is designed to elicit and highlight these competencies (de Shazer, 1985).

While stressing the solution-oriented aspects of this work, I want to emphasize that I do not suggest minimizing or denying people's pain or suffering or invalidating their views on their difficulties.

## ACKNOWLEDGMENT AND POSSIBILITY

In therapy, it is important that the therapist acknowledges people's pain and suffering as well as their points of view about their problems, but the fine balance that must be achieved is how to do this while keeping the possibilities for change open. Sometimes people have a view of their situation that makes it difficult or impossible to resolve.

One way to achieve this balance is to acknowledge people's feelings, experiences, and points of view without agreeing or disagreeing with them and to then open up possibilities for new views and new feelings and experiences. A common method for doing this is to use the past tense when reflecting the client's reported feelings and points of view that have been troublesome for them and using the present or future tense when mentioning new feelings, goals, and new points of view. For example, "So you've been afraid right before having sex. When you are feeling more comfortable before sex, what do you think you will do or say differently to your partner?"

## COMMISSION AND COMMISSION-GIVER

At an international family therapy conference in Ireland in 1989, I listened to some folks from Sweden (Mia Andersson, Klas Grevelius, and Ernst Salamon of the AGS Institute) talk about their work. They discussed the importance of finding out what the commission is in therapy and who the commission-giver is in each case. I loved that idea. In English, this word lends itself to a nice pun. What I try to discover and create with my clients is a co-mission.

The therapist also has an agenda. Some of that agenda derives from the therapist's theories, some from his or her values, and some from his or her legal, ethical, financial, or agency concerns. Out of the therapist's and client's agendas come some mutually agreed-upon goals. If we do not develop some joint, mutually agreeable goals, we will probably have a rocky, "resistant" relationship. I will be resistant to hearing them and working on their goals and they will not cooperate with my agendas.

In any particular case, there may be more than one commission-giver and more than one co-mission. The therapist's job, then, is to develop a mission statement that all concerned can agree upon and support.

## CRITERIA FOR SATISFACTION/GOALS FOR TREATMENT

Steve de Shazer of Milwaukee's Brief Family Therapy Center has a nice phrase for this: "How will we know when we're supposed to stop meeting like this?" If therapy is to come to a successful conclusion, it is a good idea to get some idea of how we will know it has been successful.

Since I have already said that I think that therapists cocreate problems with clients, I obviously don't think that having a problem is the indication for starting therapy. Many people have difficulties and never enter therapy. Therapy starts when someone is complaining about something and someone decides that what is being complained about is relevant for therapy. Of course, sometimes someone other than the person who shows up for the session is complaining (as in cases of "involuntary" treatment, such as court-ordered treatment and parents who bring their children to have therapy when the children do not perceive a difficulty).

Therapy can end satisfactorily, then, simply when whoever was complaining about something no longer complains about it. This happens in two ways: one is when what the person was complaining about is no longer perceived as a problem. The other condition for successfully ending therapy is when what the client was complaining about is no longer happening often enough or intensely enough for the person to say it is a problem.

A goal, then, is the magnetic north that can orient the therapist's compass. One of the difficulties in the field of therapy is our inability to define what constitutes successful treatment. Goals, in collaborative solution-oriented therapy, should derive mainly from the client's vision of what constitutes success, subject to some negotiation with the therapist to ensure the achievability of the goal. Measurement of success should come from clients' reports. If clients believably say that what they were complaining about is no longer happening, then therapy has succeeded.

I have compiled a chart, *Contrasting Approaches to the Treatment of the Aftereffects of Sexual Abuse*, which summarizes many of the differences between this approach and traditional models and methods.

## CONTRASTING APPROACHES TO THE TREATMENT OF THE AFTEREFFECTS OF SEXUAL ABUSE

---

### *Traditional Approaches*

- Therapist is the expert—has special knowledge regarding sexual abuse to which the client needs to submit (colonization/missionary model).
- Client is viewed as damaged by the abuse (deficit model).
- Remembering abuse and the expression of repressed affect (catharsis) are goals of treatment.
- Interpretation.
- Past-oriented.
- Problem/pathology-oriented.
- Must be long-term treatment.
- Invites conversations for insight and working through.

### Solution-Oriented Therapy

- Client and therapist both have particular areas of expertise (collaborative model).
- Client is viewed as influenced but not determined by the abuse history, having strengths, and abilities (resource model).
- Goals are individualized for each client but do not necessarily involve catharsis or remembering.
- Acknowledgment, valuing, and opening possibilities.
- Present/future-oriented.
- Solution-oriented.
- Variable/individualized length of treatment.
- Invites conversations for accountability and action and declines invitations to blame and invalidation.

*Source:* Parts of this chart were adapted from Durrant and Kowalski (1990).

## INTRODUCTION TO THE SESSION

This session took place during the third day of a workshop I was doing on "solution-oriented hypnosis." The day was devoted to using hypnosis and solution-oriented therapy with people who complained about the aftereffects of sexual abuse.

I offer this case to show the possibility that the treatment of the aftereffects of sexual abuse can be brief and does not necessarily involve catharsis or long-term work. This woman, S, a therapist attending the workshop, had in the past few years remembered having been sexually abused in her childhood. She had connected her experience of detachment (dissociation) during sexual activity and her compulsive and unsatisfying sexual activities (often involving dangerous sex, such as being beaten or having sex with a stranger in a public place) with the abuse. Consequently she had stopped the dangerous sex, but she still had the experience of being detached and afraid before and during sex. We were both aware that we had only this one session to help her achieve her goals.

As you shall read, we negotiated two main goals for our work. The first was to help her be more present and less fearful before and during sex. The second was to remember more of her younger sister, who had recently died of cancer. S speculated that when she had forgotten the abuse, she had also forgotten many other things from her childhood, including good memories of time she spent with her sister. Because her sister was now dead, those lost memories were more precious and she wanted help in recalling them.

I started, where I usually start, with getting an initial statement from the person about what they want.

*William O'Hanlon* [WOH]: So how may I help you? I want to start a complaint-land. Tell me so I can be oriented toward recent concerns or complaints and how you'll know when you get there, when you've achieved your goal. *[I try to orient toward recent concerns. The implicit message is that the past is not all that relevant. I also want an initial statement about a complaint so we can begin the process of focusing on creating a solvable problem and achievable goals.]*

*S*: The most recent complaint I would say would be intermittent lack of sexual desire, and, then, I'll still have sex, but I don't . . .

*WOH*: You won't be there totally. You won't be into it.

*S*: I feel afraid right at the moment, right before, and then I can kind of push through it sometimes and then other times I go into the numb state, where I'm not really there but I'm there. And still having fairly severe menstrual cramps and . . . Hmmm. . . .

*WOH*: So how will you know when you get there? *[S starts to add more complaints and I try to focus by asking about goals.]*

*S*: How will I know when I get there? Well . . .

*WOH*: When you get through it, when you leave that behind, when that's taken care of. *[S hesitated, so I restated my request for a goal statement.]*

*S*: Yeah, leave that behind and . . .

*WOH*: Okay, less severe menstrual cramps—that seems to be related to you or you don't know that it's related? *[I'm not sure that the menstrual cramps are relevant to the intermittent lack of sexual desire and her not getting involved when she's having sex, so I gently challenge their relevance to the problem we are to work on.]*

*S*: Well I know that. . . . I guess just to give you a little background for up until the last five years I couldn't remember from 0–11 years of age. And my memory went to 11 years of age and my memory started when I had my first kiss with a boy and then through hypnosis in the past five years little by little and flashbacks . . . the memory of a sexual abuse when I was 6 years old by a cousin who was 16. It was interesting because I was just reading a *People* magazine article about this woman who disassociated and that was when, you know, like you said, you read a book or something and that is when it just all flooded back up that that is what I have done all of my life is just, you know, disassociate either in sex or I have all these different parts—I can be the perfect professional, the perfect daughter but still then running out and screwing a stranger in an elevator or something like that. You know, that kind of thing.

*WOH*: Right. Okay, so you recognized that when you read that it was like . . . WOW. *[S responds with some history. I did not ask for this history, but since she has provided it, I'd better include and acknowledge it.]*

*S*: Right. That was kind of what she had done and it hit me and also it has just come up that maybe there was some pleasure involved and that's what made me perhaps forget the whole thing was the fact that maybe I had caused it. . . .

*WOH*: That you couldn't deal with that.

*S*: And I have always kind of had that my whole life—appearing to be very sexual and . . . I have always called myself the elephant man because on one (hand), I look this way on the outside, but inside I have always felt I was a different person looking out and couldn't really get too much of it. . . .

*WOH*: Acting out.

*S*: So I could act things out really perfectly and pretend that I was the great seductress and everything, but really I was. . . .

*WOH*: Inside.

*S*: I was either not there or a scared little girl or pretending or acting. So I guess another thing would be if some memories could come back. Now I remember the abuse, although I never confronted the abuser. But I lost my youngest sister to cancer about two years ago, and I would kind of like to bring back some memories just to have more of. . . .

*WOH*: Sense of what growing up with her was like?

*S*: Right.

*WOH*: So to have the nicer parts of that too.

*S*: That would be another thing is to have the good memories come back too.

*WOH*: Okay, good. And so just to summarize for me: the work you have done over the five years or whenever through hypnosis. You remembered some things, a lot of the abuse, you think, or most of it, or part of it, or . . . ?

*S*: Well, actually, I remember I had a boyfriend in high school, that I was laying there on a couch one time, and I opened my eyes and he was standing above me with an erect penis right above me and I screamed at the top of my lungs and he couldn't understand. It was sort of that same reaction, like the woman who screamed at you. *[This was a reference to a story I had told earlier about a co-worker who had yelled at me but was really yelling at someone else she was angry with who wasn't in the room.]* Where are you coming from kind of thing.

*WOH*: Right.

*S*: Then as time went on all of the sudden it was the flash of like somebody turning around and I would have been probably waist level of him, and I think that's what happened—that he in kind of a gentle way came over and said, "this is my pee-pee and this is yours" and kind of made it like a game and "let's do something." And I think I had a fairly dominated childhood by my mother, so doing something she didn't know about—that was maybe like an adult and feeling old and so, I don't really remember, you know. I'm pretty sure there was penetration because I never had uh . . . when you . . .

*WOH*: A hymen.

*S*: Right, a hymen or anything. And I always talked myself into the fact that I must have done it doing gymnastics or something. [*WOH*: Yeah, that's the sort of . . .] And then again I don't know, because then why didn't I have some kind of physical ramification that I went and cried to? Also I had one flash of actually seeing my father—it happened in a barn, so maybe we would go away (it was on a farm) and play in the barn and I would see this vision of my father walking up past the door on the outside and there were windows on the outside. . . . Like there were windows on the barn door. . . . Like something was happening—we were engaged in sex and then I saw him. Then for many years I hated him. For a long time I thought he was the one maybe that had and I felt like maybe it was sexually abuse but I then I thought I was making this up and then all . . .

*WOH*: Right.

*S*: . . . of these ramifications, these problems

*WOH*: So, it's still not totally clear for you all that happened, but you have a sense of what happened.

*S*: Right, right.

*WOH*: Okay.

*S*: And I don't really know how to totally resolve it. I would like to resolve it within myself whether I ever confront him about it or not.

*WOH*: That is something different and you may or may not do that. I just thought of something though that may be helpful for you. Sometimes I have people write a letter, not so that they are going to send a letter to that person—to the cousin or to whomever it may be—not so they were going to send it, but write it as if they were going to send it, but not sending it. And write this whole letter. Everything you would say from what you know right now or anything you . . . yell at them or apologize—whatever you feel moved to do. Whatever it is. And write it all out and then if you ever did decide to actually write a letter, to save that letter or else get rid of it but to save the pieces of it that you would actually send in a real letter.

*S*: I did think of, in a nice way saying, "Look, you know, I have worked all through this but could you just confirm . . . ?"

*WOH*: Yeah, "Could you just tell me what happened?"

*S*: Like circle *yes* or *no*.

*WOH*: Check *yes* or *no*. I did this on this day . . . (*laughter*)

*S*: Not to tell the family or hurt anybody else or anything.

*WOH*: Right. Just to remember this and, "Did this happen?" and "Am I remembering it right? Was there any stuff I didn't remember?"

*S*: Right.

## SOLUTION-ORIENTED HYPNOSIS

Here I start to do hypnosis. Solution-oriented hypnosis is a collaborative venture. As you will be able to read, it is a permissive, empowering, rather than authoritarian, approach to hypnosis.

The purpose of this type of hypnosis is different from traditional approaches as well. In traditional hypnosis, the hypnotherapist attempts to uncover repressed memories and feelings, to get the person to abreact or remember the sexual abuse. Or the hypnotherapist tries to counteract the negative injunctions and beliefs established during the abuse by substituting more positive beliefs, affirmations, and self-talk.

Solution-oriented hypnosis intends to evoke resources, strengths, and abilities and help people renarrate their situation. It is a way to help people *experience* their situation differently, not just talk about it differently.

Multiple-choice options for making changes are given and new distinctions and connections are proposed. The person will not take up all the options provided, but will pick and choose among the alternatives to find the ones that fit for her. The point is not to have people abreact and express their feelings and points of view, but to *change* those feelings and points of view.

Now to the trancework.

*WOH*: Good, so you have been in trance before lots of times.

*S*: Yeah.

*WOH*: Okay, good. So let yourself go into trance and I am going to say in a way that is appropriate for you, safe for you, as safe as possible in this particular setting—for you to go wherever you need to go to move yourself along toward those goals, toward resolving, toward remembering just as much as you need to remember and just as little as you need to remember, and you may have already done all of the remembering you need to do or want to do and somehow find a way to create the room in there—the space in there for you to validate who you are, how you are, for you to include your history, your experience, the things you have done, the things that have been done to you. . . . To be able to leave the then time in the then time and when you are in the now time to be able to know about all the then time that you need to know about as part of your background of learnings and experience and to really be in the now time *[So far I have been acknowledging the difficulties and opening up new possibilities. One of the implicit ("history") and explicit ("leave the then time in the then time") suggestions is to put the past in the past, where it belongs.]* and to be able to give yourself permission. . . . That's right *[She started to nod her head]* . . . to have felt the things you've felt and separate that from blame or approval and find some way to reconcile and connect in a way that is meaningful to you the past to the present to the future and to disconnect any parts that are not meaningful to you or useful for you—to know about consciously and bring into the present and the future. As we've talked all day, you have abilities, skills, resources and strengths, coping mechanisms, ways of dealing with things, ways of not dealing with things, and you can just rearrange those in any way that you need to rearrange those. And your hand may start to lift up *[Here I am using her difficulty, dissociation, as her solution. In order to lift the hand automatically, one must dissociate it. As it continues up, I link it to the changes she is making. So, dissociation leads to integra-*

*tion and healing now.]* and that may be one of those things you have done in hypnosis before and it could lift up and as it starts to lift up to your face, you can be doing the work that you need to do. It may be in terms of resolving, and it may be in terms of remembering, and it may be in terms of remembering to forget the things that are interfering with your good memories—the memories you would like to keep more present and future. As that hand continues to lift up, and it can lift up to your face, it doesn't have to, and it might be lifting up to your face, and as it comes in contact with your face—as it does—that can be the signal for you to do whatever it is that you need to do to include within that work—any emotions or experiences you have had and that you have, that you need to have, whatever you need to know, experience at the rate of that which you could know that, and you can change time to do that in a way that is right for you. You can come up with something that lets you know that these changes have occurred. And when it is time in that process, as that hand continues—up toward your face—in an appropriate way you can find the resources you need to resolve that in a way that's right for you. And after it touches your face you can, at some time—when you are ready, maybe right away, maybe in a minute or two, three minutes—open your eyes and look at me when you are ready and I'm going to talk to you just briefly and find out from you if there is anything that I need to know or what I need to know. Now is there anything I need to know or to tell you to do inside or to talk to you about while you are in trance? So what is happening right now?

*S*: I see little boxes.

*WOH*: Little boxes?

*S*: With the then and the now, with a minus sign and an arrow taking all the hurtful experiences and leaving them and they kind of pass through the now and there were little like addition signs and they were kind of shifting around the boxes and they would superimpose on each other . . . and realizing that I am who I am because of them. *[After she came out of trance, in response to a question asking her to elaborate on this experience, she replied: "Yeah I saw that as the sexual abuse experience as well as other poor sexual choices that I had made through the years all caught in this little box. Then I saw my present life, all the good parts of it and strengths and coping mechanisms and they were like almost an addition—kind of like this little plus, and the future as good. But I knew I couldn't just keep it separate, so that's why I kind of moved it so it went on top of it like a superimposition."]*

*WOH*: Right and it has made, in a weird way, it has made a contribution to who you are. That is not all bad and good in a lot of ways. Okay, good. All right, so you close your eyes and find a way to put those things in their place and have them to be the platform upon which you stand to see farther into the future, to step off into the future, in a safe way so that you can feel solid grounding underneath you. And also I think it would be nice while you are in that trance to be able to find a way to make arrangements with yourself to be there for the pleasurable parts when it is safe and when it is a situation that you trust . . . to be there for the pleasurable parts of having sex—when it's appropriate for you—to be able to be fully in your experience and to know that what happened then was then and it had all sorts of ramifications then, had all sorts of meanings for then and as you were growing up. With the resources you have now and the understanding you have now and that you are getting as moments go on, minutes, days, months, and weeks and years go on, that you could come to a new understanding and even appreciation of your history.

One of the things for me is that I used to be real depressed and real shy and very miserable and I think that kind of sensitivity to that kind of pain has been one of the things that has made me very sensitive as a therapist to other people's pain and discomfort, also to the possibilities of change. Because, with me, I thought I was a hopeless case and now I realize I wasn't a hopeless case and that somewhere deep inside I knew I would make it through . . . that somewhere deep inside there was a strength and resilience even in the midst of what looked like fragility to me like I couldn't handle anything and that I couldn't deal with anything and I was full of fear, but I came to appreciate the sensitivity that gave me and to tap into the strengths. And that's one way I have come to reconcile myself with those experiences and those hurts. *[Here I offer a new frame of reference for her painful experience: that pain can lead to sensitivity to others' pain. This is relevant for her as a therapist.]*

I think it'd also be nice while you are in trance to really have something come to your mind that's pleasant from your childhood, from your growing up, maybe something to do with your sister—I think that'd be nice—maybe just a flash or maybe a full blown memory or experience or maybe just a feeling. I remember my sister and I as we were little, climbing in the middle of a bunk bed that was folded up. It was real tight and it felt like our fort. I don't really remember what it looked like or where it was, I just remember the feeling of that foldaway bed. And I think the body remembers those good feelings too in sort of a connection and a legacy that your sister left behind in your experience, your feelings and memories of her.

I was watching television last night, or the other night, and someone was saying, "It's amazing—I watched my grandchild and I can see some of the things that he does are just like my father, although he never met my father and isn't it interesting how these legacies get passed on." So your sister, even though she is not around, probably influenced people that you influence, that you are in contact with and connection with through the spirit and the memory of her, through those feelings. And you can bring those forward into the present and the future as well, and have a little more choice about that. Now in a minute I am going to suggest that that hand either starts to drift down or you can just put it down very deliberately, whatever is most comfortable for you. And that as it goes back down to your thigh . . . that's right . . . you can begin preparing to complete this experience in trance knowing that each trance experience completion is also the beginning of other things and the opening of other things. So do that in a way that's right for you when you are ready to come all of the way out of a trance leaving behind in trance the things that are for trance. Good. Thanks.

*S*: That was good. I saw her clearly.

*WOH*: That's great. Good. Good job.

*S*: A good memory just came back. *[S experienced some vivid memories of her sister while in trance.]*

*WOH*: That's nice. Okay. Good.

*[In the discussion afterward, S told me that the reason she had wanted to do the session right at that time was that she was getting married in a week. She had had a string of terrible and abusive relationships with men over the course of her adult life and had finally gotten into a good relationship with a man who was not abusive and seemed pretty healthy and supportive. He knew about her abuse history and was sensitive to her fear and discomfort with sex. She wanted their marriage to start out, however, without being dominated by her abuse history and the aftereffects.]*

S wrote me a letter a month later.

Dear Bill,

Just a short note to update you on my progress since our session. The first thing I noted when my husband and I had sex on our honeymoon night (one week after the seminar—the first chance we'd had to have sex all week with all the family in for the wedding) was that I did not dissociate. I was able to feel the physical enjoyment without having to retreat. I have also noticed a total extinguishing of the presex fears. All my goals were accomplished automatically.

Although I did not remember a lot of what you said specifically while in trance, I do remember you saying, "I used to be shy and depressed." I remember thinking for days later, "He used to be shy? Wow! It sure doesn't show."

I haven't written the letter to my abuser yet, but I will. I'm still floating in marital bliss.

Sincerely and affectionately,

S

Follow-up done nine months and 21 months later indicated that the results have held. S said that she realized that resolving what happened to her is a continuous process, but she recalls this session as the time when she turned the corner in that process.

We worked together to cocreate a new view and experience for S. She had been living a life that was in many ways determined by her history, by what someone who had abused her had done to her in the distant past. She was living *his* story. We collaboratively opened the possibility for her to start to live *her* story, to take back her life, and to create new chapters in the future. In summary, I offer some principles for using collaborative solution-oriented therapy with survivors of sexual abuse.

*Collaborative Solution-Oriented Therapy With Survivors of Sexual Abuse*

- Find out what the client is seeking in treatment and how she will know when treatment has been successful.
- Ascertain to the best of your ability that the sexual abuse is not current. If it is, take whatever steps necessary to stop it.
- Don't assume that the client needs to go back and work through traumatic memories. Remember that everybody is an exception.
- Use the natural abilities the client has developed as a result of having to cope with abuse (e.g., being facile at dissociating). Turn the former liability into an asset.
- Look for resources and strengths. Focus on underlining how she made it through the abuse and what she has done to cope, survive, and thrive since then. Look for nurturing and healthy relationships and role models she had in the past or has in the present. Look for current skills in other areas.
- Validate and support each part of the person's experience.
- Keep focused on the goals of treatment rather than getting lost in the gory details.
- Do not give the message that the person is "damaged goods" or that her future is determined by having been abused in the past.

## REFERENCES

de Shazer, S. (1985). *Keys to solution in brief therapy*. New York: Norton.

Durrant, M., & Kowalski, K. (1990). Overcoming the effects of sexual abuse: Developing a self-perception of competence. In M. Durrant & K. Kowalski (Eds.), *Ideas for therapy with sexual abuse*. Adelaide, Australia: Dulwich Centre Publications.

O'Hanlon, W. H., & Weiner-Davis, M. (1989). *In search of solutions: A new direction in psychotherapy*. New York: Norton.

O'Hanlon, B., & Wilk, J. (1987). *Shifting contexts: The generation of effective psychotherapy*. New York: Guilford.

Chapter 13

# Fragments for a Therapeutic Autobiography

**Bill O'Hanlon**

When I first began writing this piece, I thought of many ways to approach it. Each way I considered seemed to have merits and each way seemed (somehow) incomplete, only part of the story. What we leave out and what we include influence the story/outcome/tale/narrative so much. Any version of our past is necessarily distorted, warped in a certain direction. As some pundit said/suggested, "It's never too late to have a happy childhood." The best we can do, I believe, is make up a story/tale/narrative/allegory about the past, based on our faulty reminiscences. As I wrote, various memories occurred to me and I thought eventually they would come together as a unified whole. Instead, I find myself with fragments, short vignettes. I decided to leave them as pieces and let the reader make his or her own story/conclusion from them. What follows is the rather fragmented story/accounting of my path to becoming a therapist and trainer.

## LIVING IN THE WORLD

I decided to kill myself in 1970. I was a very shy, sensitive young man who was having trouble making it in the world. I was in my first year of college and going through those existential and value crises that young people often go through. After a friend talked me out of killing myself I was left with a question which has guided my personal and professional life since. "What makes a life work?" I was determined that since I had decided to live, I wanted to have a life that worked and I wanted to be happy.

This article originally appeared in *Journeys: Expansions of Strategic and Systemic Therapies* (Brunner/Mazel) edited by Don Efron in 1986.

Psychotherapy seemed a good place to start the inquiry. It was concerned with personal change and growth and related issues. How do people get in difficulties and how do they get out of them? How do people get their lives to work and how do they attain happiness? What can people do that can make a difference in the quality of their lives and in their circumstance? Various schools of psychotherapy claimed to have at least some of the answers and most were actively engaged in the inquiry.

At first I read and read voraciously. I read mainly self-help and psychotherapy textbooks. I found some useful information. Two things particularly influenced me. The first was Albert Ellis' idea: You can influence your happiness with your beliefs and by challenging your beliefs. That was something I could do on my own and did. I challenged my dramatizing of my misery and my powerlessness.

The other influence was from Gestalt and Ram Dass. The idea that all it took to be happy was to give up the struggle to be happy and to let yourself BE where you are had a powerful impact that has stayed with me. I remember being struck with the rather obvious insight that the way to be "self-actualized" was to continue to be the way I was. I had often longed for the oasis of self-actualization and it always seemed like a mirage, because I never could actually reach it even though I could see it in the distance. When I gave up trying to reach it, it was right under my feet.

Okay, so I had left misery behind and was now okay the way I was. I was content with who I was, but my life still didn't work. I was disorganized, chronically in financial straits, always late for things, painfully shy, and didn't seem to have the discipline to achieve my goals. I "had potential." But it wasn't clear whether I was a dreamer doomed to constantly have unrealized potential or whether I would turn out to "be somebody."

The ultimate test for whether I had mastered this life would be, I thought, when the results in the "real world" reflected that mastery—when, instead of dreaming about and longing for the things I didn't have and hadn't accomplished, I would have accomplished those things and have those things in my life. I decided I wanted a few things. I wanted to love and experience (love) and to know that I was loved. I wanted to make a contribution to other people, to the world. I wanted fame and fortune, not necessarily for themselves but because they would give me the influence and credibility to have an impact on people and on the world, and because that would be a good testing ground for the inquiry and experiment that I was conducting. If I, as messed up as I was, could make good, anybody could!

## CLARITY BEGINS AT HOME

I have a confession to make. I have never been in therapy. Worse than that, I'm proud of it. I know that may sound like heresy, but I'm of the persuasion (with

Haley and others) that therapy is the problem to be solved and it is best to avoid it if at all possible. I certainly don't view therapy as something that everyone (or even every therapist) should have. I think of therapy as analogous, in some ways, to getting my car repaired. At times it may become necessary, of course, but one hopes it doesn't. If it does become necessary, one wants it to be over soon and as inexpensively as possible. Human beings aren't cars, of course. I think that humans have self-repair mechanisms that require even less service and repair than autos.

I used to be a seeker of sorts. I searched religions, therapies, self-help groups, philosophies, etc., for THE ANSWER. Some years ago I went through the infamous est training. Much has been said in praise and damnation of est. I enjoyed it quite a bit and managed to avoid being an "esthole." One wonderful result for me in attending the est training was that I stopped searching for THE ANSWER, not that I stopped being intellectually curious or trying out new philosophies or anything like that. I just finished the search for something that would finally make me whole and complete and at peace. I don't seek therapy to get fixed, because I'm not broken!

I much prefer to sort out difficulties within my natural contexts, my family and friends. I'm wary of therapy for all the iatrogenic problems that it can give rise to. One can seek therapy for some very simple difficulty and leave with all sorts of esoteric psychological problems one never knew one had.

## LIVING WITH THE ROBOTS

For many years I had really long hair (down to the middle of my back) and I remember very clearly when I decided to cut it short. I was on my way from Phoenix to New Orleans, riding with two close friends to attend a psychotherapy conference. My two friends drove and talked all night while I dozed fitfully in the cramped back seat. As the sun was coming up, I began to awaken and heard one friend say to the other, "You know, people are robots. They see Bill with his long hair and 'hippie' clothes and they make all sorts of assumptions about him that aren't true—that he does drugs, that he's irresponsible, has no money, etc. They see me (my friend looked as if he had just stepped out of a college fraternity, very clean-cut, but he lived much more of a hippie life than did I) and make all sorts of conclusions that aren't accurate. I have instant credibility with most people, whereas Bill has a strike against him at the start." As I lay there (in hypnogogic state), I thought, "He's absolutely right, people are robots, and what am I doing pushing the wrong buttons?!" When we arrived in New Orleans, I shaved off my beard and when I arrived back home, I got my hair cut short.

Two things I noticed right away: (1) store employees stopped following me while I was grocery shopping (and I had always thought I was just being paranoid) and (2) I was much looser with my language and behavior in therapy. I no longer felt the need to act so "straight" to gain rapport in therapy. People did respond differently to me.

## OUT OF THE SEA OF PSYCHOLOGY

One of the things that has emerged for me in the past several years is the utter
uselessness of explanations and analysis of motives and meanings in being able
to get happy and make a life work. This seems especially true in psychotherapy.
We have already gone down the road of psychology and down the road lies no
results. Psychotherapy has notoriously been shown to make no difference with
people's problems overall. I grew more and more skeptical of explanations as I
went along in psychotherapy. Each theorist and school have their own pet explanations for why people change and why they stay the same. But what ultimately
makes an impact in therapy is what the therapist does and says.

I like Bandler and Grinder's early (pre-neurolinguistic program [NLP]) work
(1975a, 1975b) because it was long on action, flexibility, and observation and
short on explanations and hypotheses. The Milan folks are fond of saying that
one shouldn't "marry" one's hypothesis, but I'm more inclined to say one shouldn't
even go out on a date with one. I think hypotheses are mere distractions at best
and at worst become self- (or other-) fulfilling prophecies. One of my coauthors,
Jim Wilk, and I had a joke we told in our trainings. We said that we think we have
regressed to analytic or psychodynamic approaches; however, we assure you that
the couch is not for the client, it is for the therapist to use whenever he gets a
hypothesis. He should lie down until it goes away!

The radical shift I have gone through after working in a strategic, systemic,
Ericksonian, contextual way for some time is that I am not concerned with how
problems arise (not much new here, most modern therapist avoid the search for
etiology), nor with how they are maintained in the present (this is somewhat
radical, as most therapies these days are concerned with discerning and altering
what currently maintains the problems). I am even unconcerned with what functions the problem might serve for the person or the system (and this is perhaps the
most radical stance of all, as most therapists are convinced that there is a function
for the symptom and that it must be taken into account if the symptom is to be resolved and no other problems are to arise). I am only concerned with what will create
the conditions for change, what will resolve the symptom, dissolve the problem.

Therapy has been stuck in a sea of explanations, mostly derived from psychology and medicine, the main disciplines from which psychotherapy emerged.
No matter which direction we move in this sea of what the evolution of psychotherapy involves, it will always be in the realm of possibilities allowed to sea
creatures. I propose that it is time to emerge from the sea of psychology, from the
realm of explanation, into the realm of action. New possibilities, as undreamed of
as eagles and elephants are to the creatures of the sea, are possible when we
emerge from the sea of psychology onto the dry land of action.

## ENTERING THE REALM OF ACTION

Therapy has, I think, been pretty good at helping people accept themselves the
way they are, with the feelings, thoughts, and experience they have or have had.

This, however, is not enough much of the time to solve the problems that were brought into therapy, although people usually feel better when they come to accept themselves the "way they are." Where therapy has fallen short of the mark has been in the area of getting people to take action to solve their problems, to make changes by DOING something.

This is not to imply that internal experience (thoughts, feelings, and the like) do not exist or have an impact on people's lives. Of course they do. But what ultimately makes a difference in people's lives are the actions that they perform. Analysis and explanation rarely further the action in people's lives and is often what they do instead of action.

Of course, this view about therapy is very much influenced by what I have been experiencing in my personal life. I decided at a certain point that I wanted to be an international trainer and publish several books. I had my doubts about whether I could do that and so did other people. Look at all the things that were stacked against me: I had a master's degree in a field that accords status mainly to doctoral level practitioners and physicians; I was from NEBRASKA, not exactly the hub of therapeutic innovation ("Do you practice your therapy on cows or something?"); no one had ever heard of me, etc. At a certain point in my development, I decided to stop just dreaming and wondering whether I could accomplish my goals; I started to take actions toward them AS IF they were going to be accomplished and then let the world teach me where the limitations were.

One time I was on a teaching trip to England, where I stayed with Jim Wilk, who was coauthoring a book with me. I told Jim that I would like to complete the whole first draft of the text while I was in England, since we write much better when we are face to face. Jim was quick to point out that there was no way for us to complete the draft in the time available. I got very upset and we had quite a row, until I said, "Look, Jim, what I want is for you to do action and then tell me what's possible. Don't decide beforehand what's possible and what's not!" He agreed and we set to work. I think that clients and therapist alike often decide beforehand what's possible and what's impossible, closing an issue that I would rather have left open. I like to work from the assumption that what I am trying to do is possible and then let the world inform me (by the success or failure of the actions to bring about the goal) what to do next or whether it is possible.

## THE ONE-SESSION CONSPIRACY

I remember hearing about the beginnings of family therapy, where several individuals and groups had independently started seeing whole families together in their offices but didn't know that anyone else was doing so. This was such a radical idea at the time that therapists didn't talk about it with their colleagues, fearing censure and derision. At national meetings, over late night drinks or in conversations in the halls, people started to mention, tentatively, that they had been seeing the whole family together. As they discovered kindred colleagues, who were also doing family therapy, they grew emboldened and started writing and teaching others about family therapy. From that emerged a growing national movement leading to the widespread acceptance of the approach around the world.

I feel somewhat the same way about writing and talking about my "one-session cures." At first, I thought them to be lucky flukes and dismissed them. But as they happened more frequently, I started to think I might have something and wanted to talk to others about the phenomena. I was concerned that I might lose my credibility with people and be seen as a braggart or merely fooling myself. I mentioned it to my colleague Jim Wilk on my first visit to England in 1982 and he confessed that the same thing had been happening to him on occasion. I have found that it happens occasionally or often for others in the field, but no one has been able to offer a good formula or approach for making it happen more often or more predictably. Jim and I decided we should give it a try, which led to our collaboration on a new book (O'Hanlon & Wilk, 1987). We figured that the key must be in the assessment process, because in these cases we rarely got a chance to do any formal "interventions," as the client knew that the problem was gone before we got the chance to do any "tricks." My assessment process has changed over the years and now seems to reflect an entirely different set of assumptions than I previously held (when I never got one-session results). We decided to articulate those basic assumptions and those presuppositions deeply embedded in all of psychotherapy.

## GROWING WITH ERICKSON

I met Milton Erickson in 1973. I worked in the Arizona State University art gallery and he came with his wife and daughter to buy a Seri Indian ironwood carving. After I had carried the art piece down to their car, someone at the art gallery told me about Erickson and showed me an article that was in *Time* magazine that week about him. I read that article and went out immediately to buy *Uncommon Therapy* (Haley, 1973). I was intrigued and read all that I could find on his work. It took me until 1977, as shy and as much of a procrastinator as I was, to finally contact Erickson to study with him. I wrote him a letter in early 1977 telling him that I'd come up with several schemes to visit him (I'd write an article or a biography to expose him and his work to a wider audience, I'd trade him gardening for teaching, etc.), but that in the end I really just wanted to visit and learn and I didn't have much money. I went away for the weekend and when I returned my roommate said, "The strangest guy has been calling early in the morning, asking for the O'Hanlon Gardening Service. He won't leave his name or number, just says he'll call back."

The next morning, right on cue, came the call for the O'Hanlon Gardening Service. I took the phone and said that this was Bill O'Hanlon. He asked, "Don't you think you ought to survey the territory before you decide to take the job?" I answered yes, and asked if this was Dr. Erickson. He answered that it was and we arranged a time for me to come visit. He showed me his garden and set me to work in it. I had thought we were speaking only in metaphor, but noooooo! I actually worked in the garden. Working with him was very disconcerting and I left after several months more confused than when I started. From that experience, I vowed that I would figure Erickson out. I knew that I was on my own with that. He didn't clarify what he did at all when I studied with him, but I became convinced that what he was doing was very powerful.

In 1980, I started a private practice. As those of you who have done the same know, one has a lot of time on one's hands when one starts a practice. I went back and reread everything that Erickson had written and what others had written about him and listened to tapes. What emerged after a time was a clarity about Erickson's approach that has been the basis of the things I teach in workshops and has made a profound impact on my therapeutic results.

## WORKING THE PSYCHO JET SET: BECOMING A THERAPY TRAINER

The workshop leader was a well-known practitioner and teacher of Gestalt therapy and he was attempting to teach the (then-new) techniques developed by Bandler and Grinder (later to be called NLP). As I sat there in the workshop, I grew more and more frustrated. Although a novice therapist, I could tell the presenter didn't know his subject. I had read several books on the subject and been to a workshop with Bandler and Grinder earlier in the year. This man was pitiful! I was appalled.

Something inside me snapped. I had for the past several years been a "workshop junkie" and was disgusted with attending disappointing training after training. While driving home from that workshop with a colleague, bitter about wasting my time and money, I rashly declared, "I could have taught that workshop better and charged less money!"

Later, I thought to myself, "Okay, big shot, if you think you're so terrific, go out and teach a workshop!"

Currently, I teach workshops all over the country and occasionally around the world.

### Blissful Ignorance: Getting Started

Okay, so I was going to do a workshop. The only problem was that I didn't have a clue as to how to do that. A friend suggested that I talk to a friend of his who had just started a graphic design business, as one of the first things I would need was a brochure. They kindly guided me through my first brochure, pointing out that before I could do the brochure, I would need to secure a place to teach the workshop (generally a church hall, college classroom, auditorium, or hotel meeting room). I called hotels, expecting to be quoted outrageous prices, but was pleasantly surprised to discover that a smallish room (holding 30–50 people) generally ran $40—$70. I chose a date and reserved a room. Next came the brochure preparation. I used brochures I had received in the mail as guides for writing mine. The graphics people designed and printed the finished product (for about $75). I put together a mailing list from the yellow pages in the phone book and from a social services directory. I hand addressed, hand stamped, and mailed out several hundred brochures (about $40), as well as handing out many to friends and colleagues.

Lo and behold, about 20 people showed up at the first workshop (at $20 apiece) and I made a small profit. More that that, however, I discovered that I *loved* to teach and that I could put together a workshop. I was hooked. During the next year or so, I taught several more workshops, each one showed a modest profit, and I became more proficient in both the teaching and coordination of workshops.

I have had my ups and downs along the road. I have had workshops where only two people showed up, as well as some where several hundred showed up. I have met some wonderful people, some of whom have become good friends.

When I was teaching at a family therapy conference in Germany several years ago, I had dinner with Boscolo and Cecchin, from the Milan group. After I was introduced to them and told them that I taught workshops around the United States and lately in Europe, they said, "Welcome to the Psycho Jet Set!"

I currently teach about every weekend and see about 10 clients per week during the week. With my writing and editing work, as well as my family and social life, I keep quite busy.

## RIGHTEOUS INDIGNATION

Some people ask me how can I keep such a hectic teaching and traveling pace going. If I did it just for the money, I don't think I could. I have this burning sense of righteous indignation when I hear of some of the things being done in the name of healing. People drugged out, people told that they will never change or that it will take a minimum of a year to solve their problems, people sexually abused in the name of therapy, etc. I have made a resolve to alter the course of modern therapy and the energy of that keeps me going. My quest is paralleled by that of many former "hippie radicals" who have now gone on to become professionals but have not lost their revolutionary fervor or desire to make a contribution.

Buckminister Fuller (one of my heroes) had a metaphor that he used to explain how one person could make a difference. There is a little rudder on the big rudder of modern ships that is call the "trimtab." Turning the trimtab, which takes relatively little effort, makes a larger difference in the rudder, which would have taken a lot more effort to turn. In this way the ship is turned with relatively little effort by a small difference that makes a big difference. Fuller said, "Just call me trimtab!" Me too. I want to make a difference in the larger field of therapy and I have plans about how to get to that trimtab. One of them is through writing. This article is part of that process.

I had some friends who had a musical group when I was in college. They had one song that had a line that has stayed with me: "We are all flutes through which the breath of God should pass." While I'm not a religious person, I am very spiritual. I feel as if the Universe (or God or whatever) is using me as an instrument.

My job is to get my self and my life as clear as possible so that the notes will sound pure. My job is to get my life to work and make a contribution to other people.

I had a psychiatrist friend who had a theory of the world that he called "benevolent paranoia." He thought the world was set up to work absolutely and our job was to discover what the world wanted us to do. When we did, it would reward us (with little pieces of paper which we could trade in for things we want, with life, with status, etc.). I hold a similar view. The analogy I use is that this planet and our species are like an ant colony in some ways. Each ant has its own life experience and individual urges, yet somehow they are all working in harmony and get the job done at a social level by following their individual paths. I think each of us has a part to play in making our planet work and our species a success. To discover that requires only a sensitivity to what works and what doesn't work for you (no one else can decide for you, intuition is your rudder), a commitment to integrity, and a willingness to try many things to discover what the universe needs at this moment. The Mel Brooks movie *Blazing Saddles* has a line which I remember from time to time and use as a criteria for deciding whether this path is right for me or not. The villains ask the preacher to say a prayer before they go into battle and the preacher says, "Dear Lord, is what we're doing really important or are we just jerking off?"

I think that the contextual/strategic/systemic/Ericksonian approaches can make a difference for individuals, groups, and societies. What we're doing is important. We're not just jerking off.

## REFERENCES

Bandler, R., & Grinder, J. (1975a). *The structure of magic: A book about language and therapy*. Palo Alto, CA: Science and Behavior Books.

Bandler, R., & Grinder, J. (1975b). *The patterns of the hypnotic techniques of Milton H. Erickson, M.D.* (Vol. I). Cupertino, CA: Meta Publications.

Haley, J. (1973). *Uncommon therapy: The psychiatric techniques of Milton Erickson, M.D.* New York: Norton.

O'Hanlon, B., & Wilk, J. (1987). *Shifting contexts: The generation of effective psychotherapy*. New York: Guilford.

# Chapter 14

# Debriefing Myself

## When a Brief Therapist
## Does Long-Term Work

**Bill O'Hanlon**

For years I've been a brief therapy evangelist, going around the country several times a month teaching therapists how to accomplish the goals of therapy in the shortest possible time. These days insurance companies and other third-party payers are on my side. I have been getting more and more calls from hospitals and mental health centers asking for in-house workshops in brief therapy. Whether it is because clinics are trying to offer services to a growing number of people or because insurance companies are trying to increase their profits by limiting the length of treatment, the pressure is on therapists to reduce the length of treatment.

You'd think I'd be happy that my side seems to be winning, but something about the newfound popularity of brief therapy worries me. After all, the real question is not how long therapy takes, but how effective it is and whether it serves those who seek it. I believe effective therapy is usually brief, but not in every case.

Although I see clients on the average of about five sessions, I occasionally do long-term work. Sometimes I see people for several years. I've had some of my long-term clients come in for sessions waving brochures they have found in my waiting room describing brief therapy workshops I teach. "What is this brief therapy stuff?" they demand to know, "I've been seeing you for two years!" I even had one long-term client jokingly threaten to sell an exposé about me to the *National Enquirer*.

This article originally appeared in the March/April 1990 issue of the *Family Therapy Networker*.

It is important to distinguish between the therapist assuming that therapy must be long term to be effective and the client teaching the therapist that therapy should be long term. Sometimes therapists induce an expectation for long-term therapy. At times this is as simple as saying, "This is a serious problem and it will take a minimum of two years to resolve it." At other times, the induction is more subtle.

Last summer I got into a conversation with the woman seated next to me on an airplane. When she found out I was a psychotherapist, she told me she had started therapy that year for help with her lifelong obsessions. She had been favorably impressed with the therapist at their first meeting but was confused and slightly mystified when he had announced at the end of the session, which took place in February, that his vacation was in August. "Why is he telling me this?" she thought to herself. "I'll be long gone by then." In July, when I met her, she was still in therapy with the man and had decided to take her vacation at the same time he had his. She now realized, she said, that her initial view had been naive and that her problems were much deeper than she realized. Since she liked her therapist and was glad she had found him, I didn't rain on her parade. Nevertheless, I thought she had probably been seduced into long-term therapy when she may have gotten results sooner if she had found someone who worked briefly. In fact, toward the end of our conversation, she asked me if I could give her a referral for a hypnotist in the Boston area. She wanted to keep going to her therapist, she explained, but she thought hypnosis might help her get rid of the obsessions that had originally brought her to therapy.

Whenever I give workshops on brief therapy, someone usually stands up sometime during the workshop and asks, "But what about borderlines? Does this brief therapy stuff work on them?" The question strikes right to the heart of the differences between most brief therapists and their long-term therapy colleagues. Brief therapists typically see the problem as negotiable. We focus on changeable aspects of people's lives and on clear, obtainable results. Latent schizophrenia and borderline personality disorders are not on the brief therapy menu. I should also add that they are not on clients' menus either. Clients usually don't come seeking treatment for their personality disorders unless they have learned the concept from some psychotherapist or from the media.

Brief therapists don't usually attend to personality diagnoses, because personalities don't usually change or certainly don't change rapidly. I help people to act, think, and feel differently. I have never changed anybody's personality and think it is unlikely I ever will. A woman in one of my workshops told me that she had recently started working at a clinic where most of the staff talked about personality disorders. Her response was to challenge them to show her an ordered personality.

I had a client once who came to therapy because she felt inadequate in her job, often cried when she talked to other people, got angry at her parents and family much of the time, and felt as if she were just generally crazy. When I started my standard approach, focusing behaviorally on how she did all this and what she could concretely do differently, it sent her into a tizzy. She told me she couldn't possibly carry out the homework tasks we were discussing. Just talking or thinking about them made her feel like curling up into a ball. Then she said that she felt terrible because she had shown me she wasn't a good client. It took me several sessions to learn how to say things to her so she wouldn't freak out. I asked her to be patient with me because I was a slow learner. I assured her that I was trainable and would find a way to help her. Finally, I noticed that when I told stories about problems I was still struggling with that were similar to her issues, she felt empowered to do the things we had decided would be helpful. Once she began doing some new things, she was able to make rapid changes in her life.

Long-term therapists often claim that brief therapists are missing the point and that they ignore the deeper underlying problems and dynamics. But brief therapists argue back that therapy should focus on goals that are attainable within a short time period. Assessment is an opportunity to guide the problem definition in a solvable direction. I think this disagreement goes a long way toward explaining why, for most therapists, brief is brief and long is long and never the twain shall meet.

I begin therapy with new clients assuming that it will be brief, and I let my clients teach me how long it will be. I have had successful therapy be as brief as one session and as long as five years and hundreds of sessions. In my experience, the nature of the presenting problem doesn't determine whether therapy is to be brief or not, because everybody is an exception. For me it is the client's response to the therapy that is the determining factor.

I once had a woman come to her first session having had the vague sense that she was sexually abused by her father when she was a child. She asked me to hypnotize her to verify or eliminate her concern about the abuse. She went into trance quickly and remembered catching her father having sex with the maid. She was upset by the memory but soon realized that it explained many things from her childhood. She also remembered her father having approached her for oral sex, which she had refused. She scanned for other revelations, but none emerged. She intuitively felt that she had gotten to the material that had been nagging her. She thanked me for my help and that was that. I heard from a mutual acquaintance some time later that this client had been amazed that she was able to resolve the issue so quickly.

Another similar presenting problem led to long-term work. A woman came to my office referred by a friend who had seen me do a presentation. The client said that she had a history of psychiatric difficulties (she had been hospitalized on several occasions and had been on antipsychotic medication for many years). She had been seeing a local psychiatrist and, under hypnosis, had experienced something quite powerful for which she had only a vague memory. All she could remember was that she had screamed quite loudly and that it had felt as if she were being born. The psychiatrist had been quite evasive after the incident and had told her a story about a woman with whom he had worked that had remembered under hypnosis that she had been sexually abused as a child. When she pressed him for more details, however, or to confirm that she had remembered being abused, he remained noncommittal. He soon moved her to being his last patient on Saturday afternoons so she wouldn't disturb others with her screaming, and she got the distinct impression that she had freaked him out. She believed that because her husband was a psychiatrist, her therapist was daunted by the thought of the repercussions if she became psychotic again, while in treatment. In any case, she had gotten the message from him that she was too scary to handle.

She sought my help because her friend said I did hypnosis and my client thought maybe I could help her remember or finish whatever it was that had emerged in the psychiatrist's office. I assured her that I wasn't intimidated by the strong expression of emotion or her husband being a psychiatrist. She seemed pleased by my response. We did some hypnosis and she remembered a bit at a time that she had been sexually abused from an early age by an uncle and that her mother had observed and allowed the abuse. It took several years to remember, accept, and resolve the traumatic memories. At times during treatment, she would become catatonic in the session. At times she was tortured by religious delusions in which I and other people were either representatives of God or Satan and she couldn't tell which. She would become suicidal.

All through this process, I kept our work focused on the goal of resolving and ending therapy. At first, just the mention of the possibility of therapy ending would send her into panics and fears that I just wanted to get rid of her because she was so troublesome and time consuming. When she finally realized that ending therapy would be a mutual decision, she started to prepare for LIFE WITH-OUT THERAPY, a first in her adult life. We started to space sessions out and she found that the spacing we had chosen, once a month, was initially too long. We went back to every two weeks and then gradually moved to once per month, then to once every two months. She finally felt resolved that the abuse was in the past where it belonged. She stopped experiencing delusions, hallucinations, and suicidal impulses. Finally, we agreed to meet on occasion for lunch as an informal follow-up.

A couple of things about this client are noteworthy. First is that one day she called me up and said, "This is too painful. I can't do it anymore. I'm stopping therapy." I replied that her resignation wasn't accepted and that I would expect to see her at the next session. She later told me that that phone call had been a reassurance to her that I was willing to stay with her until she was finished. In brief therapy, I would never handle a client's wish to terminate in this way. In this case, however, I knew this woman well enough to distinguish between a plea for reassurance and an actual desire to end therapy.

Second, the case clarified the importance of the therapist–client relationship for me. During the break in a recent conference, one of the workshop participants approached me and remarked at the similarity between my work and the work of another brief therapist. "What is the difference between you?" she asked. "I make eye contact," I replied. (When I told the other therapist, who is a friend of mine, of this exchange, he rebutted, "Maybe that's why I can see so many more solutions than you, Bill. I'm not distracted by looking at people.")

The therapy model that I teach stresses neither the importance of history nor the abreaction of traumatic memories; nevertheless, abreact is precisely what I eventually helped my client do to get the results she sought in treatment. When I teach workshops I usually say that it is a shame that my clients don't attend my workshops because then they would know what they are supposed to do in therapy. Instead, they always do what they do and I have to adjust my approach accordingly. Milan therapists Luigi Boscolo and Gianfranco Cecchin tell their trainees to stay open to new ideas and, "Don't marry your hypotheses." But I say, "Don't even go out on dates with your hypotheses." I enter therapy with some ideas and guidelines for interventions and then let clients teach me, by their responses, what will work for them.

My first case of long-term therapy was a referral from a colleague who had seen the client for five years after she had been treated for several years by other clinicians. In the first session, I put her in trance and told her that she might get rid of her problems without ever having known what caused them. She immediately popped her eyes open and said, "No." "No what?" I asked. She told me that she had had these problems for so long that she was unwilling to get rid of them without knowing what had brought about the torment that had so profoundly affected her life.

This presented quite a challenge for me. The brief therapy model I teach holds that it is unnecessary to know the causes, meanings, or functions of problems in order to resolve them. But I also rail against therapists imposing their models on clients and urge students to really listen and respond to clients' requests. I thought long and hard and finally decided that if I believed what I taught, I should take the case on her terms. I might learn something. We ended up negotiating the point a bit. We came up with a likely explanation for her problem and continued treatment assuming that our explanation was true. Although we never found any definitive evidence about the real causes, she was still able to resolve the issues she brought to therapy.

When I supervise people, I hate to see them religiously sticking to my model or anyone else's. No model I know of works all the time. Respecting people, making contact with them, bringing your humanness to the encounter, and being able to recognize when your assumptions are getting in the way of listening and responding to what people need is essential to successful therapy. My commitment to people is more important than my commitment to my models. I go into therapy with a beginner's mind, not knowing what to do to solve the problem but confident that through a joint effort my clients and I will find solutions. Milton Erickson was once asked whether, with his creative and powerful techniques, he could sort out the situation in the Middle East. He replied, "Bring them to my office." I feet much the same way. I don't have a clue as to how to sort out the situation in the Middle East—or, for that matter, with borderline personalities—but bring them to my office and I almost always find openings and possibilities for change.

I think most people who arrive in our offices can and should be helped to get out of therapy and on with their lives in as short a time as possible. A small minority, in my experience, can benefit from and need longer term therapy. One cannot decide on the basis of a diagnosis or some insurance chart or some model of therapy how long effective therapy will take. I hope that as a brief therapy evangelist writing about longer term treatment, I can free therapists, both those attached to long-term and short-term orientations, from the shackles of their models.

PHASE III

# Possibility Therapy

# Introduction to Phase III

**Bill O'Hanlon**

As I continued to speak and write about solution-oriented therapy, I became dissatisfied with it for several reasons. As the years went by, I heard reports back from solution-focused therapy students and practitioners that crystallized my concerns. Clients complained that therapists were being too positive, ignoring or minimizing the problem or the suffering that accompanied the problem. Or students were finding it hard to identify solutions with certain clients, ones that were more challenging, more multiproblem or those who had already been through solution-focused therapy and found it hadn't helped.

And to compound matters, many people believed I was a student and follower of Steve de Shazer and the Brief Family Therapy Center in Milwaukee because my approach was similar to theirs and had a similar name. This concerned me because my approach is very different from the solution-focused model.

I thought that the solution-focused model had left out the crucial element of acknowledgment and validation of the client—the client's feelings and points of view—which was always a cornerstone to my approach. Solution-focused therapists may acknowledge them, but they don't teach it much or write about it.

I also felt that the solution-focused model became very formulaic, with a rigid set of officially approved questions and engineering-like flow charts and decision trees that bear little resemblance to the intuitive and spontaneous way I work. Clients' problems don't always fit into a rigid series of questions. To me, this model can turn into an imposition on clients rather than being responsive to clients. It is crucial to fit the model to the client rather than the client to the model.

So, to differentiate my work, I began to call it possibility therapy. That includes an orientation to the present and future and to strengths, abilities, and solutions, as well as a willingness to respectfully consider the past, problems, diagnoses, medications, etc., as relevant to therapy. As I began to teach and write about this approach, many therapists told me that they felt validated and freed from the restraints that they had found in solution-focused work.

Here are some papers that reflect and articulate this developing model.

Chapter 15

# Possibility Therapy

## From Iatrogenic Injury
## to Iatrogenic Healing

**Bill O'Hanlon**

## IATROGENICS

I had a hand in making up the faculty list for the conference from which these papers came. Over the years I had come across the work of the major faculty members and had found some commonalities in their approaches. Although they all had different ideas and methods, there was something they all had in common: they respected their clients and collaborated with them in the change process. They had views that were coconstructivist. Together clients and therapists were considered to create in conversation and interaction the focus for therapy and the view and experience that change was possible. In addition, all of the faculty members eschewed views that were pathologically based or blaming toward clients. I was discussing this idea with my friend, Tapi Ahola, a therapist from Finland, and he said, "Oh, yes, the Fourth Wave." When I asked him what he meant by that phrase, he told me, "The First Wave in psychotherapy was pathology based. The Second Wave was problem-focused or problem-solving therapy. The Third Wave was solution focused or solution oriented. The Fourth Wave is what is emerging now, only no one has a good name for it yet."

This article originally appeared in an abbreviated form in the book, *Therapeutic Conversations* (Norton), edited by Stephen Gilligan and Reese Price and published in 1993. The version in this book includes several parts that were previously deleted and, we think, noteworthy.

## Iatrogenic Injury and Iatrogenic Healing

Iatrogenic refers to treatment caused problems. The word refers to injuries that are the result of the interventions done by the healing agent. It was initially applied to medicine but has come to be used in therapy as well (Morgan, 1983). In 1961, Milton Erickson was giving a lecture in which he discussed the importance of iatrogenics. "While I have read a number of articles on this subject of iatrogenic disease and have heard many discussions about it, there is one topic on which I haven't seen much written about and that is iatrogenic health. Iatrogenic health is a most important consideration—much more important than iatrogenic disease" (quoted in Rossi & Ryan, 1986, p. 140).

Iatrogenic injury (a term which I have borrowed from my colleagues at the AGS Institute in Stockholm, Sweden) refers to methods, techniques, assessment procedures, explanations, or interventions that harm, discourage, invalidate, show disrespect, or close down the possibilities for change.

Iatrogenic healing refers to those methods, techniques, assessment procedures, explanations, or interventions that encourage, are respectful, and open up the possibilities for change.

The faculty and papers from this conference seem to me to be standing against iatrogenic injury in therapy and for iatrogenic health and healing. Taken together, I call these stances possibility therapy.

## POSSIBILITY THERAPY: A SHIFT IN THE WIND

For the past few years, I have been teaching an approach I call solution-oriented therapy (O'Hanlon & Weiner-Davis, 1989). It is a relative of de Shazer's and the Brief Family Therapy Center's work. We share an interest in exploring and emphasizing solutions, strengths, abilities, and exceptions. As I teach this method, though, I often get comments from workshop participants and supervisees along the line of, "I really like the positive approach you use. It's so refreshing." While I'm aware they are offering a compliment, I cringe when I hear this.

Of course, any approach that doesn't blame people, give them stigmatizing labels, and that emphasizes workable aspects of people's lives looks positive compared with traditional therapy approaches, but I am concerned about this word "positive." To me, it smells like either that gung-ho, "You-can-do-anything-you-set-your-mind-to" schools of sales/motivation training or of a New-Age Pollyanna view of life ("you can be wealthy if you write enough affirmations," and other such claptrap).

I don't like positive thinking because I think it minimizes the very real (you radical constructivists will excuse me for using that word) physical negative things that happen in the world and in the lives of the people with whom we work in therapy. I'm talking about things like rape, violence, poverty, malnutrition, job discrimination, etc. Positive thinking seems to me like gilding the top of a pile of manure. It looks nice, but if you poke it very hard, you'll find the pleasantness does not go very deep. All the positive thinking, reframing, paradigm shifting, or whatever doesn't directly alter these difficult/harmful conditions.

At the same time, I'm not voting for negative thinking either. Negative thinking holds that everything is manure and there's not much you or I or anyone can do to change that. People *are* born with or develop "narcissistic" or "borderline" or "sociopathic" personalities and they will *never* change. This is not a recommended stance for a change agent.

So, for now, I have settled on the label "possibility therapy" for what I do. Possibility thinking does not claim that everything is (or will be) wonderful and successful or that it is (or will be) awful and futile.

Some years ago, I read a story about Dick Gregory, the American comedian turned social and nutritional activist. When someone asked him whether he thought we could achieve his hopes for eliminating hunger and starvation on this planet by the end of the twentieth century, he replied that he had once chanced upon the scene of a building on fire. The firefighters were struggling to fight the fire. Gregory asked the fire chief whether he thought the building could be saved. The chief replied, "If there's a shift in the wind, we will. If not, we won't."

The possibility therapist recognizes the seriousness of clients' situations without taking a minimizing or Pollyanna view. She (he) also recognizes the possibility that things won't change (the building will burn down), but works to be the shift in the wind in clients' lives.

An acquaintance of mine was once accused of being a pessimist. She replied, "I'm not a pessimist, I'm an experienced optimist." I am an experienced optimist when I approach clients. I know that there is a great deal of violence in this world and that there are economic problems, racial problems, and other difficulties to be faced. My view is that there are always possibilities, even within those difficult situations.

## RADICAL CONSTRUCTIVISM AND SOCIAL/INTERACTIONAL CONSTRUCTIONISM

Radical constructivists and quantum physicists suggest that what we call reality is constructed—fabricated by our beliefs and our neurology. There is no such thing as reality (or truth, either, which is another matter altogether and a compelling reason not to hire a radical constructivist to handle your cash).

Social/interactional constructionists take a different stance. They (or I should say, "we," since I count myself in their numbers) hold that there is a physical reality out there but that our social reality, being influenced by language and interaction, is negotiable. This social reality can influence and be influenced by physical reality. For instance, if someone in a crowded hall yelled, "Fire!" it would probably affect the physical reality creating a rush for the exit. If someone was crushed to death in that rush, no amount of talking and interacting could change that reality.

This social reality is mutable, but within some limits—the constraints seem to be physical, environmental, and traditions/habits.

Traditions consist of typical ways of speaking, thinking about, perceiving, and doing things in a particular interactional group (family, subculture, culture). Habits consist of an individual's way of speaking, thinking about, perceiving, experiencing, and doing things.

One can't just waltz into a social situation and define it or reframe it as one likes. First, there is the physical environment, including our neurology and physiology, to be dealt with. Some frames just won't fit into these realities. Then there are traditions to be dealt with. Certain frames have held sway for many years and are not to be swept aside by a few clever phrases or questions. The social reality created in therapy interviews is just that—social. It is cocreated by the therapist and clients, as well as by the culture and social system traditions that influence them. This stance is called social or interactional constructionism.

## ACKNOWLEDGMENT AND POSSIBILITY

I learned much of what I do in therapy from Milton Erickson. In the way that I have come to understand it, Erickson's work reminds me a great deal of the first model of counseling I learned in depth, the client-centered model of Carl Rogers.

I do hypnosis in the Erickson tradition. It is different from traditional hypnotic approaches in that it is more permissive, more inclusive, and more validating of whatever the "subject" is doing during the induction and however he or she responds while in trance.

I remember I was working with a client of mine who had terribly intrusive obsessions. He was rarely, if ever, free of them. He had seen a psychoanalytic expert on obsessive–compulsive disorders for some time who pronounced the client had the worst case of obsessiveness he had ever seen. I used hypnosis with the man and by the second session he was starting to develop fine trances. At the third session, I started the trance induction with my usual sort of spiel, "You can be where you are, feeling what you are feeling, thinking what you are thinking, obsessing about what you're obsessing about, and experiencing what you are experiencing. There's nothing to do to go into trance, no right way or wrong way to go into trance. So just let yourself be where you are, doing what you are doing, worrying that you won't go into trance." At that point, he popped his eyes open and said simply, "That's why I come here." "To go into trance, you mean?" I asked. "No," he replied, "to hear those words." He later explained that it was the only time in his life in which he could escape from the terrible sense that he was constantly living his life incorrectly. He would also often be obsession-free during parts of the trance.

When this obsessive man said those words, it coalesced something for me—something that I hadn't been articulating during my teaching about more directive ways of working with people. That is, that you have to acknowledge, validate and include people's experience before they will be open to new possibilities and directions.

If you only acknowledge, validate, and are inclusive, however, most clients won't move on very quickly, as we have seen from decades of experience with client-centered work. Twenty-seven sessions after the intake, you'll still be bobbing your head and reflecting back the client's depression or whatever, and they'll feel valued and heard but they won't have much relief or have made many changes in their problematic situations.

So I think therapy is always a balance between acknowledgment and possibility. If clients don't have a sense that you have heard, acknowledged, and valued them, they will either spend time trying to convince you of the legitimacy of their pain and suffering or their illness or they will leave therapy with you. Someone once asked me about the place of Carl Roger's methods in my work and I replied, "That's the first five minutes. If you don't do that stuff, I don't think you're going to get anyplace with clients." In fact, I think people who work briefly generally have to be much better at acknowledging and joining people. If they are to be invited to move along rapidly, they must have the sense that you understand them.

## HEISENBERG MEETS PYGMALION

A physicist named Werner Heisenberg pointed out some years ago that there is no way that physicists can make precise observations on the subatomic level without disturbing the data they wish to study. This has come to be called the Heisenberg Uncertainty Principle. I'm not the first to make the connection of this principle to the social sciences, but I do think the principle holds true in the therapy field. In therapy, different therapists' observational tools and assessment procedures cannot help but influence the data being observed.

Unfortunately, most therapists have what I call "delusions of certainty" or "hardening of the categories." They are convinced that the observations they make during the assessment process are "real" and objective. They are certain they have discovered real problems.

I have often told my students that I'm sorry that the therapy field doesn't sell futures in therapy diagnoses like they do in other commodities. Ten years ago I would have bought a few shares of Borderline stock, a couple of thousand shares of Adult Children of Alcoholics, and a little Bulimia for a balanced portfolio. These days I'd recommend a hot investment opportunity in Multiple Personality Disorder and Adults Molested as Children. In fact, I'll share with you one sure-fire way to know when a particular therapeutic stock is about to take off: when it becomes known by its initials. How many of you know what PTSD is? What about ADD? MPD? Just a few years ago, these initials would have been meaningless to most of us.

"What about real mental/neurological disorders?" the reader may ask. By now, there have been enough books debunking and deconstructing most of the major diseases to cast doubt on the truth of such constructions (Breggin, 1991; Coles, 1987; Fingarette, 1988; Fisher & Greenberg, 1989; Goffman, 1961; Kroll, 1988; O'Hanlon & Wilk, 1987; Szasz, 1961).

## LANGUAGE IS A VIRUS: LINGUISTIC EPIDEMICS

Why can't we diagnose problems without in some way influencing them? Because we live in an atmosphere of language, which steers our thinking, experience, and behavior in certain directions. Language not only describes, it creates and distinguishes. There are certain to be other psychiatric disorders that are discovered or invented in the future. Why aren't we noticing them now? Because we haven't yet distinguished them in language. We notice things as "things" by distinguishing them in "language-land." How many pioneers crossing the plains of America suffered from stress? Probably none. Why? Because stress hadn't yet been invented as a problem for the pioneers. They may have had stress, but they never knew it, so it didn't bother them and they never felt the need to see a counselor about it. The same holds for low self-esteem. Cavemen never worked on their self-esteem, because they didn't have any to work on.

Problems do not exist in a vacuum. They exist only in a context—a linguistic, social, cultural context. They are spoken and interacted and presupposed and metaphored. In therapy, we must acknowledge the therapist as part of the problem context. The therapist helps to create therapeutic problems by the way in which he or she carries on the therapeutic interview and endeavor.

## SEEING IS BELIEVING: PYGMALION ON THE COUCH

I maintain that there are no such "things" as therapy problems. I think therapists, for the most part, give their clients problems. That is, therapists negotiate problem definitions out of the raw material of clients' concerns by conversing with clients. They either come up with a problem definition that is agreeable to both client and therapist or they try to convince the client that he or she has a problem of the type the therapist says he or she has.

It seems more than a coincidence that when clients have seen Gestalt therapists for more than a few sessions, they usually have Gestalt-type problems and start to use Gestalt-like jargon. Likewise, analytic therapies seem to engender analytic-type problems. Behavior therapists always seem to identify and treat behavioral problems, neurologists usually find neurological problems, and biological psychiatrists almost always discover biochemical imbalance and disorders. Michael White and followers always find oppressive symptoms/practices and ideas that are external and dominating the person.

Clients do not usually decide which theory will work best for them and then seek out that kind of practitioner. They come in complaining about something, concerned about things, and the therapist helps shape those complaints into therapy problems, i.e., some problem that therapy can solve and some problem that this particular therapist with this particular approach knows how to solve.

We advertently or inadvertently influence the descriptions our clients give us of their situations. We do not enter therapy neutrally, finding the "real" problem or problems. We usually only elicit or allow descriptions of problems that fit our theories, that we know how to cope with, make sense of, or solve.

Pygmalion refers to the story of a sculptor in Greek mythology who created a sculpture of his ideal woman that was so lovely he fell in love with it. The gods were impressed and brought her to life for him. In a similar way, we fall in love with our theories and bring them to life in our clients. I call this "theory counter-transference." Robert Rosenthal did some extensive investigation of the phenomenon and called it the Pygmalion Effect (Rosenthal & Jacobson, 1968).

So, combining the uncertainty principle with the Pygmalion phenomenon, we come to the idea that there is no way to discover what the "real" problem is in any therapeutic situation. The therapist influences the data and the description in directions that are biased toward his or her theoretical models.

I propose that the papers in this book and the faculty are creating a new tradition in therapy. Because therapy conversations can have different emphases and components, I will detail some of the components of traditional therapy conversations and some of the components of the new tradition that this conference represents.

## A NEW TRADITION

Traditional models of therapy create a climate for certain kinds of conversations. The approach detailed here, as well as others at this conference, creates a climate for other kinds of conversations.

First, I'll discuss the conversations engendered by traditional theories and then I'll list the conversations engendered by the new tradition.

## TRADITIONAL THERAPY CONVERSATIONS

### Conversations for Explanations

When I first went to study with Milton Erickson, I was a "true believer" in family systems theory. At the time, I worked in an agency in which the dominant model was psychodynamic. I was regularly getting into arguments with my colleagues during clinical case staffings. I would try to convince them that doing individual therapy was useless because they were just sending their clients back into their symptom-inducing systems, where they would again develop problems. I never seemed to sway them, though, as they would argue back just as vociferously that I was missing the clear, underlying psychodynamics of the situation.

Erickson had a way of pulling the rug out from under one's cherished theories. As I studied with him, he did that very effectively with me. He would bring up a clinical problem and ask me how I would handle it. I would usually spin out some impressive-sounding systems psychobabble involving "entrenched coalitions," "enmeshment," and "triangulation." He would chastise me for attending to my theories more than the client's and reorient my attention back to what the clients were showing and telling me. He was big on observation and disdained theories. (I once asked him why he did not think that more people came to study with him, as I did not have to wait in line to see him in 1977. He replied, "Because I have no theory and some people think that's very wrong.") By the time I finished studying with Erickson, I was no longer a true believer in systems theory.

Unfortunately, my colleagues at the agency had gotten the family therapy religion and again this led to clinical disagreements. They would try to convince me that people's problems were functions of systemic processes and I remained unconvinced. I was not a psychodynamic therapist, I was not a family systems therapist, what was I? I was warped. I realized that I no longer believed any particular explanation of why people had problems. They all had some credibility, but they now seemed irrelevant to me. I went around for some years telling people I had no theory of psychotherapy. People would challenge me, of course. Just as you cannot not communicate, you cannot not have a theory. You have a theory, they would say, you have the theory of not having a theory. That didn't ring quite true to me and it seemed a little too precious. So I finally figured out that I had no explanatory theory, but I did have an intervention theory.

Typical conversations for explanations in traditional therapy include discussion and pursuit of the function of the symptom. Depending on the theory, the function is either benevolent or malevolent. The explanation is often pathologically oriented, maintaining that the presenting concern is evidence of some pathology, dysfunction, or illness. Again, depending on the theory, the dysfunction is either individual or social (familial, cultural, etc.) or some combination of both.

Often traditional conversations focus on categorization according to some schema such as the *DSM-III-R*. Of course, not all categorization is iatrogenically harmful. I remember a time in therapy that I call B.B.—before borderlines and bulimics. When I first practiced therapy, neither of these were common problems and one (bulimia) had not even yet been invented. I mention them because I think that these two labels show a contrast between labels that empower and labels that disempower and make the problem more difficult to resolve.

When I first treated someone who binged and vomited, I had never heard of bulimia. A woman came to therapy and asked me if I could help her stop this compulsive eating and vomiting pattern that she did. We worked out some ways for her to change and after a relatively short time, she stopped eating such large quantities and making herself vomit. Some time later, I came across a book that named this disorder "bulimarexia" and distinguished it from anorexia (Boskind-White & White, 1983). I became interested in this problem and advertised in the local university newspaper describing the problem and announcing the formation of a treatment group for it. In the next few days, I received about 50 phone calls from young women regarding the group. Most cried on the phone and told me they had never known there was a name for what they did, they never knew anyone else did this, and they were relieved to find there was treatment for their problem. Many found by the time they entered the group, the knowledge they were not alone and that there was help had enabled them to stop bingeing and vomiting or taking laxatives. This was a label that empowered and helped people to change.

When I first started hearing widespread reports of the epidemic of borderline personality disorder (Masterson, 1976), I was perplexed. I was traveling frequently to the East Coast of the United States and teaching workshops. Participants in the workshops started asking with more and more regularity about how my approach would work with people diagnosed with borderline personality disorder. I had heard of the disorder, but when I learned of it, it was an obscure analytic concept that meant the person wasn't quite neurotic and not quite psychotic but somewhere in between, on the borderline. A therapist at the clinic where I had worked in Arizona had seen one person with the disorder and the client had killed himself in the course of treatment. In Nebraska, where I worked at the time, there weren't any people diagnosed with borderline personality disorder that I had heard about and nobody ever asked questions about them in workshops. Since that time, of course, people diagnosed with borderline personality disorder have become ubiquitous in the therapy field. Many books and workshops have spread this epidemic around the globe. We even have them in Nebraska now. There is a problem with the diagnosis, though. Most therapists have the idea that these are very difficult "patients" to work with and that treatment necessarily takes years. When one gets a person diagnosed with borderline personality disorder, one's colleagues commiserate and tell one not to expect much and not to get too many on one's caseload or one will burn out. This pessimism is often communicated to the client and can become part and parcel of the difficulty.

Sometimes traditional therapy conversations focus on a search for or discussion of causes and deterministic ideas. Current concerns are thought to be caused by past events or situations or by current events or situations, either inside or outside of the person.

## Conversations for Expression of Emotion

Traditional therapy approaches often put an emphasis on the expression of emotion as a curative factor. The classic question is, "How do you feel about that?" I rarely, if ever, hear possibility therapists utter this question. A therapist colleague of mine, who works in this new tradition, once had a client come in and appear very uncomfortable during the session. The therapist had seen the woman for some time and knew something was up. The therapist asked the woman what was going on and the woman told her that she had something she needed to talk about but was afraid to say. After much prompting, the woman still had not revealed her secret, so my colleague started to guess. "Is it about sex?" The woman nodded. "Do you have a man?" The woman shook her head. "Is it a woman?" Again the woman shook her head. Perplexed, the therapist asked jokingly, "Well, what have you got, a big dog?" To my colleague's surprise, the woman nodded. The therapist was so shocked that all she could do was utter that timeless counselor phrase, "Well, how do you feel about that?" Usually, however, this phrase and others like it are more suited to the traditional therapist.

## Conversations for Insight

Most therapists strive to give their clients insights, understandings into the nature, causes, and associations of their concerns. This idea, like the idea that expressing emotions is curative, is thought to be related to change in the presenting concern. This process is often guided by the therapist's interpretations or leading questions.

## Conversations for Inability

Traditionally therapists have seen clients as somehow damaged or having deficits or inabilities. Clients are said to have an inability to tolerate ambiguity, conflict, or their feelings. They are said to be unable to assert themselves, to get in touch with their feelings, to control their violent actions, or to live "normal" lives. Whatever the particulars, the overarching concept is that of inability and that is communicated implicitly or explicitly to the clients or their families or both.

## Conversations for Blame and Recrimination

If you've ever worked in a traditional psychiatric clinic or hospital, you've experienced the amount of blaming of patients/clients that goes on in these settings. The blaming is sometimes subtle but sometimes very blatant.

"This patient likes his/her illness." "She is playing a game with us, manipulating us." "He doesn't really want to change." "She's a borderline, don't expect much change."

Blame takes two forms. One attributes bad or evil intentions to people (they don't want to change, they like their illness, they want to control or manipulate others, etc.). The other attributes bad or evil characteristics (narcissistic, selfish, sociopathic, resistant, etc.) to people.

## Adversarial Conversations

Closely related to conversations for blame and recrimination are adversarial conversations. If the patient is resistant or has defenses that block him or her from cooperating or changing, the therapist must either confront those defenses (breaking through the denial, a specialty of drug and alcohol abuse treatment but used in other treatment as well) or somehow find a way around the defenses. This can lead to trickery or deceit on the part of the therapist. If the therapist is open and above board about his/her thoughts or agenda for therapy, the client may sabotage or thwart it.

This stance in therapy conversation arises in part from the idea that the therapist is the expert and the client is the nonexpert or amateur in psychological/emotional matters. The therapist knows best not only how to solve the client's concerns but about what is really going on within the client. In addition, if the therapist's theory has a normative model within it, the therapist is then an expert on what "normal" is and how the client should live after therapy is over. For example, the idea that one should always express one's feelings was a popular idea for many years in therapy. Not only would this solve the present concern of the client, but also it was in general a good rule for how to conduct one's daily life.

## POSSIBILITY THERAPY CONVERSATIONS

### Collaborative Conversations

In possibility therapy, clients and therapists are both considered experts. Clients are experts on their own experience, including their pain, suffering, and concerns. They also have the expertise about their memories, goals, and responses. Therapists are expert at creating a conversational and interactional climate for change and results in therapy. Clients and therapists are partners in the change/therapy process and collaborate on deciding the focus for therapy, the goal to be sought, and when therapy should come to an end. Therapists attend carefully to clients' responses, both during the session and between sessions, to ensure that the therapy fits for the client.

### Conversations for Change/Difference

Therapists, because they are not living the lives of their clients, are able to notice and ask about differences and changes that may not at first be apparent to clients. The possibility therapist, like the solution-oriented therapist, highlights changes, exceptions to the problems, even changes that made the situation worse. In addition, the therapist introduces new distinctions into the conversation and attends carefully to notice which distinctions show up in clients' experience or actions or both. The possibility therapist also creates a sense of expectancy for change by his/her language and nonverbal behavior.

### Conversations for Competence/Abilities

The possibility therapist presumes client competence and pursues evidence of it, always being careful not to invalidate clients or minimize their pain, suffering, or own view of their concerns. This competence can be directly related to clients' concerns or perhaps from a different domain of clients' lives. For example, a golfer may find some golf knowledge that will help him approach his marriage in a new and more successful way.

### Conversations for Possibilities

Possibility therapists focus the conversation on the possibilities of the future rather than on the problems of the past. The past may be discussed, but the emphasis will usually be on clients' goals and visions of the future. I teach workshops on working with people who were sexually abused. Once Steve de Shazer was hassling me for teaching them, saying that by focusing on the problem I was inadvertently being problem focused. "I don't do therapy with people who have the problem of having been sexually abused, " he told me, "I only do therapy with people that want things to happen in the future." He had a good point. The fact that they were sexually abused is certainly important background information, like the fact that they grew up in a rural or urban environment or that they were shy or outgoing, but the ultimate emphasis in therapy is on where the person wants to go in the future.

In addition to focusing on future possibilities, possibility therapists spend time searching for new possibilities in the past and the present as well. Some wit has said, "It's never too late to have a happy childhood." While that, perhaps, overstates the case, it points to the idea that one can change one's selection and interpretation of events in the past and thereby create a new sense of where one came from: a new narrative, in the current parlance.

New possibilities are introduced into the present by getting clients to change their actions (the doing, as I have called it) and their frames of reference and attention (the viewing) about their current situations and concerns.

## Conversations for Goals/Results

Closely related to conversations for possibilities is focusing on how clients will know that they have achieved their therapeutic goals. Getting clear on when therapy should end according to the client not only minimizes the imposition of the therapist's ideas on the client but often hastens the achievement of those goals. This also leaves the therapist with a clear sense of accountability for therapeutic results. If the goal is not achieved, the client is not blamed for lack of results. Goal setting was mutual and responsibility for results is mutual.

## Conversations for Accountability/Personal Agency

A strong thread that runs through many of the faculty members' work at this conference is the idea that people are accountable for their actions, in philosophy talk, that they have personal agency. Mental disorders, terrible childhoods, etc., do not excuse people from accountability for their actions. This is distinct from blaming clients, which was detailed in a previous section. Holding people ac-countable says nothing about their intentions or character in performing those actions.

## THE DISTINCTION BETWEEN EXPERIENCE, ACTION, AND STORIES

I make a distinction between three domains in people's lives.

The first is the domain of *experience*. That includes everything that seems to just happen inside the person's "bag of bones" (as Gregory Bateson used to call people's bodies). This includes feelings, sensations, automatic thoughts, fanta-sies, neurology, and physiology. My stance about experience is that there is noth-ing to change about it in therapy. The therapist should acknowledge and validate clients' experience without trying to rid the clients of those experiences directly. This is basically the Carl Rogers stance. Let people know that who they are and what their "organismic selves" experience is acceptable and can be valued.

This validation consists of the following:

1. *Acknowledging*—Letting people know that you have noted their experience and points of view.
2. *Validating/valuing*—Letting people know that their experiences and points of view are valid and valued.
3. *Giving permission*—Letting people know that they can feel, experience, think, or do things.
4. *Inclusion*—Incorporating whatever concerns, experiences, objections, and barriers people show/express into the conversation without it becoming a block to moving on toward solution.

In this validating process, it is important to filter out blaming/invalidating questions, statements, and labels. As we have discussed above, blaming is attributing bad, sick, or evil intentions or character traits to oneself or others. Some labels blame and invalidate and some empower. It is also important not to invalidate the person or his/her experience. Invalidating means minimizing, denying, or undercutting a person's felt experience, sense of self, or point of view in a way that devalues them.

I was consulting for a psychiatric inpatient unit and did an interview with a woman who I later learned had the label "borderline." After the interview, when I asked her how the interview had been for her, she told me that she had expected to be crucified and had been pleasantly surprised to find that she wasn't. Afterward in the discussion with the staff of the unit, I asked about her feelings of being crucified and they told me that she had made quite a scene after she was offered the wrong medication during the night shift. She complained to the nursing supervisor, who told her that it was a therapeutic issue and she should go confront the nurse. When the staff asked me what I would recommend, I said that first I would apologize to her for making the mistake. They all nodded and agreed, but previously her complaint had seemed a symptom of her borderline personality. They had invalidated a legitimate complaint due to her diagnosis. She had also been encouraged to talk in group therapy and then when she did, she was confronted about dominating the group. It's no wonder she felt crucified.

The second is the domain of *action*. Action consists of what people do that is actually or potentially under their deliberate influence. Whereas in the domain of experience I give the client the message that everything is okay, in the realm of action, I take a stand against actions that are harmful to the client him/herself or that do not lead in the direction of results in therapy or both. After initially acknowledging the actions that clients have done or are doing, I start to sift between the ones that are okay (not harmful, ethical, and lead toward the stated goals) and the ones that are not okay (are harmful, unethical, and lead away from the stated goals). I do my utmost to oppose not okay actions and lead clients and their intimates to okay actions.

The third domain is that of *stories*. This consists of the ideas, beliefs, frames of reference, and habits of language that the client and his/her intimates show in reference to the presenting concern in therapy. Again, I take a stance that some stories are okay (those that lead toward clients' goals and do not invalidate or close down possibilities for clients) and some that are not okay (those that lead away from the goal, block access to the goal, invalidate clients, or close down possibilities for them). I encourage okay stories and filter out, create doubt about, or gently challenge stories that are not okay.

I prefer not to introduce explanations into my therapy sessions. My clients, of course, often introduce explanations into the conversation. I typically respond in several ways to such explanations. I either validate them as possible or create a little doubt as to their adequacy, relevance, or truth. If the explanations are not ones that blame them or their loved ones, invalidate them or their loved ones, or close down possibilities for change for them or their loved ones, I validate them. If they contain any of those elements of blame, invalidation, and closing possibilities, I create some uncertainty about them.

During a marital therapy session, a woman told me that, after ending an affair, her husband suggested that she call him anytime he was at work to ensure he was where he said he would be. She wondered aloud whether he was saying that because he didn't trust himself and wanted her to keep tabs on him or whether he was trying to show her that he was now trustworthy and hoped she would check to find out he was not having affairs. Later in the session, when we discussed the matter again, she said, "I always look on the negative side of things." I replied, "Wait, I'm not so sure about that. I heard you say you had two ideas about why he suggested you check on him. One was positive and one was negative. It seems to me that you are a person who looks at both sides." I was inviting her not to blame herself.

Since most of the interactions in therapy take place in the therapy session, conversation (both verbal and nonverbal) in the session then becomes the main fulcrum for influencing clients to develop stories and actions that further their goals and empower them. The session becomes like a filter, a colander, separating the empowering from the disempowering, the useful from the harmful. This is why we called the conference "Generating Possibilities through Therapeutic Conversation."

The task of the possibility therapist, then, is threefold:

1.   to *validate* the person and his/her experience;
2.   to *change the doing* of the problem;
3.   to *change the viewing* of the problem.

Possibility therapy is a method by which the client as a person, with all his/her past and current experiential realities, is validated and valued, as well as invited to change by cocreating new stories and opening the possibilities for new actions. All this is designed to empower clients, to remind them of their power. Possibility therapy seeks to avoid iatrogenic injury and to maximize iatrogenic healing and health. I hope that the reader has found both validation and possibility in *reading* this paper. I suspect that a lot of readers are working this way already and I have attempted in this paper to articulate and organize this emerging view.

## REFERENCES

Boskind-White, M., & White, W. (1983). *The Bulimarexia binge-purge cycle.* New York: Norton.
Breggin, P. (1991). *Toxic psychiatry: Why therapy, empathy, and love must replace the drugs, electroshock, and biochemical theories of the "New Psychiatry."* New York: St. Martin's Press.
Coles, G. (1987). *The learning mystique: A critical look at "learning disabilities."* New York: Pantheon.
Fingarette, H. (1988). *Heavy drinking: The myth of alcoholism as a disease.* Berkeley, CA: University of California Press.
Fisher, S., & Greenberg, R. (Eds.). (1989). *The limits of biological treatments for psychological distress: Comparisons with psychotherapy and placebo.* Hillsdale, NJ: Lawrence Erlbaum Associates.
Goffman, E. (1961). *Asylums: Essays on the social situation of mental patients and other inmates.* New York: Doubleday Anchor Books.
Kroll, J. (1988). *The challenge of the borderline patient.* New York: Norton.
Masterson, J. (1976). *Psychotherapy of the borderline adult: A developmental approach.* New York: Brunner/Mazel.
Morgan, R. (Ed.). (1983). *The iatrogenics handbook: A critical look at research and practice in the helping professions.* Toronto: IPI Publishing.
O'Hanlon, W. H., & Weiner-Davis, M. (1989). *In search of solutions: A new direction in psychotherapy.* New York: Norton.
O'Hanlon, B., & Wilk, J. (1987). *Shifting contexts: The generation of effective psychotherapy.* New York: Guilford.
Rosenthal, R., & Jacobson, L. (1968). *Pygmalion in the classroom: Teacher expectation and pupils' intellectual development.* New York: Holt, Rinehart & Winston.
Rossi, E., & Ryan, M. (1986). *Mind-body communication in hypnosis.* New York: Irvington.
Szasz, T. (1961). *The myth of mental illness: Foundations of a theory of personal conduct.* New York: Hoeber-Harper.

# Chapter 16

# My Guess Syndrome

## Bill O'Hanlon

I remember a particular case in which the client and I mutually gave up after about a year of regular visits and effort. The client was a doctor in a small rural community who had developed a most severe and unpleasant clenching of his facial muscles. He appeared as if he had just eaten something distasteful. He experienced it as involuntary and the problem persisted from the moment he awakened until he went to sleep. At times it would diminish somewhat, but it never entirely went away until he went to sleep. He was initially convinced that it was neurological and organic, but several years of visits to specialists far and wide had given him the idea that it might be psychosomatic.

Indeed, this man's problem had started around the time that his daughter had become engaged to and married a young man of whom the doctor and his wife had thoroughly disapproved. He had thought this through and decided that it may have been a reaction to those events and his inability to effectively prevent his daughter from marrying this distasteful man. It had been several years since then, and the man had turned out to be a better match for his daughter than he had seemed at first, but the facial grimace had persisted. He was quite embarrassed by the problem and avoided telling people in the small town what he had, allowing most of them to assume he had some degenerative muscular disease such as multiple sclerosis.

The man was referred to me because his therapist knew that I had studied with Milton Erickson. Therapists in my area tend to refer some "impossible" cases to me, thinking I might work some magic like Erickson was said to have done. Well, the magic eluded me. Even slow, steady progress eluded me. I tried and persisted in using (sequentially) hypnosis, marital therapy, family therapy,

---

This is an unpublished paper that was originally titled, *Not All My Cases of Long-Term Therapy Have Ended Successfully.*

paradoxical interventions, positive reframing, negative reframing, and a few other techniques. He was a nice man and cooperated with all procedures, but none of it seemed to have any impact. His wife was enlisted to watch for any minute sign of change, but she could see none. The only curious aspect of him coming to see me was that the grimace disappeared as soon as he entered my waiting room (it sometimes reappeared during hypnosis, which is the only way I was able to observe it happening). His best explanation for this disappearance of the symptom was that he knew I knew about it, so maybe he felt more comfortable around me and it went away.

Regardless, we finally mutually agreed that what we had done together hadn't been successful and I referred him to a colleague who worked much differently than I. That colleague saw him for about four sessions, usually conjointly with his wife, and got no further than I had. Several months later, while I was out of the country, the doctor called back to talk to me and when he found out I wasn't available, talked to my colleague. He reported that he had finally found a neurologist that had diagnosed his problem. It was called *Myges syndrome*. My colleague asked whether he had obtained relief after getting the diagnosis. "No," the doctor replied, there was as yet no treatment, but he did want us to know that it was neurological in basis. In hearing about it after I came back, I thought that perhaps some wise neurologist, knowing that this doctor would feel much better with a neurological explanation had given him a placebo diagnosis, "My guess is as good as yours."

# Chapter 17

# *DSM-V*

## A Modest Proposal

**Bill O'Hanlon and Paul Lambakis**

With the recent release of *DSM-III R*, the revised version of *DSM-III*, we were reminded that there will be future revisions of this august bible of psychiatric diagnoses. We wanted to be able to put our 2.5 cents worth in to influence these future versions of *DSM*. Realizing that our suggestions may be a bit radical for the current clinical climate, we are aiming for the revision after next, *DSM-V*, in the hopes that the field will be ready for our input by then. Our proposal aims to radically simplify the diagnostic categories by limiting them to three classes and a few variations.

### Category 1000.X

**Iatrogenically Induced Ailments.**   This category, which would make up the bulk of diagnoses in *DSM-V*, specifies disease processes that are initiated or made worse by contact with mental health professionals.

### Category 1001.X

**Iatrogenically Induced Chemical Dependence.**   This category is reserved for patients of psychiatrists who have been convinced they need to be taking drugs when there is little or no evidence to support such a need, and when those drugs seriously impair the functioning of the person.

This is an unpublished paper that seemed to somehow never make it into publication. It represents Bill and Paul's suggestions for the *DSM-V*. It is generally in its original form but was slightly revised by Bob and expanded during the process of editing.

## Category 1002.X

**Iatrogenically Facilitated Suicide.** This includes people who are given enough prescription drugs by physicians to commit suicide or are given enough prescription drugs to muddy their thinking enough or discourage them enough to commit suicide or both.

## Category 2000.X

**Psychiatric Syndrome of the Month (or the Donahue/Winfrey Disease).** This category is for popular psychiatric syndromes that come and go as fads with the time. Remember when, in Freud's Vienna, hysteria was a popular disease? Where have all those hysterics gone—the same place all the people who had inferiority complexes went; the diagnostic fads left them a historic artifact. Some diseases would be created and abolished by referendum (as homosexuality was in the 1970s). Others would be created by popular demand. After your fifth patient brings you *Women Who Love Too Much*, you could nominate the category for inclusion as "Psychiatric Syndrome of the Month." The syndrome with the most votes at the end of the month would be chosen and published in the newsletters of major clinical organizations.

## Category 2001.X

**Patient Whom It Is Acceptable to Hate.** Mental health professionals are people, too; they have their feelings, after all. In the days of overt rampant male chauvinism, this category was occupied by schizophrenogenic mothers (Where have they all gone?). Nowadays it is occupied by incestuous fathers and wife batterers. We propose that tomorrow's occupants of this category be determined by the same process as "Psychiatric Syndrome of the Month," outlined above.

## Category 2002.X

**Theoretical Resistance.** This diagnosis is reserved for those patients who have failed to adequately read their attending mental health professional's articles or books. Had they done so, they would have understood how to respond to the ingenious interventions bestowed upon them. Therefore, they must be deemed resistant to treatment.

## Category 3000.X

**No Mental Disorder.** We expect this to be a major category by *DSM-V*, if the third-party payers can be persuaded to cover them. If not, this category will remain to reassure the third-party payers that it is possible to have no mental disorder, but it should never, repeat never, be used with anyone who uses third-party payment methods.

## Category 3001.X

**Dormant Mental Disorder.**   For years, mental health moguls and other social control agents have known it is wise to keep all one's bases covered (cf. Orwell, George). Thus, we offer this category for those who are not currently eligible for third-party payments but are contemplating a new job with a good benefit package.

## Category 3002.X

**Arrested Mental Disorder.**   This category includes health maintenance organization referrals who have exhausted the allowed number of sessions for the current year. Of course, good protocol demands a follow-up appointment at the beginning of the next year so that an exhaustive assessment may be performed to detect any possible reemergence of mental disorder.

## Category 3003.X

**Masked Absence of Mental Disorder.**   This diagnosis describes those who are quite crazy but can neither afford treatment nor use third-party payment methods.

In addition to the categories, there are axes that can further specify the diagnosis and give indications as to the prognosis. The higher the number following the decimal point, the worse the prognosis. These are:

.1 = The clinician likes the patient. The patient is in the same social class, dresses like, talks like and acts like the clinician. The patient is of the gender and race the clinician prefers. Prognosis is excellent.
.2 = The clinician does not like the patient. The patient is not like the clinician. Prognosis is poor.
.3 = The patient cannot afford to pay for services and has no third-party payment option. Prognosis is dismal.
.4 = The clinician's secretary, nurse, or spouse does not like the patient. Prognosis is hopeless.

# PHASE IV

# Inclusive Therapy

# Introduction to Phase IV

## Future Directions

**Bill O'Hanlon**

My work is very much still in flux and development. I never really know where I am going until I get there. My ideas coalesce as I speak and write about them. I would say I am developing a more "inclusive therapy," because it includes many things that I had previously left out of my articulation of my work (although I think my actual therapy contained many of these elements for years). For example, I had the reputation of always doing brief therapy, but I have done therapies that have lasted for many years. I also wanted to include approaches that I had previously disdained, such as psychodynamic therapy. Very bright people have been using these approaches for years and some clients have found them to be immensely beneficial, but I came from a tradition that was trying to challenge the dominance and truth of psychodynamic therapy, so I had either ignored it as irrelevant in my writings and workshops or derided it in some way. Also, because of the minimalist tradition in solution-based approaches, considerations of politics and gender have been left out of many of my writings. I have also mellowed regarding the harm caused by diagnoses and medications, as I have had more life and clinical experience and wanted to soften my previous writings on those subjects. The last element of a more inclusive therapy is a consideration of the spiritual component of therapy and clients' and therapists' lives.

I have always been strident about standing against approaches that seemed to me disrespectful or ineffective, perhaps a bit too strident to make a more dramatic and forceful point. Perhaps the years have mellowed me. Perhaps the years have humbled me. Perhaps I am continuously aware of the gap between what I describe and what I do with clients. So stay tuned for further developments in the articulation of a more inclusive possibility therapy.

Chapter 18

# Frozen in Time

## Possibility Therapy With Adults
## Who Were Sexually Abused as Children

**Bill O'Hanlon**

I was sexually abused by my paternal grandfather when I was about 8 years old. I never forgot it. When I first began doing psychotherapy, I would occasionally hear from one of my clients that she (or more rarely he) had been sexually abused in childhood. The main idea at the time in the field of therapy was that these reports were probably based on fantasies or on Oedipal or Electra impulses. Because I had been abused, I did not hold such views. I knew abuse happened, because it had happened in my life. In recent years, with more publicity, more clients have been presenting with sexual abuse aftereffects as the main problem. I began to get more interested in this problem at about the same time many clinicians did and had my share of successes and failures. As I started to learn more about how to successfully work with abuse survivors, I became curious about how the experts (the folks who were writing books and teaching workshops) were doing treatment. What I found when I investigated surprised me, because most of the models and methods I discovered in the literature and workshops were very different from what I was doing. Because my clients generally seemed to benefit from the methods I was using, I thought it was important to start teaching and

*This manuscript was originally published in the 1993 edition of the edited series, *Innovations in Clinical Practice* by Leon VandeCreek, Samuel Knapp, and Thomas L. Jackson (Professional Resource Press). It is a summary of Bill's work with survivors of sexual abuse. Along with *History Become Herstory: Collaborative Solution-Oriented Therapy of the Aftereffects of Sexual Abuse,* this article preceded the book (with Bob Bertolino), *Even from a Broken Web: Brief, Respectful Solution-Oriented Therapy for Sexual Abuse and Trauma* (Wiley).*

writing about an alternative approach to mainstream treatment conceptions and methods.

In this contribution I will offer a clear simple model for understanding the aftereffects of sexual abuse, which fits with the traditional view but clarifies it. Next, I will talk about a major departure in treatment philosophy and method that can be used with sexual abuse aftereffects.

## FROM BUDDHISM TO DISSOCIATION:
## A THEORY OF RESPONSE TO TRAUMA

I earned a master's degree from a family studies department and in the process studied several theories of human development, even though I was only interested in learning marriage and family therapy at the time. I quickly forgot most of it as soon as I had passed my comprehensive exams. I studied Piaget as part of that human development literature and I did retain one thing from my studies. I remember that Piaget had demonstrated experimentally that all children are born Buddhists.

What do I mean by this? Piaget (Gruber & Voneche, 1977) showed that young children do not distinguish themselves from their environments or from others. They are one with everything. They have diffuse self-boundaries. Over time, however, we change them from happy Buddhists into people with distinct and separate personalities. Most of us develop a sense of identity and boundaries. We learn that we are living in a body that is separate from our environment and from others. We learn that our feelings and experiences are different from those of other persons. We may have various feelings, thoughts, sensations, and experiences, but we consider them to be *ours*. We have internally diffuse boundaries and generally fairly solid external boundaries.

## THE MISSING ROOMATE:
## THE THREE D'S OF SEXUAL ABUSE AFTEREFFECTS

Most abused people develop rather differently. When they have been intruded upon and their body or self-boundaries have been regularly violated, they often develop fairly solid *internal* boundaries. In the case of multiple personality disorder (Kluft, 1985; Braun, 1986), people have usually been intruded on severely and consistently enough before they develop much of a sense of self, so they divide themselves internally even more distinctly. Their external boundaries remain quite diffuse, though. Even in cases in which there was not severe and persistent enough abuse to create the splintering of self into multiple personalities, abuse survivors' external boundaries are still diffuse, giving rise to a diagnosis such as borderline personality disorder.

The solid internal boundaries represent the dissociated nature of the traumatic memories and other aspects related to the trauma.

It is as if a bunch of roommates get together one day and decide to banish one of their group from the house. They throw him out and change the locks. He bangs on the door for awhile, creating quite a ruckus, but the other roommates ignore him and hope he'll go away. For a long time, he can think of no way to get back in the house, so he waits outside. One day, desperate to get back inside, he crashes in through the front window.

Flashbacks are like the crash through the front window. Impulses to mutilate oneself are like the crash through the front window. When an aspect of one's experience has been dissociated, disowned, and devalued, it goes "underground" for much of the time and then intrudes in a destructive and unpleasantly surprising way into an abuse survivor's experience.

Recall the movie, *Dr. Strangelove or How I Learned to Stop Worrying and Love the Bomb*. Peter Sellers plays a Cold War scientist, Dr. Strangelove, who is talking about winning a nuclear war and pushing the button to drop the bomb. His gloved hand (the one that would push the button presumably) keeps reaching for his own throat throughout the movie. His hand seems to have a mind of its own and becomes involuntarily destructive.

## INTRUSION AND IDENTITY

People who are intruded upon physically and experientially usually react by dissociating—splitting off from themselves or parts of their experience. This seems to be a natural response to traumatic stress (Dolan, 1991; Herman, 1992). People who are severely or sexually abused not only dissociate the traumatic experience but disidentify with it. The feelings, memories, or perceptions seem to be outside their sense of themselves, outside their self-image or self-concept. It is ego-dystonic, not integrated into the ongoing self-story or life narrative that we create to compose or make sense of our lives.

Sexual abuse survivors dissociate and disidentify with the experiences, memories, or perceptions involved with the sexual abuse and also devalue them. The memories (or feelings, or perceptions, or whatever) are not only "not me" and they are distant from me, but they are bad or wrong. If I identify with them or experience them, I am bad or wrong or evil. Many people who are suffering from post-traumatic stress in general do not have such severe problems with believing that aspects of themselves are bad or that they themselves are bad in general. Almost everyone who has suffered severe sexual abuse thinks they are bad.

These then, are the three "D's" of sexual abuse aftereffects: dissociation, disowning (disidentification), and devaluing.

## INTRUSION AND INHIBITION: OR, HOW CAN YOU BE IN TWO PLACES AT ONCE WHEN YOU ARE NOT ANYWHERE AT ALL?

The result of the dissociating, disowning, and devaluing processes is paradoxical. On the one hand, the survivor is intruded upon by memories, sensations, and perceptions that are painful and unwanted. On the other hand, pleasant memories, sensations, and perceptions from the past or even involving in the present or the future are absent. Judith Lewis Herman (1992), commenting on this dichotomous experience, writes:

> In the aftermath of an experience of overwhelming danger, the two contradictory responses of intrusion and constriction establish an oscillating rhythm. This dialectic of opposing psychological states is perhaps the most characteristic feature of the post-traumatic syndromes. Since neither the intrusive nor the numbing symptoms allow for integration of the traumatic event, the alternation between theses two extreme states might be understood as an attempt to find a satisfactory balance between the two. But balance is precisely what the traumatized person lacks. She finds herself caught between the extremes of amnesia or of reliving the trauma, between floods of intense, overwhelming feelings and arid states of no feeling at all, between irritable, impulsive action and complete inhibition of action. (p. 47)

In a similar vein, here is Kardiner and Spiegel (1947), writing about a traumatized combat veteran: "He had, in fact, a profound reaction to violence of any kind and could not see others being injured, hurt or threatened. . . . [However] he claimed that he felt like suddenly striking people and that he had become very pugnacious toward his family" (p. 128). This man felt both repelled by and compelled to violence.

Judith Herman (1992) again states: "Trauma impels people both to withdraw from close relationships and to seek them desperately. . . . The traumatized person therefore frequently alternates between isolation and anxious clinging to others. A rape survivor describes how the trauma disrupted her sense of connection to others: . . . 'I was terrified of being with people and terrified of being alone'" (p. 56).

The theme that runs through these quotes and examples is that trauma survivors seem to be in two contradictory places at once, with seemingly opposing experiences: intrusion and inhibition. In the next section, I will propose a model to explain these troubling simultaneous polarities and a way to reconcile them.

So far, what I have written is compatible with the views of most of the experts on treating sexual abuse. Next, however, I will show how this approach starts to diverge from traditional treatment models. It will become apparent that the focus for this model is on the present toward the future, and the focus for the traditional model is on revisiting the past in order to resolve the aftereffects of sexual abuse.

## AN ALTERNATIVE TO THE ABREACTION/CATHARSIS MODEL FOR HEALING FROM SEXUAL ABUSE

### Challenging the Unexperienced Experience Model

A traditional view of why people have aftereffects of sexual abuse is that when the person went through the original trauma, he or she dissociated and therefore did not experience the trauma. This model has been aptly called the "unexperienced experience" model. Therefore, treatment is aimed at having people recall the original experience if they have forgotten it or to relive and experience the original emotions and sensations involved in the experience. Only then is the person truly able to move on from the unfinished trauma.

This is an interesting idea but certainly not a scientific truth. It derives from the psychodynamic assumption that when unconscious (repressed) material is made conscious, healing can occur and symptoms are resolved. It also includes more recent conceptions that in order for a symptom to be resolved, one must express emotions (experience catharsis). This model has *certainly* been useful to some people, but close examination reveals a few potential problems with it.

One problem is that some people suffer a great deal through the process of remembering their abuse and reexperiencing the emotions and sensations involved with it. These clients have already suffered a great deal in their lives. We should avoid adding to their suffering if it is possible for them to resolve their symptoms and reach their therapeutic goals without such additional suffering.

Also, some clients become much more self-destructive during this difficult process. There is often an initiation or increase in self-mutilating or self-hurtful behaviors such as cutting on arms, suicide attempts, or bulimia. Their relationships often deteriorate, as partners, family members, and friends are overwhelmed and alienated by the intensity of the pain or struggle and by the negative effects on the client's everyday functioning. Severe sexual difficulties often begin, although the client may have had some sexual dysfunction prior to the regressive, cathartic work.

Often clients are heard to say things such as, "This is too hard," "I won't be able to make it through this," and so on. Sometimes they do not make it through the process and kill themselves before treatment is complete. If we as therapists can find a less difficult and potentially lethal process to help people heal from sexual abuse aftereffects, I think it is incumbent upon us to use it.

## Frozen in Time: Symptomatic Trance

The clients that I see not only report that they experienced the abuse the first time it happened, but that they continue to experience it again and again. It is as if they are frozen in time, continuing to repeat the experience as if today were yesterday again and again.

Why don't most survivors of trauma experience the aftereffects all the time, then, if they are frozen in time? It is because they disown and dissociate those traumatic experiences and effects. The aftereffects only emerge in an intrusive way when they are called forth or triggered by something that reminds the survivor of the original traumatic experience.

It is as if the survivor enters a trance (dissociated) state in which she keeps repeating old painful memories, experiences, and perceptions. This state could be called symptomatic trance (Gilligan, 1987; O'Hanlon & Martin, 1992). Like therapeutic hypnotic trance states, it feels involuntary and involves focused attention and the experience of perceptual and experiential distortions. But in these symptomatic trances, people experience invalidation, devaluing, and a sense of no choice.

Possibility therapy is concerned with inviting people out of these symptomatic trances in a compelling way using the processes of acknowledgment, validation, and opening possibilities. One of the concerns about traditional models of post-trauma treatment is that clinicians might inadvertently be part of an invitation into symptomatic trance by focusing the client on reliving the past and on their pathologies rather than on his or her abilities.

## Beware of Theory Countertransference; Or, Where Did All These Multiple Personalities Come From?

Clients who have diffuse external boundaries may be especially vulnerable to being influenced by their therapist's pet theories and diagnoses. Because the usual theories involve regression and catharsis, most therapists become convinced of the necessity of this approach and, either subtly or overtly, convince their clients of the necessity and truth of regressive and abreactive approaches. I think we must be very careful to guard against what I call "theory countertransference" (Hubble & O'Hanlon, 1992). Like emotional or psychological countertransference (the process of projecting feelings, motives, or traits onto our clients during therapy), theory countertransference involves projecting our theories onto our clients.

Take as an example the amazingly rapid rise of diagnosed multiple personality disorder (MPD) in the past 20 years. Advocates of this diagnosis claim that there are many undiagnosed cases of MPD and that the rise in diagnosis is due to better education of clinicians in this complex disorder. Surely that is partially the case. MPD may resemble many other disorders in its initial presentation, so education is bound to increase the frequency of the diagnosis. But there is another, more insidious, side to this increased awareness. Some clinicians start to find clients with MPD entirely too frequently. In my town, there is a psychiatrist who is well known for "producing" cases of MPD. Almost any client that gets referred, regardless of initial presenting complaints or symptoms, emerges from a few hypnotic sessions with this psychiatrist with a diagnosis of MPD. Of course, as he specializes in the disorder, he is bound to get more cases referred, but the frequency with which he "discovers" or "uncovers" the disorder stretches the bounds of credibility.

We must be careful not to subtly or overtly impose our models on our clients, because they are especially vulnerable to such impositions. It is important to let clients teach us how to work with them, to be flexible in our methods and theories, and to occasionally challenge our own treasured beliefs and assumptions in working with adult survivors of abuse. It is important to individualize our treatment.

Of course, even the model proposed in this paper might be used in an intrusive way to impose these ideas on clients. The easiest way to avoid such coercion is to use "possibility language," taking care to include permissive words and phrases such as, "might," "could," and "can" in questions and comments. It is also crucial to respectfully respond to the clients' verbal and nonverbal responses to those questions and comments and make adjustments when the responses indicate discomfort with the direction the therapist is taking.

Of course, if the client needs to go back to the past, remember and abreact, we should support him or her in doing so. My experience and that of others who have worked in nontraditional ways (Dolan, 1991; Durrant & White, 1990; Gilligan, 1987) has shown that many clients, when given the choice, find other ways to resolve their abuse issues and symptoms. In the following section, I will detail a model that invites clients to resolve their sexual abuse issues in some of those "other ways."

## TREATING THE AFTEREFFECTS OF SEXUAL ABUSE: A SIMPLE, CLEAR MODEL

According to this model, there is a way to work in the present toward the future to resolve the abuse. This involves first acknowledging the facts and current and former inner experience of the abuse. Next it focuses on the presenting complaint or symptom to help clients value, own, and associate with discarded aspects of themselves. Last, it helps clients develop a clear sense of a future with possibilities.

There are three general strategies, then, in possibility therapy with survivors of sexual abuse:

1) Acknowledge past and present experience without closing down the possibilities for change.
2) Help the person value and associate with dissociated, disowned, devalued aspects of experience or self.
3) Rehabilitate a sense or vision of a future with meaning and possibilities.

### Acknowledgment and Possibility: Finding a Balance in Treatment

*Telling the Truth: Acknowledging What Happened and What Followed.*   One of the first ways to acknowledge is to get the client to describe, in factual ways, the abuse and his or her experience of it. This does not entail inviting the person to regress or abreact and cathart (express a lot of emotion), just to report the facts of the abuse and their own and others' responses to it. Most clients can do this without much direction, but some find it helpful to have some guidance from the therapist in this recounting.

To this end, I have listed questions that I sometimes use to help clients articulate and acknowledge their experiences of abuse. They can be given a list of these or similar questions and asked to respond to them as much or little as is appropriate.

---

**Facts/Descriptions of the Abuse**
How old were you when you were first sexually abused?
How old were you when the sexual abuse stopped (if it ever has)?
How long did the sexual abuse last?
How or why did the sexual abuse stop?
Who did you tell about the sexual abuse (if anyone) at the time?
How did they respond when you had told them?
Did they do anything to help or protect you or stop the sexual abuse?
How many times (approximately) were you sexually abused?
Were you abused by a member of your immediate family of origin (parent(s), stepparent(s), brother(s), sister(s))?
Were you abused by a member of your extended family (aunt(s), uncle(s), grandparent(s), stepgrandparent(s), cousin(s))?
Were you abused by a friend of the family or person whom your family trusted?
Did the person or people who abused you touch your breasts/chest during the abuse?
Did the person or people who abused you touch your vagina during the abuse?
Did the person or people who abused you touch your penis during the abuse?
Did the person or people who abused you touch your clitoris during the abuse?
Did the person or people who abused you touch your anus during the abuse?
Did the person or people who abused you put his/her fingers inside your vagina during the abuse?
Did the person or people who abused you put his penis inside your vagina during the abuse?
Did the person or people who abused you put his/her fingers inside your anus during the abuse?
Did the person or people who abused you put his penis inside your anus during the abuse?
Did the person or people who abused you put his penis inside your mouth during the abuse?
Did the person or people who abused you have you touch his penis (or her vagina) during the abuse?
Did the person or people who abused you masturbate in front of you during the abuse?

Did the person or people who abused have you masturbate in front of him/her/them during the abuse?

Did the person or people who abused you put anything besides parts of their body inside your anus/vagina or mouth during the abuse?

Did the person or people who abused you tell you not to tell anyone about the abuse?

What did they say would happen if you told about the abuse?

Did the person or people who abused you threaten you if you told?

Did the person or people who abused you say anything to you during the abuse? What?

Who have you ever told about the abuse?

How did the people or person you told about the abuse respond?

**Feelings/Experience/Perceptions During and After the Abuse**

Did you think at the time that the abuse was okay?

Were you confused during the abuse?

Were you scared during the abuse?

Did you feel physical pain during the abuse?

Did you feel physical pleasure during the abuse?

Did you enjoy the attention that the abuser gave you during the abuse?

Did you (do you) think the abuse was your fault in some way?

How do you feel about the abuse now?

When clients aren't clear about having experienced abuse, perhaps they are reporting dream or fantasy images or bodily memories and want to discover whether they have been abused. I acknowledge that these experiences could or could not be indicative of having been abused and there is no way to determine with certainty which is the case. I redirect them to what is bothering them, what brought them to treatment. (Uncovering memories is not a presenting problem in my estimation.) I explain to clients in this situation that there is a concern that I could lead them to believe that abuse occurred when it may not have. If we do the work on what is bothering them, whatever memories are needed and relevant come forth. By valuing the devalued, shut off aspects of experience or unclear or forgotten memories often follow.

*Acknowledging Without Closing Down the Possibilities for Change.* The first model of counseling I learned in depth was the client-centered model of Carl Rogers. What was so valuable to me about Rogers' model was the emphasis on the importance of acknowledgment and validation as cornerstones of the therapy process. In the ensuing years, however, I learned many other ways of doing therapy that were much more directive and showed practical ways to help people move on more quickly from being stuck. Working with people who have been abused has brought these two seemingly disparate approaches together and showed a way to combine the best of both nondirective and directive approaches.

I do what I call solution-oriented hypnosis. It is different from traditional hypnotic approaches in that it is more permissive, more inclusive, and more validating of whatever the "subject" is doing during the induction and however he or she responds while in trance.

I remember a client who had terribly intrusive obsessions. He was rarely, if ever, free of them. He had seen a psychoanalytic expert on obsessive–compulsive disorders for some time who pronounced him the worst case of obsessiveness he had ever seen. I used hypnosis with the man and by the second session he was starting to develop fine trances. At the third session, I started the trance induction with my usual opening: "You can be where you are, feeling what you are feeling, thinking what you are thinking, obsessing about what you are obsessing about, and experiencing what you are experiencing. There's nothing to do to go into trance, no right way or wrong way to go into trance. So just let yourself be where you are, doing what you are doing, worrying that you won't go into trance." At that point, he popped his eyes open and said simply, "That's why I come here." "To go into trance, you mean?" I asked, a bit surprised since he had been so skeptical about hypnosis at the start of treatment. "No," he replied, "to hear those words." He later explained that it was the only time in his life in which he could escape from the terrible sense that he was constantly doing everything wrong.

When this obsessive man said those words, something coalesced for me. It is crucial to acknowledge, validate, and include every bit of people's experience, especially the aspects of their experience they themselves have had trouble valuing and including, before they will be open to new possibilities and directions.

If one only acknowledges, validates, and is inclusive, however, most clients won't move on very quickly, as has been shown by decades of experience with client-centered work. Twenty-seven sessions after the intake, the therapist will still be bobbing his or her head and reflecting back the client's pain or feelings, and the clients will feel valued and heard, but they will not have much relief or have made many changes in their problematic situations.

Therapy is always a balance between acknowledgment and possibility. If clients do not have a sense that you have heard, acknowledged, and valued them, they will either spend time trying to convince you of the legitimacy of their pain and suffering or they will leave therapy with you. In the case of abuse aftereffects, it is important to acknowledge the facts of the person's abuse and his or her feelings and reactions to the abuse, but it is equally important not to wallow in the experience or to get stuck endlessly exploring the gory details of the past.

## Helping the Person to Value and Associate to Dissociated, Disowned, and Devalued Aspects of Themselves

*Permission, Valuing, and Inclusion as Antidotes to Devaluing, Dissociating, and Disowning.* Sometimes clients have come to the conclusion, consciously or unconsciously, that they are bad or that parts of themselves are bad. They might say, "If you only knew what I am like inside, you would see that I am evil."

They might have the sense that anger is bad and they should not feel it or show that they are angry. If they do, they think they are very bad or that anger is very bad. One way to counter this self-devaluing is for the therapist to first value those devalued aspects and then to invite the client into a valuing relationship with them.

How does one know which aspects of the person have been devalued, disowned, and dissociated? The symptom gives the clue. As discussed previously, whatever is inhibited or intruding can be seen as the devalued aspect.

A client who had been abused by older brothers in two separate incidents said that the only aftereffects that were apparent to her were in the area of anger. When her children were arguing, she could generally let them work out the matter, but if one of them asked for her protection, she would fly into a rage.

This case illustrates two important concepts: triggers for symptomatic trance and dissociated, disowned, and devalued experience as symptomatic.

When this woman was growing up, she was both overprotected by her parents and not protected (as she had been abused by her brothers), so the external event that cued her into symptomatic trance was being asked for protection. It was enough of a reminder of the abuse to revivify it for her. Once it was revivified, the experience she had was rage, way out of proportion to the current situation. Usually in everyday life, she had no feelings of anger.

Part of the treatment, then, was to invite her to let anger be an accepted part of her life. The following example shows one way to accomplish this:

> Janet had been angry for months. She was afraid, however, that her rage would be so out of control that it would damage her husband and children and others who came in contact with her, so she kept a tight clamp on those angry feelings. After we discussed the stance of just acknowledging your experience and letting your feelings be the way they are, she decided to experiment with that idea. One weekend, her husband and older son went out of town and she was at home with her 12-year-old. She decided to give herself permission to get into her anger and rage but set the limit that she wouldn't show any of it to her son, who was in and out of the house all weekend. She was amazed to discover that she wasn't "out of control" when she felt the rage, rather that she felt, in a strange way, more in control. All weekend she indulged in angry fantasies and rageful imagined conversations with her husband and others with whom she was angry. "The anger just came and went all weekend, sometimes it was very strong and sometimes almost totally gone," she reported. By the end of the weekend, she had a different sense of the anger—it just didn't run the show anymore like it used to.

The idea is to invite clients to allow and value all that they feel, think, perceive, sense, or experience. This can be done with actions, by having them journal or dialogue with those devalued aspects of themselves, or by giving them permissive messages. For example, you might have them close their eyes, focus inside, and say to them, "Just let yourself feel what you feel, think what you think, perceive what you perceive, sense what you sense, and just be where you are."

*The Inclusive Self; Or, How You Can Be in Two Places at Once.*   Some
time ago, Martin Orne (1959) and associates did some experiments in which a
phenomenon they called "trance logic" emerged. Deeply hypnotized subjects were
trained to negatively hallucinate a chair (meaning not to be able to see a chair).
While hypnotized, they were led to be in a room with a chair and not be able to
see it. Then they were given a task that would cause them to bump into the chair,
but somehow they avoided it. When questioned closely, they reported that they
avoided the chair, but they did not see it. It seemed as if they were both seeing the
chair and not seeing the chair at the same time. This ability to hold two contradictory perceptions was called "trance logic."

This kind of logic seems to be available to people on a different level from
their normal processing. That level can be called the "inclusive self." That level
of self can hold seemingly contradictory ideas, perceptions, and feelings in a way
that integrates or allows both to exist and to be valid. It is at that level that survivors both remember and do not remember their abuse, or, as one client said, "My
mind didn't remember, but the cells of my body did." It is at this level that the
person can have room to both feel sexual and not feel sexual and have neither of
those feelings invalidate or cancel out the other.

> A client reported that she never really experienced everyday life. She always saw it
> as if it were being displayed on a movie screen before her. Her inner experience was
> dominated by memories of the sexual abuse she had suffered in childhood. I invited
> her to close her eyes and focus inside and suggested that she could allow both the
> memories and everyday life to be included in her experience. She could remember
> and not remember at the same time. After she opened her eyes, she reported that she
> had instantly begun to see everyday life on one side of a split screen and the abuse
> memories on the other side of the screen. When she emerged from trance, she said
> that for the first time she could remember, the abuse memories were not dominating
> her experience.

There are several methods for inviting clients to process their experience at
the inclusive self level:

1)   Suggest the possibility of having seeming opposites or contradictions
coexist without conflict.

> A client told me that she felt compelled to tell me about her abuse but at the same
> time felt that she could not, as she was terrified to do so. I invited her to go inside to
> the deepest levels of herself and suggested, "You can tell me and not tell me about
> the abuse." She sat quietly for a moment and then her hands began to move in an
> almost poetic and artistic manner, weaving an intricate dance in the air above her
> lap. I encouraged her to continue to move through what she was experiencing and
> after a time she opened her eyes and told me with a smile, "I did it—I told you and
> didn't tell you at the same time. My hands told the story of my abuse. Now I think I
> can tell you in words."

2)    Give the person permission to and permission not to have to experience or be something. For example, "You can feel angry and you don't have to feel angry," or "It's okay to feel sexual sensations and you don't have to feel sexual." Remember that I am recommending that you invite the person to include and have permission about experience, not actions. So I would never suggest, "It's okay to kill yourself and you don't have to," or anything that might be construed as permission for harmful or unethical behavior.

## REHABILITATING A SENSE OR VISION OF A FUTURE WITH MEANING AND POSSIBILITIES

### Orienting to the Future: Viktor Frankl Meets Shakti Gawain

A few years ago, I heard the psychiatrist Viktor Frankl give a talk. He was describing one of the experiences he had while imprisoned in a Nazi death camp during World War II. He was being marched through a field one day to a work detail. He had inadequate clothing on, holes in his shoes, and he was very weak and ill from mistreatment and malnutrition. It was a cold winter day with snow on the ground. He began to cough and developed a coughing fit during which he sank to his knees. He could not seem to stop coughing or get up from the ground. A guard began to beat him with a stick and tell him that he would be left to die if he didn't get up and start walking immediately. Frankl thought he was going to die. In the next moment, he found himself giving an imaginary lecture on "The Psychology of Death Camps" to a rapt audience. In the lecture, he was describing precisely what was happening to Viktor Frankl there in the field in Poland, but he was not really experiencing it. It was as if he were detached from it and merely recounting what *had* happened. He described how, against all odds, he arose from the ground and kept walking, surviving yet another impossible-to-survive day. He went on to describe to his (imaginary) audience how he and some other of his fellow prisoners had psychologically survived the death camp experience. At the end of this imaginary lecture, he received a standing ovation from the audience. When I saw him over 40 years later, he gave a lecture to over 7,000 people and received a standing ovation.

What did Viktor Frankl do that most trauma victims do not do? He projected himself into a future with possibilities. Most trauma victims dissociate, as Frankl did, but usually they imagine a future that is a repeat of the past or the present or they project themselves into a future that is even worse than the present or the past.

In possibility therapy, one of the tasks of the therapist is to resurrect, excavate, or create the trauma survivor's vision or sense of a future with possibilities. One can assume there is at least some semblance of a future with possibilities in our clients, because they have come to our offices. If they had no sense of the possibility of a different and more satisfactory future, they probably would not have bothered seeking or accepting therapy.

One way to do this is to ask survivors about their vision of a future without their current problems or symptoms (O'Hanlon & Weiner-Davis, 1989). This is akin to what Shakti Gawain, the New Age writer, does when detailing the technique of creative visualization (Gawain, 1978). She helps people create a sense of the possibilities for being where and how they want to be in the future by coaching them to develop specific visual, auditory, and other sensory-based imaginings of such a future.

Solution-oriented therapy employs many strategies for helping people orient to meaningful and preferred futures (O'Hanlon & Weiner-Davis, 1989), including asking people what they would notice as a first sign that they were moving in the right direction and asking them what they would notice if their problems were removed by some miracle or magic wand. Next I will detail a few ways to use language to create compelling invitations into better futures.

*The Moving Walkway: Creating Compelling Invitations Into Possibilities.* I travel quite a bit and often encounter moving walkways in airports. These "people-movers," once you are on them, can transport you toward your destination even if you do not take a step on your own. I use language in a similar way in therapy. I help people start moving in the direction of their preferred futures before they have even taken any actions of their own. I do this by reorienting their attention to a better future and by introducing possibilities through questions and statements. The technique of asking questions to introduce rather than elicit information has been detailed before (O'Hanlon & Martin, 1992; O'Hanlon & Weiner-Davis, 1989; O'Hanlon & Wilk, 1987). Here I will mention several techniques that can be used to create compelling invitations to clients to leave the past in the past and to begin to feel a sense of moving on toward their hoped-for goals.

### Technique 1: Introducing Possibilities into Past and Present Reports

1) When clients give generalities about their problems, introduce the possibility that the problem is not so general. Reflect clients' problem reports with qualifiers, usually of time (e.g., recently, in the last little while, in the past month or so, most of the time, much of the time), intensity (e.g., a bit less, somewhat more), or partiality (e.g., a lot, some, most, many).

*Client:* Everything is going wrong for me.

*Therapist:* A lot has been going wrong lately.

*Client:* I've been really depressed.

*Therapist:* You've been depressed most of the time in the last little while.

2) Translate clients' statements of the truth into statements of clients' perceptions or subjective realities.

*Client:* Nobody is on my side.

*Therapist:* Sometimes it has seemed to you as if nobody is on your side.

*Client:* From the things she has said and done, it is obvious she doesn't care for me or our marriage.

*Therapist:* Some of the things she's done have given you the impression she doesn't care.

### Technique 2: Introducing a Future With Possibilities

1) Assume the possibility or likelihood of clients finding solutions.

   *Client:* I just can't seem to be comfortable around people.

   *Therapist:* So you haven't found a way to be as comfortable as you'd like around people yet.

   *Client:* I do better sometimes, but then I seem to slip back.

   *Therapist:* So you haven't quite mastered the ability to stay on course most of the time.

2) Reorient from a focus on the past to a focus on the preferred future.

   *Client:* I've been upset about every little thing.

   *Therapist:* Then it seems to me that you'll know you've gotten what you came here for when you let some of the little things slide.

## SOME GUIDELINES FOR POSSIBILITY THERAPY WITH SURVIVORS

What follows is a list of principles that summarize and extend the main points of this paper in the form of suggestions for treatment.

- Find out what the client is seeking in treatment and how he or she will know when treatment has been successful.
- Ascertain to the best of your ability that the sexual abuse is not current. If it is, take whatever steps necessary to stop it.
- Don't assume that the client needs to go back and work through traumatic memories. Some people will and some won't. Remember that everyone is unique.
- Look for resources and strengths. Focus on underlining how they made it through the abuse and what they have done to cope, survive, and thrive since then. Look for nurturing and healthy relationships and role models they had in the past or have in the present. Look for current skills in other areas. Have the person tell you how they stopped themselves from acting on destructive impulses, got themselves to seek therapy, and so forth, despite having the aftereffects of sexual abuse.
- Validate and support each part of the person's experience and self.

- Make provisions (e.g., contracts) for safety from suicide, homicide, and other potentially dangerous situations if necessary. Make these mutual.
- Keep focused on the goals of treatment rather than getting lost in the gory details.
- Do not give the message that the person is "damaged goods" or that their future is determined by having been abused in the past. Remember that change can occur in the interpretations and actions or interactions associated with the event(s).
- Gently challenge self-blaming or invalidating identity stories the person has or has accepted from others.

## CONCLUSION

What I have tried to do in this article is to introduce a new model for doing therapy with survivors of sexual abuse who present complaining about some aftereffects of their sexual abuse trauma. The model involves acknowledging and valuing all aspects of clients' past and present experience; inviting them to value and embrace dissociated, disowned, and devalued aspects of themselves and their experience; and inviting them to rehabilitate their sense of being able to look forward to and move into a future with possibilities. The model is, then, present and future oriented and eschews the standard past orientation.

## REFERENCES

Braun, B. (Ed.). (1986). *Treatment of multiple personality*. Washington, DC: American Psychiatric Press.
Dolan, Y. M. (1991). *Resolving sexual abuse: Solution-focused therapy and Ericksonian hypnosis for adult survivors*. New York: Norton.
Durrant, M., & White, C. (1990). *Ideas for therapy with sexual abuse*. Adelaide, Australia: Dulwich Centre Publications.
Gawain, S. (1978). *Creative visualization*. Mill Valley, CA: Whatever Publishing.
Gilligan, S. G. (1987). *Therapeutic trances: The cooperation principle in Ericksonian hypnosis*. New York: Brunner/Mazel.
Gruber, H., & Voneche, J. (1977). *The essential Piaget*. New York: Basic Books.
Herman, J. L. (1992). *Trauma and recovery: The aftermath of violence—From domestic abuse to political terror*. New York: Basic Books.
Hubble, M. A., & O'Hanlon, W. H. (1992). Theory countertransference. *Dulwich Centre Newsletter,* 25–30.
Kardiner, A., & Spiegel, H. (1947). *War, stress and neurotic illness* (rev. ed. of *The traumatic neuroses of war*). New York: Hoeber.
Kluft, R. (Ed.). (1985). *Childhood antecedents of multiple personality*. Washington, DC: American Psychiatric Press.
O'Hanlon, W. H., & Martin, M. (1992). *Solution-oriented hypnosis: An Ericksonian approach*. New York: Norton.
O'Hanlon, W. H., & Weiner-Davis, M. (1989). *In search of solutions: A new direction in psychotherapy*. New York: Norton.
O'Hanlon, B., & Wilk, J. (1987). *Shifting contexts: The generation of effective psychotherapy*. New York: Guilford.
Orne, M. (1959). The nature of hypnosis: Artifact and essence. *Journal of Abnormal Psychology, 58,* 277.

# Chapter 19

# Possibility Therapy With Families

## Steffanie O'Hanlon and Bill O'Hanlon

In family therapy often only one or two family members are very motivated for treatment and the rest are along for the ride at best and are conscientious objectors at worst. However, less-than-motivated family members can be the best collaborative therapy trainers. They will notice if the therapist hasn't heard and acknowledged all the points of view, whether he is allowing unhelpful interactions to proceed too long without interruption, if he is more eager to have the family in treatment than they are to be there and, finally, if he knows anything about how to solve the problem with which they came in. Possibility therapy offers a collaborative approach, which allows the therapist to ally with even the most reluctant clients. Possibility therapy also offers an effective way to address the additional challenges that occur in family therapy: Figuring out who should show up and what they should change. There are multiple and sometimes conflicting perspectives, experiences, and goals. When Steffanie took her first job in the family unit of a community mental health center, she had a next-door officemate, Gary, who would drop by between sessions and recap the progress of his latest case. His usual refrain was "*veni, vidi, vici*" (loosely translated as *they* came, *they* saw, *they* conquered). Steffanie and Gary, despite their advanced training in psychodynamic psychotherapy and family systems treatment, felt stymied about how to proceed. "Okay, so the family is triangulating. Do we do a structural or strategic intervention or do we talk about projective identification? And what about the fact that the family was referred by the social services, doesn't really want to be here, and is resentful of almost anything we say or suggest?" In this paper, we will show how the collaborative process of possibility therapy allows one to work even with reluctant family members, to decide which treatment strategies are right,

This article was written by Stephanie and Bill in the process of editing this book.

solve problems in a timely and effective manner, and actually to have fun in the process.

## WHAT MAKES THERAPY COLLABORATIVE?

We start by creating a collaborative context by recognizing the expertise of family members and giving their expertise as much weight as our professional training and expertise. We view our role as consultants. We have lots of ideas based on our education and experience to bring to the family, but family members are the only ones who know what is happening in their lives, what they are concerned about, what ideas and actions will work for them, what feels respectful, and what feels disrespectful.

Families frequently come to therapy prepared to be blamed for or rescued from their difficulties. We try to move them from these unhelpful postures and empower them to be active participants in bringing about change. We assume the family has strengths and look to utilize and incorporate these rather than focus on pathologies and deficits. On the other hand, we acknowledge that families can damage one another through abuse, neglect, and other interactional processes. At these times we confront and intervene in destructive patterns. We endeavor to do this in a way that doesn't blame or presume bad intentions but invites family members to alternative behaviors and interactions.

Families are an active part of the treatment planning process. They are consulted about goals, directions, and their reactions to our methods of therapy throughout treatment. We make the process of therapy clear and accessible. This includes making diagnostic procedures, conclusions, and case notes understandable and free from jargon or theoretical or technical terms.

We try to ask questions and make speculations in a nonauthoritarian way, giving families ample room and permission to disagree or to correct us. For example, if we were going to talk to the family about clear lines of authority and decision-making, we would bring up the idea as a possibility, rather than a truth. We might say, "One of the theories of family therapy has an idea that it is very important for the family hierarchy to be clear. If it isn't, according to this idea, it tends to generate problems. For example, if grandparents are somehow taking over for the parents or undermining parents' rules or policies with kids, it can cause problems with either the marriage or the children. Do you think the rules and lines of authority are clear in your family? We have seen some things that make us think there may be some confusion in the hierarchy. Is it important to you that they be clear? Some families and some cultures do it differently; there is no one right way. What do you think?" We give multiple options and let the family coach us on what fits for them. If we have an idea, strong personal opinion, or perception, rather than keeping it hidden and unspoken, we make it public by noting it in the conversation, but clearly as our personal point of view or perspective and not as a statement of fact about the family. We are wary of what we call "theory countertransference" (Hubble & O'Hanlon, 1992), imposing our beliefs and therapeutic values (and favorite diagnoses) on the family. We don't view ourselves as having special knowledge about the best way for the family to live life after therapy is concluded or the manner in which they should resolve the concerns that brought them to therapy.

We also extend this collaborative stance to our work with other helpers who may be involved with the family. We respect their treatment and contribution and invite them to cooperate by inquiring about their views of the situation and the outcomes they expect from treatment. If they are willing, we ask them about how we might help or at least not interfere with their treatment. We want to note that this does not mean that we always accept or support everything other helpers do. Our first loyalty is to our client(s). If we feel that the other therapist/helper is imparting harmful or discouraging ideas, what we typically call *impossibility stories*, to the family, we gently and subtly challenge those unhelpful ideas by first acknowledging their possible validity and then introducing alternate perspectives. For example, "So the discharge planner at the hospital said Johnny would always need to live in a structured setting because of his schizophrenia. You agree for right now that he should be in residential treatment following discharge, but lots of things can happen down the road (medication changes, independent living programs, and so on) that may make other living situations more workable."

## WHO TO SEE

A primary and crucial question in family therapy is which members to see. When family therapy was new, there was a rigid insistence on seeing *all* the family members or refusing to take the case. This has softened over the years, so therapists are now faced with the dilemma of deciding when they should agree to meet with part of the family and when it is important to hold out for everyone to attend. We prefer to see whoever is motivated to seek therapy or make change, or whoever is upset. Typically this is the person who is making the phone call, but it may include a large supporting cast as well. We ask ourselves a number of questions to ferret out the most likely participants: Who is complaining or alarmed? Who thinks there is a problem? Who is willing to pay for therapy or do something to effect change or both? Whose concerns will constrain or affect therapy? Who is pushing for change?

Sometimes we start with one person and end up with many. Sometimes we start with a whole family and break down into smaller subsets. If a mother is calling and is concerned about appropriate limit setting with her 14-year-old daughter and says no one else in the family is concerned or wants to come, we would be willing to meet with the mother alone to do "family therapy." Later we might try to involve other family members if it seemed important. Or, in another family, if the father says he doesn't like the way he responds to his son's "mouthing back," we might just see the father. Of course we prefer, if possible, to see whoever is affected by the complaint. For example, if a father were calling about conflict between mother and daughter, we would like to see all three because although mother and daughter are fighting, the father is concerned about the escalation of the conflict.

We can and often do family therapy with only part of the family, usually with the motivated part of the family. It isn't necessary to have the whole family attend therapy to bring about a change. Who will attend is often determined by the goals or agenda that has been set. The more the agenda includes the various members' concerns, the more likely reluctant family members will attend. We will talk more about how to set inclusive goals a little later.

And what to do about those clients who are mandated/required to attend therapy? We see them even if it seems they are not motivated and then we negotiate goals or a focus that is relevant to them. Steffanie used to work in a psychiatric hospital with adolescents. Most of them did not want to be there, let alone comply with the rigorous rules. What they did want was to get out of the hospital as quickly as possible. Treatment would focus around what the teens needed to do to demonstrate to and convince hospital staff, family members, and whoever else was involved (school personnel, youth services, parole officers, and so on) that they were ready to leave the hospital and handle their problems in a different way. It is important to acknowledge up front that the client doesn't want to be there and also to hear the reasons behind their not wanting to participate in therapy. This approach also works with parents who are being forced into treatment. Bill saw a parent whose child had been removed from the home by child protective services. She was accused of having burned her son with cigarettes. She maintained her innocence. She had seen a variety of helpers, but none had in her view listened to her. Bill listened to her experiences with protective services and the various therapists and her frustration about wanting her child back in a way that the *client* perceived her position was acknowledged. Then Bill and the client were able to come up with a plan that allowed her to both maintain her innocence and fulfill the requirements for safety that protective services had set.

There seems to be an inverse effect in that the more motivated certain family members are the less motivated the others will be. In her private practice, Steffanie became known as a specialist in adolescents and therefore she saw this phenomenon quite frequently. One or both of the parents would be eager about therapy and the teenager was miserable about being dragged in. The teen didn't want to speak and either communicated this through sullen glances or direct pronouncements of his unwillingness to participate. Steffanie would casually commiserate (a.k.a. acknowledge) that he didn't want to be there or speak. She would tell him that it was okay with her. The teen could just hang out and be silent if he wanted, and Steffanie would speak with whoever had brought him (typically a parent) as they were clearly the most concerned. And if something came up that the teen wanted to clarify or add, he could speak up but he didn't have to. At this point there would be a sigh of relief and the tension/hostility meter would drop significantly. Usually within five to ten minutes the adolescent was jumping in to rebut the parent's description of the problem. If, on the other hand, the teenager was reluctant to attend treatment and refused to even attend one session, Steffanie would suggest the parent go home and tell the teen that part of what was going to happen in therapy was renegotiating rules and consequences in the house. They would also explain that the therapist (Steffanie) was concerned about offering the teen an opportunity to represent himself and to talk about other changes he would like to see happen in the family as well. Usually the teenager would show up for the next session. To make therapy palatable for the reluctant attendee, find out what motivates him and link therapy to that. Also important is to find out what turns the reluctant family member off and stop doing that (e.g., giving him the sense that he is to blame, repeatedly asking him about how he is feeling, etc.). What makes therapy relevant and interesting for him? Since he may be feeling dragged there to begin with, the therapist needs to be careful to structure the session to minimize the likelihood he will feel misrepresented or blamed and not to allow prolonged unhelpful interactions to occur. If the reluctant client is a child or teen, he or she can often be motivated by the possibility of having a say in renegotiating rules and consequences, discussing other changes that he or she would like in the household, and of course, the possibility of increased privileges. This often motivates the reluctant spouse as well. If he or she has a sense that real change can occur and that it isn't just going to be a gripe session, the reluctant client is usually a more willing and, often, more enthusiastic participant.

Many people ask whether we see children individually. Generally we don't see children in individual therapy. Steffanie began her career doing play therapy and working under the child guidance model (children are seen separately from parents; often each family member has his or her own individual therapist). The change that happens with this approach tends to be long in coming, if at all. And when a child is able to make change in individual psychotherapy, it does not always transfer into the family context unless the family members have changed their interactional patterns. We have both found it more effective and respectful to coach parents and families to develop strategies to directly solve their own problems than to rely on a third party to influence the emotional and behavioral lives of their children. When we meet with a family for the first session, we may speak with the child or children separately briefly to provide them with an opportunity if there are things they have to say privately and to get a sense of their resources outside of the direct family context.

We do tend to see adolescents in a combination of individual and family therapy, usually because most adolescents have individual concerns and express some desire for more individual sessions after they become engaged in treatment. Rarely do we see younger children in individual treatment, again mostly if the child wants to be seen alone and has a specific personal problem on which to work. For example, we both may see a child individually to do hypnosis or eye movement desensitization and reprocessing (EMDR) for a focused problem such as a school phobia or bedwetting or a trauma. We also see children individually when parents, school, or court insist on it and our efforts to dissuade the parents from individual sessions have been futile. (Sometimes a parent just won't believe that change is possible and will be sustained unless we see the child individually and discuss Little Ken's anger.) When we do meet with children individually, we talk with them about whether they think there is a problem and get their ideas about the problem. We say things like, "We are meeting because your parents are concerned about your anger. They think it's a problem. Do you think it's a problem? Does it make things hard at school or with friends? Or does it cause you to lose out on things you want to do? Do you want to do it differently or is it okay for you?" We typically use these sessions to build rapport and gather information to build interventions for the family.

## WHAT DO YOU WORK ON?

When families come into therapy, they are typically demoralized and entrenched in a process of speculation and blame about the causes and reasons for their difficulties. Traditional family therapy sometimes inadvertently reifies the situation by initially replicating these same conversations (pathology/blame-based). Further, traditional family therapy sometimes requires that the first three sessions be used for gathering information about family history and etiology of the problem before one can begin intervention. Families are often frustrated by this process and the therapist feels hamstrung, unable to act until all the information is collected. This is akin to checking into a hospital with acute appendicitis and having the staff tell you that they want to gather a lot of insurance information and history before giving you treatment. Possibility therapy focuses on clients' goals for treatment and almost always starts the intervention process in the first session.

### Complaints and Goals: Focusing and Finding Mutually Agreeable Directions

The focus of treatment in possibility therapy is the family's complaints and goals. It is vital that the focus comes *from* the family, not from our theories or from some normative model. We get that information from the family. For example, a family may come in complaining of a child's temper tantrums and we may observe "triangulation" in the family interactions, but if it is peripheral to the problems and goals on which we are trying to focus, we wouldn't bring it into the spotlight or challenge it. *Many families triangulate but do not have problems that bring them to therapy.* Unless the family members are concerned about triangulation or it is part of the problem as they express it, we do not pursue such "theoretical" problems.

To determine the complaint, again we ask the family members and ourselves a series of questions. What is bothering someone enough to get them to seek or get sent to treatment? What are they complaining or alarmed about? When has the complaint occurred? Where has it occurred? What are the patterns surrounding or involved in the complaint? How does the person, the customer, or others involved in the situation explain the complaint?

With families and couples typically there are multiple complaints, usually at least one per person and sometimes several per person. We try to acknowledge and address each complaint and combine them into mutual complaints and goals on which to focus our inquiries and interventions.

We ask each person what they are in therapy for and what they want to accomplish. Needless to say each person has a slightly or vastly different perspective on the situation. So finding or creating mutual goals is a way to harmonize multiple complaints.

Acknowledging, tracking, and linking are ways to coordinate complaints and goals. We acknowledge each family member's perspective by restating it in the least inflammatory way possible that still acknowledges and imparts the meaning and feeling. We link these statements by using the word "and," as it builds a common concern rather than opposing or competing needs and goals. For example, "Dad, you become concerned that Pete is getting depressed and may make another suicide attempt when you see him hanging out in his room. So you go and check on him. And Pete, you feel like you're on 'fifteen minutes checks' and want your Dad to back off. And so you guys get into it. And then Mom you hear them winding up and feel like you need to cool things down. So Dad, you want to be reassured that Pete is okay. Pete, you want some space. And Mom, you don't want to have to be in the middle of these fights." We not only acknowledge and link but also track the complaint by giving descriptions of actions or sequences of behaviors that are occurring. The intent is that the family members jump in and clarify any misperceptions or areas of discomfort until a mutually agreeable description emerges. Once we have a commonly agreed upon description, we begin to flesh out the direction and goals for treatment.

It's important to acknowledge the difficulty the family members are experiencing without allowing them to become too discouraged in the process. There is nothing more demoralizing than going to a therapist's office and having the same old arguments with no better outcome (and paying a lot of money to do so). One of the ways we do this is by going back and forth between getting descriptions of concerns and problems on the one hand, and eliciting descriptions of better moments (exceptions to the problem and more compassionate, helpful ways of viewing the situation) on the other hand. We also usually ask clients what methods they have already tried to solve the problem, so we don't reinvent a broken wheel. We also acknowledge their efforts and expertise, as well as how seriously stuck and discouraged they are.

In gathering information, it is important not to crystallize or reify the problem. Feelings and concerns are not set in stone. We notice that in the process of gathering information and filtering out problematic stories, family members' feelings or ideas about the complaint often change, sometimes radically. One of the ways this transformation occurs is by getting people to translate vague and blaming words into action descriptions (videotalk) (O'Hanlon & Wilk, 1987; Hudson & O'Hanlon, 1992).

If "poor self-esteem" is the complaint, get a specific description of what "poor self-esteem" and "good self-esteem" looks like in that family. Does it involve eye contact when speaking, a certain tone of voice, asking for what you want, or other components? The key here is to get a description of the actions or processes involved in the expression of "self-esteem." If someone is complaining about a "messy house," find out what that means for that person or that family. Is it papers in piles or no piles of paper, passing the white glove test, clothes on the floor or clothes on the bed/chair instead of hung in the closet, or something else altogether? Families (and many therapists, we might add) tend to use words like "communication," "self-esteem," "depression," "trust," "behavioral problems," and "underlying anger," which are very general.

In addition, we like to find action correlates for feelings ("Tell me what kinds of things she does when you get the sense she's upset with you," or "How does he show you that he is sad but hiding it?").

Another element of involving family members in setting the direction and focus of therapy and in developing mutuality is to collaboratively define goals for the therapy and for the family. How will family members know when therapy has been helpful enough to terminate or when the agreed-upon results have been achieved? What are the first signs that will indicate (or already have indicated) progress toward the goal(s)? What are the final actions or results (in videotalk— seeable, hearable, checkable terms) that will indicate that this is no longer a problem? How will therapists know when therapy is done, when it has been successful? It is important, if possible, to get goal descriptions in specific videotalk terms. This helps to ensure that goals are achievable, not utopian. Achievable goals consist of clients' actions or conditions that can be brought about by clients' actions (for example, parents could ask that the child spend two hours per night doing homework or that the child raise his or her grade to a B in a particular subject). These goals include time elements: how often (frequency), when (date/time/deadline), and how long (duration). We help guide the family to define the goal to achieve agreement of what constitutes final resolution of the therapy concern or enough progress to terminate or take a break from therapy. We also help family members translate labels or theoretical concepts into action descriptions. If we are unable to define goals in action terms, we attempt to get the family or family members to rate the problem on a scale and then select a target number that will indicate success on that scale.

Sometimes supervisees or participants in trainings ask us how to get family members to be specific when they persist in stating the problem or the goals in vague language despite the therapist's efforts to be specific. We often "prime the pump" by providing multiple choice answers that are slanted in the direction of being more specific. That usually leads to family members either choosing one of the provided options, which is specific, or giving a similar specific that has not been provided.

We also want to note that certain circumstances dictate that we superimpose our goals on the family instead of letting them set the agenda. In situations where there is indication of homicidal or suicidal plans or actions, sexual assault or violence, and certain other legal and ethical issues, stopping these activities becomes the immediate treatment goal regardless of whether family members see that goal as crucial or relevant. For example, if in the course of discussing her depression, a client discloses that her son has been sexual abusing other children, safety for those children becomes a primary focus of treatment at least temporarily. We continue to work collaboratively, explaining our legal and ethical responsibilities, and engage our clients in taking the necessary steps to report offenses, develop safety plans, arrange hospitalizations, and so on. However, we will act unilaterally if they are unwilling to work collaboratively. Both of us, however, have had good success in having families call and report their own abusive behavior to child protective agencies when invited to do so in a respectful and nonblaming way.

## Intervening: Acknowledging Experience and Changing Views, Actions, and Contexts

Next, we will address how we organize our thinking for intervening in families. We use four areas for intervention in family therapy. These are *experience*, *views*, *actions*, and *context*. The chart below summarizes these areas.

Within *experience* lies all the inner aspects of people's lives, their feelings, fantasies, sensations, and their sense of themselves. All these are things that happen inside our experience that are unavailable to others unless we somehow communicate it to them through words, art, or gestures. We suggest that therapists just acknowledge, value, and validate experience. Let people know their experience has been heard and not judged as wrong or invalid. Let them know that they are valued as people and they have valid experiences. This is the realm of accep-

| Experience | Views | Actions | Context |
|---|---|---|---|
| Feelings | Points of views | Action patterns | Time patterns |
| Sense of self | Attentional patterns | Interactional patterns | Spatial patterns |
| Bodily sensations | Interpretations | Language patterns | Cultural background and propensities |
| Sensory experience | Explanations | Nonverbal patterns | Family/historical background and propensities |
| | Evaluations | | |
| Automatic fantasies and thoughts | Assumptions | | Biochemical/genetic background and propensities |
| | Beliefs | | |
| | Identity stories | | Gender training and propensities |

tance, not change (although communicating that acceptance may, of course, lead to change).

We always begin by acknowledging what the family is experiencing. The family needs to know that the therapist understands not only the content of the problem but also the emotional weight or resonance it has for them. This is fundamental for the rest of the treatment process, and for some families this *is* the treatment. Steffanie had a client that came in for one session to tell her about a rape that she had experienced several years before. She had never spoken about it and just wanted someone to hear her experience. In a follow-up phone call the woman said she went home and told her husband as well. She felt able to move on with her life. Most clients, however, need more than acknowledgment. They not only need to be heard and validated but then given help to begin actively making changes to solve the problem. Acknowledgment may last anywhere from five minutes to many sessions. If clients don't feel heard and understood, the therapist will not be able to move on to the other stages in therapy. If acknowledgment is all a therapist offers, it won't be enough for most families. But if we feel as therapists that we are starting to experience lack of cooperation or hostility in the treatment, we stop and move back into acknowledgment.

> Steffanie saw a family where the 9-year-old son had been referred by his family physician for behavior problems. The family agreed with the physician that Joe's temper tantrums were a problem, and they wanted to change his behavior. However, when we began to discuss ways for the family to respond to temper tantrums, the father would begin to shift around in his chair. After observing this several times, Steffanie told the father that she felt she wasn't being helpful in some way and asked for his comment. The father said that the discussion was about things that they could do to manage Joe differently, but that he thought that there was something Steffanie could do to "fix Joe." That opened up a discussion about how the father saw the problem and what he thought needed to happen. Steffanie explained that she was using the family as a way to, as they said, "fix Joe." Once the father's expectation was acknowledged and responded to, therapy proceeded quickly and smoothly, with the father's full cooperation. If Steffanie had continued on without acknowledging the father's discomfort or had she interpreted it as a resistance, therapy might have stagnated or become bogged down.

The next three columns in the chart define the realm in which change occurs. Here, we focus on three areas of change: *changing the viewing of the problem, changing the doing of the problem*, and *changing the context surrounding the problem.*

In these three areas, we search for patterns, both the problem and solution patterns. What are the problematic views that family members hold about themselves, their family, and each other? For example, are there patterns of blame that persist in the family view of the problem situation? What are more helpful, supportive, change-enhancing, or change-inviting views? What are the problematic action or interaction patterns that occur within the family, between family members, or with others? What are more helpful action and interaction patterns? And, finally, what are the aspects of the context that are conducive to change and results and what aspects of the context hold people back or continue their problems?

We try to change the habitual ways people think about, attend to, or see the problem—changing the "viewing" of the problem—and to change the habitual ways people have been acting and interacting in the problem situation, changing the "doing" of the problem. Some years ago the brief therapist John Weakland told Bill, "Life is just one damn thing after another. Therapy can't change that. But people who seek therapy are no longer experiencing that—life for them has become the same damn thing *over and over and over.*" Our task as possibility therapists, then, is to help people get from a situation in which life has become the same damn thing over and over back to a life where it's one damn thing after another. People will always have some problems, but what discourages and disempowers them is struggling unsuccessfully with the same problem over and over.

To the ideas of assessing and changing the "doing" and the "viewing," we have added changing the context of the problem. We as therapists have become much more aware of the influence of culture, gender, biochemistry, and other contextual aspects on people's problems. Problems do not occur in a vacuum. We believe that contextual aspects are influences (not causes) and that there are both problematic and helpful contextual influences. A family member may have a biochemical context that suggests a predisposition toward obsessiveness or schizophrenia, but that does not *cause* him or her to act in a particular way. For example, one may be subject to hallucinations, but that does not *cause* one to run down the street naked or hit someone. Or just because a man is from a cultural tradition where males are trained not to express feelings doesn't mean he is or will always be unable to express feelings.

We search for helpful contextual patterns as well as identify problematic contextual patterns. For example, we might say, "So there has been quite a history of alcohol abuse and dependency in your family. Dad, three of your uncles died from drinking in their thirties. Mom, your mother was a secret drinker until a few years ago. Tell us this: How did your mother stop drinking, Mom? And Dad, who in your family didn't succumb to the invitations of alcohol?" Or "Since we don't know much about Pakistani culture, perhaps you can help us with this. When there has been violence between a couple, how does it typically stop, if it does, in Pakistani culture? What aspects of the culture support violence between couples and what aspects of the culture challenge or restrain violence in those situations?"

## CHANGING THE VIEWING OF THE PROBLEM

When family members enter therapy, they often have stories (ideas, beliefs, hypotheses) about each other or the problem. These stories tend to be rigid and

## How to Intervene in the Four Areas

| Experience | Views | Actions | Context |
|---|---|---|---|
| Give messages of acceptance, validation, and acknowledgment. There is no need to change or analyze experience, as it is not inherently a problem. | Identify and challenge views that are Impossibility-oriented<br><br>Blaming<br><br>Invalidating<br><br>Nonaccountability- or determinism-oriented<br><br>Also Offer new possibilities for attention. | Find action and interaction patterns that are part of the problem and that are the "same damn thing over and over." Then suggest disrupting the problematic patterns or find and use solution patterns. | Identify unhelpful and helpful aspects of the context; then suggest shifts in the context around the problem (e.g., changes in biochemistry, time, space, cultural habits, and influences). |

divisive. Stories are unhelpful when they get in the way of change or get a bad reaction from other family members. When families come for therapy, we typically find that someone in the family has unhelpful stories that have become part and parcel of the problem.

We have identified four typical problematic stories. These beliefs may be held by anyone interacting with the problem: the family, the therapist, or the referral source.

### Impossibility Stories

In impossibility stories, clients, therapists, or others in their lives often hold beliefs that suggest that change is impossible.

> *Example:* He has ADHD and can't control his behavior.
> *Example:* She'll never change.
> *Example:* She is just like my mother.

### Blaming Stories

Stories of blame assume or view oneself or others as having bad intentions or bad traits.

> *Example:* He's just trying to get attention.
> *Example:* It's all my fault.
> *Example:* They are trying to drive me crazy.

## Invalidating Stories

Ideas of invalidation lead to a client's personal experience or knowledge being undermined by others.

> *Example:* He needs to express his anger about his father's death.
> *Example:* He's too sensitive.
> *Example:* You're too emotional.

## Deterministic Stories

Stories of nonchoice or deterministic stories suggest that someone has no choices about what he or she does with his or her body (voluntary actions) or has no ability to make any difference in what happens in his or her life.

> *Example:* If that teacher knew how to handle a classroom, Kate wouldn't have these problems at school.
> *Example:* I was raised in a home where silence was the way to express anger, so when I get angry, I stop talking and go my own way.
> *Example:* If she didn't nag me, I wouldn't hit her.

We challenge or cast doubt on problematic stories in three ways:

**1. Transform the Story by Acknowledging and Softening or by Adding Possibility.** Validate the current or past problematic points of view, but add a twist that softens a bit or adds a sense of possibility. For example, a mother may say of her son, "He doesn't care about our family. He just wants to do anything he feels like doing, regardless of the pain it causes us." One could respond by acknowledging the feelings and point of view of the parent, but reflect it back with a softer, less globalized sense to it. "So a lot of the things he's been doing have given you the sense he cares more for himself than for you or the family." Or another reflection could add a sense of the possibility that things could change in the situation in the future: "So you'd like to see him doing more things that show that at times he can put the family above his own interests."

**2. Find Counterevidence.** Get the family or others to tell you something that doesn't fit with the problematic story. For example, "Gee, you tell me that he's out of control, but now you're telling me that his teacher said he kept his cool when another boy taunted him in class," or "So, you tell me that you were raised in a family in which the only way to express anger was violence. But I'm curious, when you get angry, you typically hit your wife and your son, but when you get mad at work, do you hit your boss or the customers?"

**3. Find Alternative Stories or Frames to Fit the Same Evidence or Facts.** Give the facts a more benevolent interpretation. "You get the sense he just wants to do anything he wants when he wants to do it, but my sense is that he's trying to find a way to be independent and make his own decision. When you come down hard on him, the only way he can see to show he's independent is to rebel and resist you, even if it gets him in trouble," or "You think your father hates you because he grounds you, but I wonder, if he didn't care for you, he'd just let you do what you want as long as it wasn't a hassle for him."

## CHANGING THE DOING OF THE PROBLEM

*Insanity is doing the same thing over and over again and expecting different results.*
—Rita Mae Brown

There are two main ways to change the "doing" of the problem:
1) Identify and alter repetitive patterns of action and interaction involved in the problem.
2) Identify and encourage the use of solution patterns of action and interaction.

**Identifying and Altering Repetitive Patterns of Action and Interaction Involved in the Problem.**   The first way to change the "doing" of the problem is to interrupt or disrupt repetitive patterns involved in or surrounding the problem. Ways to do this are as follows:

1. Change the **frequency/rate** of the problem or the pattern around the problem.
2. Change the **duration** of the problem or the pattern around the problem.
3. Change the **time** (hour/time of day, week, month, or year) of the problem or the pattern around the problem.
4. Change the **intensity** of the problem or the pattern around the problem.
5. Change some other **invariant quality** of the problem or the pattern around the problem.
6. Change the **sequence** (order) of events involved in or around the problem.
7. **Interrupt** or otherwise prevent the occurrence of the problem.
8. **Add a new element** to the problem.
9. **Break up** any previously whole element of **the problem into smaller elements**.
10. Have the person **perform the problem without the usual accompanying pattern** around it.
11. Have the person **perform the pattern around the problem** at a time **when he or she is not having the problem**.
12. **Reverse the direction of striving** in the performance of the problem (paradox).

13. **Link the** occurrence of the **problem to** another pattern that is **a burdensome activity** (ordeal).
14. Change the **body behavior/performance** of the problem.

Bill had a family come to see him that was having a classic problem: the father and daughter would argue, while the mother felt caught in between, trying to get both of them to be reasonable and occasionally finding herself called on to be the judge of who was right. After some discussion, we decided that the next time there was an argument between father and daughter, they would have to go out into the backyard with water pistols, stand back to back while the mother counted ten paces for each of them to walk and then turn and fire until the gun was out of water. The mother was then to tell them who was the winner of the duel. This led to much laughter and good-natured dissipation of tension that allowed them all to sit down and have much more helpful discussions about the problem at hand.

**Identifying and Encouraging Solution Patterns of Action and Interaction.**   In addition to disrupting the problem pattern, usually we seek to discover and highlight solution patterns. These are efforts and behaviors that any or all family members have done in the past to solve the problem or to make the situation better. It is important to evoke a connection to the solutions, not merely convince families that they are good competent people by pointing out to them that they have at times acted in resourceful ways in the past or that they must have the best of intentions. We are not trying to be cheerleaders for the family but to ask questions and gather information in a way that convinces us and highlights for them that they have the resources to solve their problems. To this end, we have used a variety of methods for evoking solution patterns.

*One of the ways is to ask families to detail times when they hadn't experienced their problems when they expected they would.* This includes asking about exceptions to the rule of the problem. It is important to ask about this area in a way that both helps the families notice that there are exceptions and to make it likely that they will increase the solution patterns in the future. In part, that means asking about what anybody *did* differently in the exception situation. Otherwise, one might find out about exceptions but in a way that implies that there is nothing anyone can do to make it happen again, such as, "I was in a better mood that day." Asking questions that evoke action descriptions is more helpful in this regard: "So usually his coming home after curfew would lead to a big argument. How come it didn't go that way last night? What did anybody do differently last night from the usual drill?" "What is different about the times when you are getting along (there are dry beds, he does go to school, and so on)? How do you get that to happen?" "Have you ever had this difficulty in the past?" If yes, "How did you resolve it then? What would you need to do to get that to happen again?"

*Another way to evoke solution patterns is to find out what happens as the problem ends or starts to end.* What is usually the first sign the family or family member can tell the problem is going away or subsiding? What will the person or the family be doing when their problem has ended or subsided different from what they are doing when the problem is happening? "What happens or what did you do to *get* her to stop the temper tantrum?" "What did you do to *get* the fight to end?"

***We also search for other contexts of competence for the family members or the family as a whole.*** We ask about areas in the family's life that they feel good about, including hobbies, areas of specialized knowledge, well-developed skills, or places and time when they get along or solve problems. The therapist could ask, "What subjects do you like best in school?" "What kinds of things do you do for fun?" "What do you do for a living?"

For example, we might find out that when they are on family trips, things go better. "What is different then," we may ask. Everyone has clearly assigned roles and tasks; Jimmy plans the route and is the navigator. The mother makes the hotel reservations and coordinates meals. The father is the driver and Sue is the game master. She organizes games to play that everyone likes and that pass the time. Then we see if we can translate any parts of this situation to the problem that brought the family for therapy. "So, could we use the same team effort with everyone having an assigned role and task to help Jimmy get along with other kids better, without getting into fights?"

Another way to elicit competence is to get families to tell us about others who they know who have faced similar problems and resolved them successfully. A variation on this method is to ask families to tell us what they would suggest to another family or another child troubled by the same situation. Interestingly, when asked in this one-step-removed way, many children and families have lots of good ideas and wisdom that can be tapped to solve their problems.

> Bill saw a family in which all six children were having problems. The parents had just successfully completed some marital therapy and they had decided the children could use help. The family was very religious and the kids often felt out of place in their schools and had a tough time making friends. Several were depressed and some were taunted by other children at school. As we discussed this issue, it came to light that the oldest daughter had recently begun to make friends and had become more socially skilled and happy. She had previously been shy and depressed. When I showed some interest in this recent change, the mother mentioned that her history was similar to her daughter's. She had been shy and awkward socially, not due to religion, but due to her shame regarding the severe abuse and dysfunction in her family of origin. She had never wanted to make friends with anyone for fear they would discover the terrible things that were going on in her home. She had also felt so different from others that she had been shy. I asked her how she got over it, and she said she had finally left home and gone to work, where she was forced to interact with others on a day-to-day basis. She had started to realize that she wasn't so different from others and gradually made friends and became less shy and more secure. The daughter who had recently overcome shyness chimed in that she had also made the change in the same way. She had gotten a job and had begun to be around people other than her family. That led to her making friends and overcoming social awk-

wardness and isolation. From there on, it became an easy matter to have the mother and oldest daughter become expert consultants to design a program to help the younger ones end their isolation and awkwardness much earlier than either of them had. Regular nonschool/nonchurch activities outside the family were planned for each of them.

*As a last resort, if we can't find any other way to identify and elicit solution patterns, we may ask why the problem isn't worse.* Compared with the worst possible state families or people or this person could get in, how does the family explain that the problem isn't that severe? This normalizes and gets things in perspective as well as elicits things the family does when they finally succeed in confronting the problem. "Joann has failed three of her classes. How come she didn't fail them all?" "Things get loud, but they haven't gotten violent, as far as I've heard. How do you keep things from getting physical, even though tempers are flaring?"

## CHANGING THE CONTEXT OF THE PROBLEM

By context, we mean the aspects of the person's world that surround the problem but aren't necessarily directly involved in the problem. This includes time patterns (when, how frequently, and for how long the problem happens) and spatial patterns (where the problem typically happens). Since these two patterns overlap with the categories in changing the doing, we will skip them here and focus on the other aspects of the context. These include cultural background and propensities, family/historical background and propensities, biochemical/genetic background and propensities, and gender training and propensities. We assess what kinds of patterns and views come from each of these influences that are supporting the problem or make it likely to arise. We are careful not to imply that these influencing factors are causal. That is, being from certain cultural backgrounds or families of origin doesn't determine how one turns out, in our view. Likewise, having a genetic or biochemical propensity for depression or schizophrenia does not necessarily make one depressed or schizophrenic. The situation is more complex than that. While we assess the problematic aspects and patterns of the contextual influence, as in the doing and viewing, we also assess the solution aspects of the context.

Bill was teaching a workshop in England and a participant came up after the first day's presentation to say she had enjoyed the material but had a question. "I work in a battered woman's shelter," she said, "with a mixed group of women, some British in their background and some Pakistani immigrants. I can usually get the British women to at least acknowledge that they are in a bad situation, but the Pakistani women seem resigned to their situation. They have told me that if they leave their husbands, they will be dead, either from lack of support among their fellow Pakistanis or from murder that will go unsolved. What would your solution stuff say to that?" Bill replied that *he* wouldn't have the answer, but he thought that the Pakistani women might have some answers. He suggested that when she goes to work that night, she gather a group of the women together and ask them to be her consultants. She should ask, "How does domestic violence get successfully dealt with in Pakistani society?" After much discussion (in which it was generally agreed that it rarely gets dealt with successfully), several women knew of one instance in which the violence was successfully stopped. It was sometimes stopped when the woman who was being beaten told her family of origin of the situation and her father and brothers called upon her husband and threatened to beat him if he continued to abuse the woman. Of course, it didn't always work, but when something worked, that was it. When one of the women wondered out loud how this new-found realization could help any of them, since most of their families of origin were back in Pakistan, another woman got a small smile on her face and said, "Yes, but my family is coming to visit here in Britain next month."

The point of the story is that in every cultural, gender, biochemical situation, there are problematic patterns and influences as well as solution patterns and competence. Instead of just doing a genogram to find the patterns of addiction that run through the generations, it is also important to do a "solutiongram," which can detail the strengths and counterproblematic patterns that run through the family history. "So, you've told me that all of your father's brothers were alcoholic, three of them dying in their thirties from alcohol-related diseases. What I am curious about is that other brother who stopped drinking when he was 50 and your grandfather, who stopped drinking when his wife died. How do you think they did that and do you think you have inherited any of those abilities?"

Another way we use the context is to normalize and highlight strengths. If a person starts to understand that given the context in which the problem occurred, many people would experience, think, feel, or do something similar, it often lessens shame and feelings of isolation. For example, knowing that women have been socialized to take on the emotional or physical maintenance of relationships or families is often helpful to the woman who feels guilty if she doesn't do the dishes or leaves on a business trip, when she wouldn't have the same reaction if her male partner did the same things. Or a man might be complimented for withstanding his gender training and staying home with the infant, despite his guilt for not being a "good provider" for his family.

## Promoting and Provoking Change Between Sessions

Someone once asked Bill after he had given a presentation on therapy, "I'm not clear. Are you of the opinion that change mostly takes place in the session or between sessions in therapy?" Bill's succinct reply was, "Yes," which drew a laugh but was actually quite serious. Possibility therapy uses both arenas, in session and between sessions, to promote change.

We often give clients action plans or ideas to remember to further the changes we have begun in our office meetings with them. We put a premium on getting families to do things or notice new, more helpful things in their lives. These assignments are experiments that both provide the opportunity for change and mastery and provide more information for the therapist. We design those assignments collaboratively with our clients and use carbon forms to both facilitate follow-through (suggested actions are more likely to be remembered and carried out if they are written down) and follow-up (we are more likely to remember to ask about the task if we have a copy in the chart and they are more likely to take further assignments seriously if they see that we follow up).

We heard about an experiment that a physician carried out some years ago. He dictated his medical notes after seeing each patient and then arranged for the notes to be sent to half of his patients (randomly chosen) in a letter form, and he sent only the bill to the other half of his patients. Follow-up indicated that the patients who received the letter perceived the doctor as more competent and thorough and the care they received as much better than the patients who received no letter. The care given to the patients was no different, only whether they received the letter. We recommend sending follow-up letters not only to enhance clients' perceptions of clinicians' services but to further therapeutic gains as well. The letters can summarize progress made in the session, reinforce new perceptions, and urge families to follow through on the tasks agreed upon in the session.

Another way to carry out between-session changes is to do individual sessions with one or more family members between the conjoint family sessions. When family therapy was first introduced, this was a "no no." Families were always to be seen together, both in order to assess and intervene in the systemic interactions and to avoid supporting the individual view of the problem (that the problem arises from psychological processes within an individual). We find individual sessions helpful in family therapy. Sometimes crucial information emerges (such as reports of abuse or others concerns that a family member is afraid to speak about in front of other family members). Sometimes having so many people there makes it hard to focus the conversation. We find ourselves struggling just to manage the conversation or prevent conflicts from exploding.

Individual sessions also provide an opportunity to coach an individual, whether it be a parent or child, on how to change his or her response without having to attend to the potential defensive response of another family member. We find this particularly helpful with teenagers, who often need a forum in which to discuss legitimate concerns but usually do so in such a provocative manner ("They never let me do anything, they are too *&%#ing strict.") that they are not heard.

## POSSIBILITY THERAPY WITH FAMILIES SUMMARY
Create a collaborative environment.
Determine who to see and what to work on early in the process of therapy.
Acknowledge the feelings and points of view of various family members.
Focus on changing the viewing, the doing, and the context.
Disrupt or change problem patterns of the viewing, the doing, and the context.
Evoke solution patterns of the viewing, the doing, and the context.
Keep change going between and outside of sessions with letters, tasks, and individual sessions.

Family therapy is fraught with a myriad of pitfalls and possibilities for change. Many therapists spend their careers avoiding or dreading these sessions and their characteristic flashpoints and reluctant and hostile participants. Possibility therapy offers a collaborative problem-solving approach that provides a way to transform these sessions from dreaded encounters to powerful (and enjoyable) means for effecting change with children's or family's problems.

## REFERENCES

Hubble, M. A., & O'Hanlon, W. H. (1992). Theory countertransference. *Dulwich Centre Newsletter,* 25–30.

Hudson, P. O., & O'Hanlon, W. H. (1992). *Rewriting love stories: Brief marital therapy.* New York: Norton.

O'Hanlon, B., & Wilk, J. (1987). *Shifting contexts: The generation of effective psychotherapy.* New York: Guilford.

Chapter 20

# What's the Story?

## Narrative Therapy and the Third Wave of Psychotherapy

**Bill O'Hanlon**

Marisa, an Italian immigrant to New Zealand, worked as a housecleaner. Although she was an intelligent woman who spoke impeccable English, her block against writing had prevented her from getting a job more suited to her skills. After more than two decades in an unhappy marriage, she had recently visited a psychic who told her she had lived her life as a "doormat." So she enrolled in an assertiveness training course at a nearby community college, but during a role-playing exercise, she had panicked and run from the room. She thought she was going crazy. Soon afterward, she went to see narrative therapist David Epston and within minutes of their first session announced to him, "I'm bad! I'm bad! I'm bad!"

Marisa then told Epston her life story. Born in Italy just after World War II, she was her mother's twenty-first child. It was only many years later that she learned that her true father was a 72-year-old family friend who had been close to death at the time of her birth. Although for the few remaining years of his life he had been loving toward her, her mother and her siblings viewed her as a lower form of life, telling her she was only fit to be a servant. At 13, she had been sent to work as a housekeeper for an older sister in England, where she was treated poorly and sexually abused by her sister's husband. When she was 18, she decided to escape her family and immigrated to New Zealand where she married

This article was originally titled "The Third Wave" and was published in the *Family Therapy Networker* (November/December, 1994).

205

and found menial work. Recently, she had begun to chafe against her long subservience within her marriage, and her anger sometimes frightened her.

After the session, Epston, who was then developing his narrative approach to therapy, wrote Marisa a letter:

> I take it that telling me, a virtual stranger, your life story, which turned out to be a story of exploitation, frees you to some extent from it. To tell a story about your life turns it into a story, one that can be left behind, and makes it easier for you to create a future of your own design. [Also,] your story needs to be documented so it isn't lost to you and is in a form available to others whom you might choose to inspire. They will come to understand, as I have, how you were, over time, strengthened by your adverse circumstances. Everyone's attempts to weaken you by turning you into a slave paradoxically strengthened your resolve to be your own person. This, of course, is not to imply that you haven't paid dearly for this and haven't suffered. You almost accepted your family's attitude towards you and this accounted for the doormat lifestyle that you lived for some time.
>
> You probably wondered why [your father] loved you quite so much when your mother didn't want you. She taught you a servant mentality. That is, to do for others and expect very little in return. For a mother to betray a child into servitude, she must have had to convince herself you were bad; otherwise she couldn't have been your Judas and betrayed you. You were turned into a Cinderella with other people in charge of you. Your family did the worst for you and tried to have you believe that that was the best you could or should expect because you were "bad." They tried to convince you (and were undoubtedly successful for periods of time) that you deserved their punishments and cruelties.
>
> Seeing that medium who called you a "doormat" was a turning point in your life and you started your revolution with your husband because he was closest at hand. When you were a slave, you no doubt chose a partner who would be your master and you could serve, grateful for crumbs from his table. Your husband must have been shocked by your demands for justice and equality in your relationship. You had not spent all your strength in your suffering and slavery. Instead, this marked the onset of your taking action in this family. And you started accepting and trusting your own experience. Your own power was being drawn upon to shape events in your life for the first time. You broke out of some of the things that were depressing you and keeping you down. You gave yourself evidence that your anger was righteous anger. I gather your appreciation of yourself gained you more respect in your husband's eyes.
>
> In your thirties, your own power surfaced and was accepted by you. And no one could submerge it any longer. You had so much courage, in fact, that you decided to seek justice and put things right. By doing so, you draw a distinction between your history and your future. In your history, your life was defined by other peoples' attitudes and ideas about you; in your future, your life will be defined by your respect and appreciation of yourself. Your mother's death finally freed you— you no longer had to search for a mother who could never be. You were released to go forward in your life, believing in yourself. No wonder you feel dizzy with possibility. Remember, being a prisoner can make you accommodate to your prison. To be released from it is disconcerting, and many return to it for refuge. I believe you always, always, had some sense that evil was being done to you and, for that reason,

you were never made into a real slave. Rather, you were a prisoner of war, degraded, yes, but never broken. To my way of thinking, you are a heroine who doesn't know her heroism.

Several weeks later, Marisa returned to therapy, along with her husband. She had reread the letter many times. It was, she said, "reality," there in black and white, and she could not deny it. As a result, she now saw herself as a person who had had a terrible life but had always been strong and had never submitted completely to a devalued view of herself. She saw the events that had recently alarmed her as evidence that she was finally leaving old "victim" patterns behind and creating a new life. She told Epston she didn't feel a need to see him any further at that time.

Five years later, she contacted Epston again. By then, she had launched a career as a dress designer and told him, "My life has a future now. It will never be the same again." The first session and the letter, she said, had been the beginning of a life of greater self-respect and achievement. For some time afterward, she had reread the letter, especially when she suffered from flashbacks of her brother-in-law's sexual abuse. After a while, she had not needed to reread the letter at all and had finally destroyed it.

I first saw Epston's letter to Marisa a few years ago, on a plane coming back from New Zealand, in a sheaf of materials he had given me on narrative therapy. I have read scores of exciting case histories showcasing new techniques over the years, but this was different—it made me cry. I was moved by how Marisa had reclaimed her life and I marveled at how this transformation had been accomplished.

Then, as now, I was working mainly as a brief, solution-oriented therapist. Although I had occasionally witnessed dramatic transformations, most of my work was far more modest than Epston's work with Marisa. I helped people get out of stuck patterns and move on with their lives. If Marisa had come to me, I probably would have helped her with her writing block. I might have asked her what other things she had mastered after thinking they would be impossible. Could she transfer that sense of competence to writing English? I probably would have asked how she had learned to speak and understand English and tried to use the same methods to help her learn to write. I think I would have helped Marisa. She might have gotten a better job, incrementally improved her life, and triggered further positive changes. I think she would have been satisfied. But Epston's ambitions for Marisa had been much bigger than mine would have been.

"If you come to my office," his letter seemed to say, "I'm going to help you reinvent your life. You are more than the story you have told yourself about who you are." Marisa was not only going to write, she was going to get a new life, a new chance. For Epston, it was always the stroke of midnight on New Year's Eve and each session offered the possibility of a new beginning. His work, I thought, contained the ambitions of long-term therapy within a short-term time frame. Yet there was more to it than this. And I couldn't quite grasp how it was done.

In the years since that day on the plane, I have read about or watched many

other therapeutic encounters involving David Epston and his friend and sometimes collaborator Michael White, the main developers of the narrative method.
At first, it was like watching magic. A person such as Marisa would come in,
walking a road they had been on for years, a road that seemed destined to lead to
more misery. During the conversation, a fork would appear, a path that had always been there, but somehow had gone unnoticed.

It wasn't that I'd never seen that happen in therapy before. I had often helped
people find roads they had missed, in the form of solutions and resources that
they'd previously used successfully and could apply again. At other times, I helped
them find a new destination on the map, and we bushwhacked and experimented
until we hacked out a bumpy new footpath.

But Epston and White seemed to go beyond that: they conjured up doorways
to new identities out of nowhere. It seemed inexplicable, radical, and elegant.
When people found themselves in a corner, Epston and White could paint a door
on the wall where it was needed, and then, like Bugs Bunny in the cartoons, open
it and help them walk through it. I wanted to know how to paint those doors. But
the first few times I tried to imitate what I had seen them do, I was more like
Elmer Fudd, who tries to walk through the doors that Bugs has painted and crashes
into the wall.

So a couple of years ago I invited David to Omaha, Nebraska, where I lived,
to give a workshop. He showed a videotape of his third interview with Rhiannon,
a 15-year-old girl who was close to dying from anorexia. Accompanied by her
cousin and her cousin's boyfriend, she was a skeleton lost in a large sweater,
trying to make herself invisible, curling her arms around herself and slumping
down in her chair. Smiling faintly in response to David's persistent questions, she
insisted she felt fine and had lots of energy. David, carried away by his intense
interest in her answers, could barely contain himself. He squirmed in his chair,
leaned toward the girl, and asked her question after question: "Can I just ask you
why you think it is that Anorexia tricks people into going to their deaths thinking
they're feeling fine? What purpose would it have, getting you to go to your death
smiling?"

Rhiannon still would not engage. Slumped in her chair, she kept saying she
felt fine. Rhiannon had recently been discharged from a hospital after losing 25
pounds in three weeks, and a physician was monitoring her condition three times
a day. She was literally on the brink of death. At home, she had been lying in a
fetal position and screaming until her exhausted parents took her to her older
cousin's house. As I watched the tape, I thought that even I, psychotic optimist
that I am, would have given up on engaging Rhiannon and would have focused
my interventions on the cousin and her boyfriend instead. But David seemed to
be even more psychotically optimistic than I am. He persisted: "Okay, okay, okay.
If that's how you're feeling, how's it fooling you? Most people, when they're
near death, know they're being murdered, right? How's Anorexia doing this to
you? Because if it's making you feel good, or telling you you're feeling good,
then I'd like for you to ask this question of yourself. Why does it say to you

you're feeling good? Why would it do this? Why does it want to murder you? Why doesn't it want you to protest? Why doesn't it want you to resist?"

Then, suddenly and inexplicably, Rhiannon responded. Anorexia, she said, fooled her by telling her she was fat when she was thin. "Is it telling you that right now?" David asked. "No," Rhiannon said. *"I am* too thin." She sat up in her chair.

David asked her how she knew that, and she replied that people who love her told her that she is too thin. "Do you think Anorexia loves you?" he asked her. "No," she said. "It's killing me."

Her voice grew stronger. Her body language changed. In response to David's continual stream of questions, she began to make plans for standing up to Anorexia and not letting it fool her into starving herself anymore. David enlarged the new doorway, asking her how, in the past, she had shown herself to be the kind of person who could stand up to something like Anorexia. By the end of the session, nobody in the room was talking about her hospitalization anymore. David, Rhiannon, the cousin, and her boyfriend all looked hopeful and certain. Within 10 or 15 minutes, Rhiannon had become an ally in treatment, rather than a reluctant bystander. The rapidity of this change wasn't new to me, but such turnarounds usually happen only when a client actively cooperates. Rhiannon, like many people with anorexia, did not look much like a customer for change—that is, until David got hold of her.

In the past five years, therapists around the world have become intrigued by narrative and related approaches to therapy that flatten out the familiar client/ therapist hierarchy and treat personal identity as a fluid social construct. To be sure, the interest in narrative is not client driven. People don't come into my office asking for help "standing up to Anorexia" or to have a "liberating conversation" or asking to "deconstruct their social identities." Rather, the popularity of narrative and related approaches has something to do with their appeal to therapists—they heighten our sense of the possible; they make us feel hopeful and excited again.

In Omaha, the local office of the Nebraska Department of Social Services has recently adopted a narrative approach. "It has had an amazing impact around here," says Bob Zimmerman, the director. The agency had one caseworker who had been there for years and was quite open about the fact that she was burned out in the job but hung on because she needed the job security. After she started working with the narrative approach, she experienced a sudden burst of renewed excitement. In fact, she recommended that her roommate apply for a job at the agency. "When I asked the roommate during the interview why she wanted to work at a bureaucracy like the Department of Social Services, she told me that she had heard so many exciting things from her roommate about what was going on here that she wanted to be part of this place," says Zimmerman. "Needless to say, that hasn't been the typical applicant's perception of the Department of Social Services in the past."

The appeal of narrative therapy involves much more than a new set of techniques. To my way of thinking, it represents a fundamentally new direction in the therapeutic world, a movement that might be called psychotherapy's Third Wave. The First Wave, which began with Freud and laid the foundation for the field of psychotherapy, was pathology focused and dominated by psychodynamic theories and biological psychiatry. The First Wave represented a major advance because it no longer viewed troubled people as morally deficient, and it gave us a common vocabulary—codified in the *Diagnostic and Statistical Manual*—for describing human problems. But it focused so heavily on pathology that it skewed our view of human nature. Many people ended up identifying themselves with stigmatizing labels like "narcissist," "borderline personality," or "adult child of an alcoholic."

I was never much of a fan of the First Wave. It seemed to give our pronouncements a vast and overrated authority and turn diagnoses that were little more than social prejudices or imaginative guesses into absolute and eternal truths. The absurdity and damage wrought by our delusion that we could determine what was sick or healthy, right or wrong, was amply demonstrated in the 1970s, when psychiatrists belatedly decided by democratic vote that homosexuality was no longer a disease.

Psychotherapy's Second Wave—the problem-focused therapies—emerged in the 1950s but did not entirely supplant the First Wave. The Second Wave attempted to remedy the overfocus on pathology and the past. Problem-focused therapies, including behavioral therapy, cognitive approaches, and family therapy, did not assume clients were sick. They focused more on the here-and-now instead of searching for hidden meanings and ultimate causes. Personality was no longer seen as sealed in the envelope of the skin but as influenced by patterns of communication, family and social relationships, stimulus and response, and even "self-talk."

Change was not seen as nearly so difficult in the Second Wave: influence some of the variables and the whole system will shift, including personal characteristics that looked as though they were set in concrete. Second-Wave therapists saw their clients as basically sound, just making a pit stop. The goal was to fix them up as quickly as possible and send them back onto the highway of life. They didn't try to tinker with things they hadn't been asked to fix.

Although the therapists of the Second Wave included a few more women and were not as exalted as the psychiatrists of the First Wave, they remained the experts, versed in such arcana as Gregory Bateson's double-bind theory, paradoxical interventions, or behavioral techniques. Problems resided in small-scale systems; solutions still rested with the therapists. Few saw their clients as decisive agents in their own change. In fact, many saw their clients' conscious sense of self as something that had to be worked around or outwitted.

In the early 1980s, some therapists began adopting what might be called a precursor to the Third Wave—competence-based therapies. We believed that the focus on problems often obscures the resources and solutions residing within clients. Like the Third Wave that would follow, we no longer saw the therapists as the source of the solution—the solutions rested in people and their social networks.

The philosophy underlying solution-oriented therapy is summarized in a story Milton Erickson told about his encounter with a severely depressed and suicidal woman whose nephew, a physician colleague, had asked Erickson to look her up during a lecture visit to Milwaukee. The woman, who had been confined to a wheelchair, only left the house to go to church and avoided people while she attended services. When Erickson arrived for his visit, which the nephew had arranged, he asked the woman for a tour around her gloomy house. Everywhere the shades were drawn and there was little light, until they ended the tour at the woman's pride and joy, her plant nursery, which was attached to the house.

After the woman had proudly showed him her newly transplanted African violet plants, Erickson told her that her nephew had been worried about her depression, but Erickson could now see what the real problem was. She wasn't being a very good Christian and doing her Christian duty, he sternly told her. She stiffly replied that she considered herself a very good Christian and resented his opinion. No, he responded, here she was with all this money (a sizable inheritance) and all this time on her hands, with a God-given gift with plants and she was letting it all go to waste. He recommended that she obtain a church bulletin and visit each person in the congregation on the event of some sad or happy occasion (such as births, deaths, illness, graduations, or engagements) and bring along a gift of an African violet plant that she had grown from her own cuttings.

When I was in supervision with Erickson, he showed me a scrapbook with an article from the Milwaukee paper some years after his visit to this woman that had the headline, "African Violet Queen of Milwaukee Dies, Mourned by Thousands." When I asked Erickson why he hadn't focused on what was causing her depression, he replied, "I looked around her house and the only sign of life I saw were those African violets. I thought it would be easier to grow the African violet part of her life than to weed out the depression." That, in a nutshell, is solution-oriented therapy—grow the solution-/life-enhancing part of people's lives rather than focus on the pathology/problem parts and amazing changes can happen pretty rapidly.

But unlike the Third Wave that would follow us, we kept our ambitions limited. Like the man who searched under the streetlamp for his keys because the light was better there even though he'd dropped them half a block away, we worked on small, manageable problems. We saw deep changes happen sometimes, almost as an act of grace or accident, and welcomed them when they did. But planning or expecting it to occur regularly seemed like setting up our clients for failure.

The First Wave's preoccupation with history acknowledged the reality of people's victimization and yet seemed obsessed and defeated by it. The Second Wave's minimalist pragmatism helped people cope with day-to-day issues at the expense of acknowledging the depth of their pain and the richness of their lives. Both viewpoints are clearly incomplete, and this may explain some of the attraction of the Third Wave, which is arising in many different places in the world simultaneously. That is why Marisa's story so moved me. Epston did not brush aside her history, nor did he get bogged down in it—he dethroned it. He saw her as an active resister, not a passive victim. He acknowledged the tremendous power of what she had been told about herself and separated her sense of herself from her history. And he did so without one-way mirrors or therapeutic gobbledygook, using nothing more technologically sophisticated than a letter written with dignity, feeling, and respect.

The more time I have spent reading and watching the work of Third-Wave therapists, the more I see similar patterns—a willingness to acknowledge the tremendous power of the past history and the present culture that shapes our lives, integrated with a powerful, optimistic vision of our capacity to free ourselves from them once they are made conscious. Third-Wave approaches talk to the adult within.

While the First Wave conceived of troubling forces as located within individual troubled personalities, and the Second Wave concentrated on small interactive systems such as the family, the Third Wave draws attention to far larger systems, such as the daunting cultural sea we swim in—the messages from television advertisements, schools, newspaper "experts," bosses, grandmothers, and friends—that tell us how to think and who to be. We are not sure where many of these messages come from; we go around thinking of them as our "selves," and many of them are profoundly destructive and undermining. This process of identity shaping is extremely disempowering in a mass-media culture like our own.

Therapists, the Third-Wave theory goes, can play right into this sense of disempowerment when they assume they have a right to the authority clients and the culture give them. As Irish family therapists Imelda McCarthy, Nollaig Byrne, and Phil Kearney have put it, therapists often "colonize" their clients. Like countries occupied by more powerful nations, clients learn to devalue their own language, expertise, and knowledge in favor of the therapist's view of things. Third-Wave approaches take very seriously philosopher Martin Heidegger's concept of "throwness." Like clay thrown on a potter's wheel, we are shaped from the moment of our birth, not only by our family legacy, but also by the culture that creates the way we see and talk about ourselves and the world. Third-Wave therapists are interested in bringing to light this taken-for-granted "throwness" that is the foundation of people's sense of their unworthiness.

Some Third-Wave approaches seem to blur the distinction between politics and therapy. But rather than lecturing at clients, narrative therapists bring issues of racism and sexism right down to the personal level, not pinning the blame on anyone but focusing instead on the insidious effects of oppressive ideas and "practices," habits of actions, to which all of us are subject. This is not a politics of blame—finding out who the terrible oppressors are (men, White people, wealthy capitalists, etc.)—but a politics of liberation on a very individual level, as in Epston's work with Rhiannon, in which her therapy becomes her struggle to be free of the trap of the internalized power of anorexia.

The narrative approach leads to a vastly altered view of personality itself, and therefore of therapeutic change. Many of the beliefs and thoughts we cling to most dearly are nothing but a vast cultural ragbag: lines from old love songs, *Glamour* magazine layouts, advertising jingles, romance comics, "Dear Abby" columns, stern lectures from our fathers about what it means to be a man, memories of old love affairs, childhood days swimming at the river. We may have unconsciously absorbed beliefs that we are not good enough, that worthwhile people know how to dress or cook fresh pasta, that only thin women are beautiful or worthy, that real men know how to keep a woman "in line." If we consciously learn to recognize the insidious effects of these beliefs, the Third Wavers argue, and see them as not inherent to ourselves, we can free ourselves from them. This is the kind of "liberating conversation" that Third Wavers hope to have with their clients.

A compelling, politically correct ideology is one thing; having an immediate impact on troubled people's lives is something else. For years, therapists have been engaging in heady philosophizing about topics such as "epistemology" and "social construction of reality" with little discernible impact on day-to-day practice. But narrative therapy has become the most visible of all Third-Wave approaches because of its ability to put ideology into action in a way that makes something different happen in therapist's offices. Narrative approaches seem to get therapists out of unproductive struggles and enable them to avoid one of this profession's great occupational hazards—being captured by our clients' despair.

Ericksonian psychologist Steve Gilligan describes the way some clients affect their therapists: "From the moment they come in, they start the induction," says Gilligan, "Hello, I am depression. I have always been depression. I will always be depression. When you look at me, you will see nothing but depression. Go deeply into the depression trance." Once this happens, we are likely to become as discouraged and stuck as the client. But separating clients from the labels they bring in is no easy task and the appeal of the narrative approach may stem, in large part, from its unique approach to doing just that.

For years, critics of psychiatry like Thomas Szasz, Erving Goffman, and Jay Haley have railed against the dangers of labeling people and the self-fulfilling prophecy of considering someone "borderline" or "schizophrenic." They have argued that such static and generalized labels undermine everyone's belief in the possibility of change. Family therapists and other Second-Wave therapists at first tried to ignore individual labels or tried to reframe them as arising from systemic or interactional processes. But labels do not go away just because we ignore or reframe them. It is not only insurance companies that are attached to labels; clients are hooked by them as well. While a therapist may decide it's easier to treat "a child who won't eat" than "an anorexic," or a person who is "down" than a person who is suffering from "clinical depression," sometimes clients may feel that this delabeling means the therapist does not understand them or is not listening: "My child is Attention Deficit Disordered. Are you telling me there is no such thing? He's not just energetic, he's Hyperactive!" Labels often give clients a sense that the seriousness of their problems is being acknowledged, as well as a feeling of kinship with others with similar issues: "You mean as a PTSD victim I'm not the only one who has flashbacks and feels like cutting herself? Wow! I always thought I was weird and different from everyone else."

The hallmark of the narrative approach is the credo, "The person is never the problem; the problem is the problem." Through use of their most well known technique, externalization, narrative therapists are able to acknowledge the power of labels while both avoiding the trap of reinforcing people's attachment to them and letting them escape responsibility for their behavior. Externalization offers a way of viewing clients as having parts of them that are uncontaminated by the symptom. This automatically creates a view of the person as nondetermined and as accountable for the choices he or she makes *in relationship* to the problem.

"Narrative ideas lend themselves to respect and empowerment, not only for clients, but for therapists as well," says psychologist Richard Ruhrold, clinical director of the Bowen Center in Indiana. After learning about externalization, he used it with a family whose adolescent son was identified as having a "crappy attitude. . . . So we decided to name the problem Crappy Attitude," says Ruhrold. He further states,

> Before, I would have had a more negative view of the boy, seeing him, as his family did, as the problem. Using externalization, however, the family and I found ourselves talking about how Crappy Attitude had been working to rule the boy's life and had caused many problems for the boy, his family, and others. Rather quickly, we were all caught up in a discussion of how the young man could help himself and how each family member might help him "fight Crappy Attitude." This session was very positive and productive. An atmosphere of collaboration arose from that discussion that probably wouldn't have resulted from viewing and talking about either the boy or the family as the source of the problem.

Externalization also helps therapists quickly build alliances with difficult clients. Craig Thompson, a Des Moines hospital-based therapist, works with adolescent sexual abuse perpetrators. He tells about a case with a "resistant" sex offender who was extremely uncooperative, stonewalling when others in his therapy group tried to confront him. Then Thompson began to use externalization with the boy, asking him how he had been influenced by Perpetration and how he had stood up to Perpetration. Thompson reports, "We began to notice the boy very quickly became less defensive and more cooperative in the group. He was listening to more feedback from fellow group members and acknowledging responsibility for the offenses. Before, the kid had the idea, 'I'm bad and I'm never going to be any good,'" says Thompson. "But after we started externalizing Perpetration, he got the message, 'You're okay and these are things that can help you stand against Perpetration.' That gave him and us some hope for change."

"Ironically," says Canadian family therapist Karl Tomm, "this technique is both very simple and extremely complicated. It is simple in the sense that what it basically entails is a linguistic separation of the problem from the personal identity of the patient. What is complicated and difficult is the delicate means by which it is achieved. It is through the therapist's careful use of language in the therapeutic conversation that the person's healing initiatives are achieved." One brief therapist I know unsuccessfully tried using externalization after reading White and Epston's (1990, Norton) book, *Narrative Means to Therapeutic Ends.* "I would externalize and it would fall kind of flat," he told me. "My clients would look at me blankly. 'So I'm under the influence of Depression. So what,' they would say. I knew I was missing something, but I wasn't sure where to go with it or what I was missing." What many therapists fail to understand is that, as Karl Tomm explains, "What is new about the narrative approach is that it provides a purposeful sequence of questions that consistently produce a freeing effect for people." Following the therapeutic sequence is a bit like building an arch, brick by brick. If you try to do the last step without having patiently spent time doing the first ones, your arch is not going to hold up.

Here is my understanding of the fundamental structure of the narrative approach:

## The Collaboration With the Person or the Family Begins With Coming Up With a Mutually Acceptable Name for the Problem

One might ask a child who has been having temper tantrums, "So, Anger has been convincing you to throw yourself on the floor and kick your feet, huh?" To a person who has been having paranoid hallucinations, you could ask, "When Paranoia whispers in your ear, do you always listen?" At first, the person and his or her family may persist in attributing the problem to the person, but the narrative therapist will gently persist in the other direction, linguistically severing the person from the problem label, and clients themselves soon begin to take on the externalized view of the problem.

## Personify the Problem and Attributing Evil Intentions and Tactics to It

Next, the therapist starts talking to the person or family as if the problem were another person with an identity, will, tactics, and intentions that are designed to oppress or dominate the person or the family. Often, the therapist will use metaphors or images that help bring the process to life for them and the clients. For example, "How long has Anorexia been lying to you?" or "How does the Alcoholism bully push your family around?"

This starts to free the person and those around him from identifying the person as the problem and evokes motivation to change. For example, in Epston's work with Rhiannon, if she had continued to identify herself as an anorexic, she would have had to defend herself against any attempt to change as an attack on her and her autonomy. Instead, Epston's externalizing questions both separated her identity from Anorexia and attributed bad and tricky intentions to Anorexia, so she could use that defensive energy to fight against the problem.

## INVESTIGATING HOW THE PROBLEM HAS BEEN DISRUPTING, DOMINATING, OR DISCOURAGING THE PERSON AND THE FAMILY

Before the therapist tries to change the situation, he or she finds out how the person has felt dominated or forced by the problem to do or experience things he or she didn't like. The therapist might ask anyone in the room about the effects of the problem on the person and on them. This both acknowledges the person's suffering and the extent to which his or her life and relationships have been limited by the problem and provides further opportunities to create the externalization by asking more questions. For example, "When has Jealousy convinced you to do something you regretted later?" or "What kinds of tricks does Anorexia use on your daughter to alienate her from those she loves?" or "What kind of lies has Depression been telling you about your worth as a person?" The language used here is not deterministic: The problem never *causes or makes* the person or the family to do anything, it only *influences, invites, tells, tries to convince, uses tricks, tries to recruit, etc.* This language highlights people's choices and creates an assumption of accountability, rather than blame or determinism. If the person is *not* the problem, but has a certain relationship to the problem, then the relationship can change. If the problem invites rather than forces, one can turn down the invitation. If the problem is trying to recruit you, you can refuse to join.

This step also increases motivation. The family and the person come together with the therapist in their common goal of overthrowing the dominance of the problem in the person's and family's lives.

### Discovering Moments When Clients Haven't Been Dominated or Discouraged by the Problem or Their Lives Have Not Been Disrupted by the Problem

This is akin to the solution-focused method of searching for exceptions to the problem, only instead of asking, as solution-oriented therapists might, "What was the longest time you have gone without drugs," a narrative therapist would ask, "So what's the longest time you have stood up to Cravings?" No matter how the question is answered, the assumption that the problem is separate from the person has been reinforced. Gradually, a new reality begins to be created. Typical questions during this phase of the interview are, "Can you just tell me about some times when you haven't believed the lies Anorexia has told you?" or "Have you ever seen Johnny stand up to the Temper Tantrum Monster?" This step shows that change is possible, highlighting moments when the problem has not happened or when it has been successfully overcome. Language, as William Burroughs wrote, is a virus. By now, the virus of externalizing is running quite rampant through the therapeutic system.

## FINDING HISTORICAL EVIDENCE TO BOLSTER A NEW VIEW OF THE PERSON AS COMPETENT ENOUGH TO HAVE STOOD UP TO, DEFEATED, OR ESCAPED FROM THE DOMINANCE OR OPPRESSION OF THE PROBLEM

This is where the method really gets interesting. Here, the person's identity and life story begin to get rewritten. This is the *narrative* part. The previous steps have been used to prepare the ground to plant the seeds for rewriting people's sense of themselves. Narrative therapists use the evidence of discovered competence as a gateway to a parallel universe, one in which the person has a different life story, one in which he or she is competent and heroic. To keep this from being merely a glib reframing of the person's life, the narrative therapist asks for stories and evidence from the past to show that the person was actually competent, strong, spirited, but didn't always realize it or put a lot of emphasis on that aspect of him- or herself. The therapist gets the client and the family to support and flesh out this view.

Solution-oriented therapists would quickly move on to the future once a past exception is discovered, content to use that exception to solve the problem. Instead, the narrative therapist wants to root this new sense of self in a past and future so bright the person will have to wear shades. Typical questions might be: "What can you tell me about your past that would help me understand how you've been able to take these steps to stand up to Anorexia so well?" and "Who knew you as a child who wouldn't be surprised that you've been able to reject Violence as the dominant force in your relationship?"

### Evoking Speculation From the Person and the Family About What Kind of Future Is To Be Expected From the Strong, Competent Person That has Emerged From the Interview So Far

Next, the narrative therapist helps the person or the family to speculate on what future developments will result now that the person is seen as competent and strong, and what changes will result if the person keeps resisting the problem. For example, "As you continue to stand up to Anorexia, what do you think will be different about your future than the future Anorexia had planned for you?" or "As Jan continues to disbelieve the lies that Delusions are telling her, how do you think that will affect her relationship to her friends?" This step is designed to further crystallize the new view of the person and his or her life.

### Finding or Creating an Audience for Perceiving the New Identity and New Story

Since the person developed the problem in a social context, it is important to make arrangements for the social environment to be involved in supporting the new story or identity that has emerged in the conversation with the therapist.

Narrative therapists use letters, asking for advice for other people suffering from the same or similar problems, and arranging for meetings with family members and friends, to accomplish this social validation. Some questions might be, "Who could you tell about your development as a member of the Anti-Diet League that could help celebrate your freedom from Unreal Body Images?" and "Are there people who have known you when you were not under the influence of Depression who could remind you of your accomplishments and that your life is worth living?"

The therapist keeps using this process until it is clear it has "taken" in the person's life. The person or his or her family reports that things are changing for the better out in the world in relation to the problem. The person is starting to see himself or herself in the new, more competent, choice-saturated view, even when outside the therapist's direct influence. This may happen within a few sessions, but narrative therapists do not claim by any means to be brief therapists and are willing to continue the therapy as long as both client and therapist feel it is necessary.

Sometimes, to reinforce the new view of the person as expert, the client is asked to record (on videotape, audiotape, or in a letter) his or her success in overcoming the problem, or to be a consultant to someone who is struggling with a similar issue. When I asked David Epston about confidentiality, he replied, "of course, we get people's permission before we do anything. But in this therapy, people emerge as heroes and they often want that heroism acknowledged in some social way. They are usually quite happy to communicate with others and tell their stories."

Having just given you this formula, I must give you a warning—if externalization is approached purely as a technique, it will probably not produce profound effects. If you do not believe, to the bottom of your soul, that people are not their problems and that their difficulties are social and personal constructions, then you will not be seeing these transformations. When Epston or White are in action, you can tell they are absolutely convinced that people are not their problems. Their voices, their postures, their whole beings radiate possibility and hope. They are definitely under the influence of Optimism.

Like so many other approaches to therapy, so far we have primarily anecdotal evidence and the enthusiasm of narrative therapy's adherents to support claims of its effectiveness. The only formal study I know of was done with some of the chronic psychiatric patients Michael White treated at Glenside Hospital in Adelaide, Australia. The study found that White's patients stayed an average of only 14 days in the hospital compared with a matched control group who received standard psychiatric care that stayed an average of 36 days. That is the extent of the data so far.

I should also add that I'm skeptical of the repeated claims of narrative therapists to being nondirective. In the tapes I have seen, there is a clear and consistent therapist agenda, and while I like the direction, this is clearly not a nondirective approach. When I asked David Epston why his anorexic clients speak so often about being in concentration camps and under death sentences, when not a single one of mine do, he very sincerely told me that his clients came up with those metaphors. But as I watched videotapes and read transcripts of this work, I saw time and time again the moment when the therapist introduced a metaphor or some new language to the client. I studied with Milton Erickson and can recognize hypnosis when I see it. Narrative therapists would generally bristle at the suggestion that they use hypnosis, but they can take my word for it, they do.

My biggest concern about narrative therapy is that, like most other popular movements, many therapists will use it merely as a clever device. "There is nothing so dangerous as an idea," wrote Emile Chartier, "when it is the only one you have." Because the technique is relatively easy to learn, therapists might just go around externalizing problems, like earlier family therapists who went around creating paradoxes or reframing people and expecting miracles. Inevitably, many therapists will ignore the heart of narrative therapy, its fierce belief in people's possibilities for change and the profound effects of conversation, language, and stories on both therapist and client.

Now that I have learned to open the doorway of externalization, I find I only use it with clients who have organized their identity around the problem—cases involving schizophrenia, severe depression, persistent misbehavior, or obsessive–compulsive problems. Not everybody needs an identity overhaul, and most people I see just come in for simple problem solving; their concerns have not become life encompassing or defining. But in more severe and challenging cases in which either my clients or I have become induced into seeing a person as "impossible" or chronic, externalizing can help everyone involved avoid becoming discouraged and hopeless.

Just after I learned narrative therapy, a woman was referred to me by a psychologist who did not want to continue seeing her because he was worried about the legal liability. Joanne was on several antidepressant and antipsychotic medications; the psychologist told me he felt she needed daily supportive therapy as she struggled with a compulsion to murder her boyfriend. Apparently, some of the ideas she had been exposed to while studying shamanism had been distorted into terrible delusions and compulsions. She believed that many of her actions, and even the colors of the clothes she wore, were giving her boyfriend power over her, not only in this life, but in all future incarnations. If she took a shower and then touched the edge of the shower curtain, she would be in her boyfriend's power unless she showered again. She could not break up with him; that would only confirm his hold over her in future lives. The only way she could free herself, she believed, was to kill him. She struggled very hard, night after night, to resist this impulse, but she told me she thought she would have to do it soon.

Because of my travel schedule, I could only see Joanne about once a month. She was in crisis the first few sessions, always struggling with homicide or suicide. I searched for strengths and competence like any good solution-oriented therapist, and she certainly had them. I asked her how she'd been able to go along as well as she had, and she said, "Because I'm aberrant, but I'm amazing!" and we both laughed. She'd feel better when she saw me, and said that she felt less discouraged, but things were tough. Sometimes she might be able to hold onto something after our sessions, but often her delusions were as powerful as ever. I did see her as competent, but it felt like touch-and-go. I began to worry that I might lose her to suicide.

I decided to apply what I'd been learning in narrative therapy workshops and to use a disciplined questioning process. I had tried externalizing once or twice before with clients, but it had seemed more like a language trick and had fallen flat, and I'd quickly dropped it and tried something else. This time, I stayed with it, persistently using the questions like a finely honed tool.

I kept asking Joanne how Fear, Delusions, and Compulsions worked together to convince her that she had to do the things they told her. At first, she was convinced that she was the problem and her life was going downhill. But as I persisted, she began talking about the person she had always been underneath it all, a person who was loving and wanted to be loved. She told me she had been hospitalized for and had overcome anorexia, bulimia, and alcohol and drug addiction in her late teens and early adult years. She really didn't know how she had overcome them, but I highlighted this as evidence that she was the kind of person who was able to overcome big problems. Still, she felt convinced she had to kill her boyfriend.

Then, in the middle of one night, as she struggled with the urge to get out of bed and find him and kill him, she had a conversation with herself. She felt 150 percent convinced that she had to kill her boyfriend. But at the same time, she said, she realized, "I am not the kind of person who hurts people." She decided to take it on faith that her delusions were not real. She still struggled with them, but gradually she moved out of crisis mode. She got a job at a bakery, and a few months later she was finally able to break up with her boyfriend.

She has kept her job and now supervises 12 people. I asked her about what had helped her stand up to her Compulsion to kill, and she told me about the night she had lain awake thinking about who she was. "As much as I believed the delusions and was convinced they were true, I knew that I was not a murderer," she said. "At a certain point, I made the decision that I would not harm anyone, no matter how I felt, because that is simply not who I *am.*"

In the process of our work, she had let go of her identification with her delusions. They were no longer what she thought of as her "self." And, instead, something else about her that also always had been true—her experience of herself as a loving person—had become central to her. In the weeks and months that followed, we worked together with her sense that she had come through these awful things in order to help others. And as I used the techniques I had learned from Epston—externalizing the problem and enlarging her new sense of herself—my own sense of identity as a therapist shifted too. No longer did I have to choose between working deeply and working effectively. I realized I was capable, as David Epston could have told me all along, of far more than I had realized.

# Index